How Children Learn

Education at SAGE

SAGE is a leading international publisher of journals, books, and electronic media for academic, educational, and professional markets.

Our education publishing includes:

- accessible and comprehensive texts for aspiring education professionals and practitioners looking to further their careers through continuing professional development

- inspirational advice and guidance for the classroom

- authoritative state of the art reference from the leading authors in the field

Find out more at: **www.sagepub.co.uk/education**

How Children Learn

SEAN MACBLAIN

Los Angeles | London | New Delhi
Singapore | Washington DC

Los Angeles | London | New Delhi
Singapore | Washington DC

SAGE Publications Ltd
1 Oliver's Yard
55 City Road
London EC1Y 1SP

SAGE Publications Inc.
2455 Teller Road
Thousand Oaks, California 91320

SAGE Publications India Pvt Ltd
B 1/I 1 Mohan Cooperative Industrial Area
Mathura RoadA
New Delhi 110 044

SAGE Publications Asia-Pacific Pte Ltd
3 Church Street
#10-04 Samsung Hub
Singapore 049483

Commissioning editor: Jude Bowen
Associate editor: Miriam Davey
Production editor: Jeanette Graham
Copyeditor: Rosemary Campbell
Proofreader: Salia Nessa
Indexer: Anne Solomito
Marketing manager: Catherine Slinn
Cover design: Wendy Scott
Typeset by: C&M Digitals (P) Ltd, Chennai, India
Printed and bound in Great Britain by Ashford
Colour Press Ltd

Library of Congress Control Number: 2013947121

British Library Cataloguing in Publication data

A catalogue record for this book is available from the British Library

ISBN 978-1-4462-7217-6
ISBN 978-1-4462-7218-3 (pbk)

To my brother Brian, the loveliest of brothers from whom I have never stopped learning, my mother and father who taught me how to learn, my wife Angela for her continued love and support, and our four lovely children Marty, Nat, Nibs and Hayz.

CONTENTS

LIST OF TABLES

ABOUT THE AUTHOR

 Sean MacBlain is Reader in Child Development and Disability at the University of St Mark & St John, where he now leads the Centre for Education and Applied Research, having previously held the position of Research Lead for the Centre for Professional and Educational Research. Before taking up his current position Sean worked as a Senior Lecturer in Education and Developmental Psychology at Stranmillis University College, a College of Queen's University of Belfast. Prior to working as an academic, Sean worked as an educational psychologist in Belfast and Somerset, and continues in this field in his own private practice, *SMB Associates SW*. Sean's research interests include the professional development of teachers and Early Years practitioners, and the social and emotional development of children and young people with special educational needs and disabilities. Sean is married to Angela and lives in Devon, England.

ACKNOWLEDGEMENTS

I would like to offer my thanks to Jude Bowen who was encouraging from the outset and who allowed the idea for this text to take shape. My thanks must also go to Miriam Davey who, throughout the whole process, has been most supportive and encouraging. I would also like to acknowledge the support of my colleagues at the University of St Mark & St John who allowed me the time to complete this work and especially my colleagues in Room 144, Kathy Jarrett, Karen Russell, Anne Purdy and Sharon James who triggered so much of my thinking and supplied endless encouragement, coffee and biscuits. My final thanks go to my good friend and colleague Dr Colette Gray who so readily gave of her advice and time.

KEY TO ICONS

 Chapter Aims

 Summary

 Recommended Reading

INTRODUCTION

WHY IT IS IMPORTANT TO STUDY LEARNING IN YOUNG CHILDREN

From the moment of birth, children interact with those around them and through their interactions they learn about the worlds in which they live. Though much of their learning is incidental, much is also directed by adults. Parents, for example, can often be observed playing with their babies and in doing so they are directing the learning of their children in many different but purposeful ways. The environments within which infants commence their learning are also crucial and impact greatly upon future learning and development. Too many children, however, fail to learn effectively and as a result can make the transition to adulthood with low self esteem, poor qualifications and an internalized road map that will militate against them developing their abilities and reaching their potential. Our understanding of why children fail in their learning is, in effect, sadly lacking, as is, more worryingly perhaps, our understanding of the detrimental impact that failure in the school years can have on future development and the realization of life chances.

A number of significant milestones can be located within the history of education in the UK, which have come to define the nature of learning in children and young people, for example, the introduction of compulsory education, the 1944 Education Act, the raising of the school leaving age to 16, and the improved training of teachers and Early Years practitioners. Few milestones, however, can have had such an impact as the 1981 Education Act (DES, 1981), which arose from the highly influential and seminal Warnock Report (DES, 1978) in 1978 and which, in many respects, brought about the end of an outdated way of viewing the learning of countless numbers of children. It also initiated a new philosophy of hope, but most importantly it acted as a catalyst for not only addressing the complexity of learning but also seeking to understand how and why so many children and young people fail to learn and to realize their potential.

The Warnock Report had recommended that the 11 categories of 'handicap', which were used at that time as a means of identifying children with special educational needs should be done away with and replaced with the concept of 'need' gained as a result of careful assessment. The report also called for the recognition that special educational needs should be more usefully and accurately viewed along a continuum and that many children who were being educated in Special

Schools could, instead, be educated alongside their peers in mainstream schools. This was to have a monumental impact upon education and schooling, and the learning of tens of thousands of children.

The 1981 Education Act (subsequently repealed – 1.11.1996) took the recommendations of Warnock and placed many legal obligations upon schools and Local Education Authorities (LEAs). Perhaps, most importantly, the Act shifted the emphasis away from 'diagnosing' children in order to identify 'handicaps' or disabilities, to assessing their needs. This brought about an enormous philosophical shift in how we think about learning. In particular, thinking and practice began to move away from what is often referred to as the 'medical model' where disabilities were, at that time, believed to lie solely within the child and to be responsible for the child making poor progress in their learning. The legacy of this 'medical model' with its primary emphasis on diagnosing within child factors, however, continues today with some practitioners still insisting that special educational needs are located solely within the child to the exclusion of other environmental factors such as lack of provision and appropriate teaching.

In bringing about a shift in thinking, the 1981 Education Act, unlike previous education Acts, sought to legislate for learning not only in terms of within child factors but, more importantly, the degree of appropriate support offered to children at home and in school, and a recognition that assessment and intervention should take account of children's strengths and not just their weaknesses. The following chapters explore the nature of learning in children but in doing so acknowledge that our understanding of learning can be better realized if we also try to understand why children fail to learn.

THE ORGANIZATION OF THE BOOK

This text is organized in such a way that it begins by asking the reader to reflect upon the complexity of the term *learning* before inviting reflection upon what is meant by *childhood* and whether this time in the lives of individuals is a unanimously agreed construct. Through visiting the ideas of a number of key philosophers and theorists the readers' attention is then drawn to the importance of practitioners reflecting upon how they have arrived at the stage they are at, in terms of structuring the learning of children, and, more particularly, critically engaging with their own thinking and practice. Readers are then introduced in Chapter 2 to learning theories in action, in particular the work of the Behaviourists, namely Pavlov and Skinner, the Cognitive Constructivism of Jean Piaget, the Social Constructivism of Lev Vygotsky and the more recent Discovery and Learning Constructivism of Jerome Bruner, each of whom has greatly influenced our understanding of learning.

Chapter 3 then focuses on thinking and learning in the Early Years, in particular learning and brain development, and play and language as well as recent initiatives. Chapter 4 addresses learning within the family, with a particular emphasis being placed upon families in the 21st century before focusing upon learning and schooling in Chapter 5, which examines in much greater detail the function of schooling, the nature of curricula, transitions between stages of schooling and learning within a global context.

At the heart of learning lies the whole notion of intelligence and this is examined in Chapter 6, which, as well as exploring the nature of intelligence and the concept of an Intelligence Quotient (IQ), addresses the debates that exist around giftedness. This chapter also explores the work of two influential but controversial figures, Howard Gardner and Reuven Feuerstein who have challenged our perceptions of intellectual functioning, in particular the nature of ability and potential. Chapter 7 extends the ideas explored in Chapter 6 and examines those factors that facilitate emotionally intelligent learning as well as the barriers that distort and prevent it. Chapter 8 then addresses the area of additional needs and focuses on a number of conditions: dyslexia, dyspraxia, Asperger's Syndrome, Dyscalculia and ADHD, Conduct Disorders, and English as an Additional Language (EAL). Chapter 9 explores the notion of communities of learning, including learning and segregation and key economic and social factors that influence learning. The final chapter explores how learning might look in the future, in particular the changing constructions of childhood, creativity and success, and the increasing interest in the links between learning and entrepreneurship.

HOW READERS CAN GET THE BEST FROM THE BOOK

Though this text can be read from beginning to end it can also be used as a resource. Students, for example, who are exploring play and its relevance to learning, may wish to explore issues in Chapter 4 where the role of the family is discussed, in addition to looking at issues in Chapters 7 and 8, which examine the emotional development of children and the impact of special needs and/or disabilities. An initial reading of the text will allow the reader to locate particular areas of interest relevant to their own thinking and practice.

Readers are provided with a number of examples throughout the text, which are intended to act as reference points for their own experience as well as the ideas and issues raised within each chapter. A number of exercises are also offered throughout with the intention that readers should use these to reflect not only on the content of the book but also their own observations and interpretations of professional practice.

HOW PHILOSOPHY AND THEORY HAS INFLUENCED OUR UNDERSTANDING OF CHILDREN'S LEARNING

Current practice in schools and Early Years settings has been shaped by a number of key philosophers and theorists who, throughout previous generations, acted as major influences upon the thinking of their time. Their contributions have meant that we have become more informed about how children learn and how they might be best educated. Any student of philosophy will quickly realize, however, that philosophers and theorists offer us conflicting views of learning and frequently leave us with more questions than answers. Notwithstanding, philosophers and theorists do offer teachers and Early Years practitioners a means by which they can critically reflect upon their own practice and upon the thinking that underpins that practice. This said, it also needs to be emphasized that, whilst current practice in schools and Early Years settings has evolved over the generations it continues to evolve and will change radically over the next decades as new philosophies and theories emerge.

Understanding what is meant by philosophy and by theory is not a straightforward task and though the work of all practitioners is informed to varying degrees by different philosophies and theories, much confusion and uncertainty still surrounds the whole question of what exactly philosophy and theory is, and how our understanding of these can assist us in our thinking, reflection and practice. Let us begin with philosophy. In a rather light-hearted and tongue-in-cheek way the contemporary philosopher De Botton (2000, p. 205) cited the renowned German philosopher Friedrich Nietzsche who suggested that, '... the majority of philosophers have always been "cabbage-heads"'. De Botton (2000, p. 9), however, has also proposed that:

> ... philosophers not only show us what we have felt, they present our experiences more poignantly and intelligently than we have been able; they give shape to aspects of our lives that we recognise as our own, yet could never have understood so clearly on our own. They explain our condition to us.

What De Botton is indicating here is that whilst we all experience life and reflect upon our own actions and those of others, philosophers offer us the means by which we can engage more fully in understanding how we think and what we do.

A useful entry point in exploring philosophy and its link to learning can be found in the work of Gutek (1997, p. 2) who defined philosophy as follows:

> In its most general terms, philosophy is the human being's attempt to think speculatively, reflectively, and systematically about the universe and the human relationship to that universe.

Introduction   5

In relation to education, Gutek further commented:

> Over time, a number of systematic philosophies have been developed … that guide educational processes and give substance to various curricular designs … Two contemporary approaches to educational philosophy are Existentialism and Philosophical Analysis. The Existentialist is concerned about the rise of a mass society and bureaucratic schools that dehumanize students by reducing them to objects or functions. Philosophical Analysis seeks to establish meaning in the language that we use in both common and scientific discourse. (pp. 8–9)

At the time of writing this book, the world is experiencing major economic problems, with associated social difficulties. There are those who argue that childhood is disappearing, that education should be radically overhauled, and that what children learn in schools is not preparing them to meet the challenges of the adult world. To properly explore learning in children requires that we take time to inform ourselves of the ideas of those philosophers, theorists and practitioners who have informed thinking and practice in the past. We must also, however, explore the ideas of more contemporary thinkers and so we now turn to the work of some modern philosophers.

Take for example, the ideas of the French philosopher Michel Foucault (1926–1984) who has suggested that how we communicate with one another is governed by sets of rules that are not in the main within our frame of consciousness, but rather arise from those historical contexts within which we grow and develop. Foucault believed that the rules that govern how we view the world evolve through the passage of time. This way of thinking has significant implications for how we use language to converse, in particular our use of concepts, which Foucault argues are not consistent or permanent over time. His ideas can be located within those original ideas of the philosopher Immanuel Kant (1724–1804) who challenged us to ask not what the world is made of but rather why we view it in the way we do. So, why do we view the world as we do and why do we view learning and the way children are taught as we do? To address Foucault's thesis, therefore, should we view learning and childhood as concepts that never change over time? More importantly, perhaps, should we not question ourselves as to why we continue to view these concepts as we do and should we not seek to understand and, if necessary, challenge those historical rules that have come to govern popular thinking in these two areas?

Consider also the work of the French philosopher Jean-Francois Lyotard (1924–1998) who talked of the ways in which knowledge is understood and used and how this has changed over time. His ideas, therefore, lie at the heart of learning. Lyotard draws our attention to the fact that before World War II, the pursuit of knowledge was seen as central to the pursuit of truth. However, since then it has been increasingly argued that knowledge is something that can be financially acquired and then sold within a widening and diverse range of markets, what Lyotard refers to as the 'mercantilization' of knowledge. This notion is explored further in Chapter 4 where the ideas of the French philosopher Pierre Bourdieu are discussed in relation to knowledge as capital. Such a view, of course, has major implications for teachers, and parents, who daily observe children using mobile phones, social network sites and the popular media to access information. How many children in schools, for example, have their own PCs and mobile phones that are funded by their parents as a means of them being able to 'buy' information that is 'out there'?

Further to the above, now consider the ideas put forward by the German philosopher Jürgen Habermas (1929–) who has proposed that individuals persistently seek justification for why others act and behave as they do and why they themselves also act as they do. Put in more simple terms, we persist in justifying to others why we do what we do and why we behave as we do. Whilst Habermas acknowledges that modern societies are increasingly dependent upon technology he also proposes that individuals who make up these societies also have an internalized need to question and understand the traditions that define their societies. In addition, Habermas also acknowledges the potential problems that ownership of elements of the media such as newspapers by individuals or commercial groups can pose for individuals, arguably, turning many into unthinking consumers of trivia. Here again, the ideas posed by Habermas have enormous implications for how teachers perceive learning. For example, should teachers be more active in encouraging children to embrace traditions and should they work with parents to restrict access to the media and the trivia that many children pursue?

Now let us look at the ideas of Jacques Derrida (1930–2004) who is largely associated with the notion of 'Deconstruction'. Derrida has challenged us to think differently about how we read texts. For Derrida, texts contain what he refers to as 'Aporias', which, loosely translated from the original Greek, mean something along the lines of contradictions. The way in which we read texts, Derrida proposes, needs to be challenged and considered differently. In putting forward this view Derrida has coined the term 'Différance' as opposed to 'Difference' to account for how the meanings of words we read and speak become revised as we use them. For Derrida, 'Deconstruction' is a means by which we can explore how we think, and, in particular, how our thinking can be so typically characterized by 'binary' thinking. One example of this is where complex issues at the heart of the assessment of children in schools within the UK have become reduced to two simple opposing positions; *'yes, we should have exams or no, we shouldn't'*. Because of the simplicity of this emerging bipolar debate many underlying and important issues are failing to be considered and addressed. MacLure (2003, p. 44) comments:

> In order to criticize/analyse, which for Derrida is ultimately the same thing as to *read*, you need to get your fingers caught in the threads of the ceaselessly weaving and unravelling text.

When we give consideration to the work of Derrida it becomes clear that too many of the debates that have surrounded learning and that lie at the heart of how children should be best educated are of a binary nature. Take a further example, which surrounds the current debates in the UK in regard to the opening of Free Schools. Too few discussions in this area appear to be concerned with the actual nature of the learning in these schools and how their contribution to the social and emotional development of children with, for example, special educational needs, will be assessed and evaluated. Taking Derrida's thesis, it can be proposed that we need to carefully and purposefully deconstruct what we read and to understand that many of the conversations and thinking surrounding debates at the heart of how children learn are of a binary nature and as such may mask much more important issues.

Born in Frankfurt, Germany Theodor Adorno (1903–1969), who became one of the group known as the Frankfurt School, sought to explore the growth of capitalism, and in particular the effect of the popular media, namely television. Like Lyotard and Habermas he proposed that aspects of the popular media erode intellectual functioning and the sensitivity of individuals. A consequence of this has been the lessening in individuals' capacity to think through the options that face them daily and which underpin morality. Individuals, he suggests, make choices when they prefer to watch elements of television that are mindless and that do not offer them any rational advance in thinking and sensitivity. These decisions are, he suggests, of a moral nature. The logic would be that they adversely affect society as a whole. Adorno counters the view that we can separate emotion from our ability to make judgments based solely on intellectual reasoning. He sees the sciences as playing a central role in the lessening of emotions as they aim to separate emotion from intellectual functioning. In this way, he argues, they are, in a sense, dehumanizing.

More recently the philosopher Hans-Georg Gadamer (1900–2002) has emphasized the importance that we must give to history and culture and how our perceptions are governed by these. Gadamer argued that it is not wholly possible to be completely objective in our attempts to understand the world around us. All of us have our thinking affected by the histories and cultures within which we grow up and by those elements of bias that impact upon how we see things and understand ourselves and others. Gadamer's philosophical approach lies within the field of 'hermeneutics' or the art of interpretation.

Before commencing the next chapter in which key philosophers and theorists are introduced, consideration needs to be given to the notion of 'theory'. This has been well managed by Newby (2010, p. 71) who has drawn an important distinction between *Education Theory*, which deals with such areas as learning and child development, schooling and curricula, and *Research Theory*, which specifies procedures. Newby has offered the following:

> In summary, education theory shapes our understanding and gives us choice when making educational decisions. Research theory is a rule book whose legitimacy stems from principles accepted by the academic community and whose coherence owes as much to custom and practice as to any overarching theorisation. (2010, p. 71)

Newby goes on to indicate two types of Education Theory – Normative Theory, which explains, '… how things *could or should be organised or what goals should be achieved* and Explanatory Theory, which, "… explains *how things work*"'. With the second, for example, the Behaviourists sought to explain learning by generating a theory built upon their assertion that all behaviour is learned. Newby emphasized that Education Theory plays a crucial role as it provides a framework through which we can develop our understanding and knowledge of particular things. In seeking to understand Education Theory Jarvis (2005, p. 204) has offered us a most useful starting point, but in doing so he has also raised what readers might consider to be a rather worrying assertion:

> Education differs from comparable professions, such as medicine and psychology, in that although there is a thriving field of professional research, it takes place largely in isolation from professional practice. It is a rare doctor that does not peruse the medical research literature at least occasionally, and it would be unusual for a psychologist not to at least dip into current psychological literature – this is a requirement if they have chartered status … but teachers largely ignore education research.

REFERENCES

DeBotton, A. (2000) *The Consolations of Philosophy*. London: Hamish Hamilton.
Department of Education and Science (DES) (1978) *Special Educational Need* (Report of the Warnock Committee). London: HMSO.
Department of Education and Science (DES) (1981) *Education Act*. London: HMSO.
Jarvis, M. (2005) *The Psychology of Effective Learning and Teaching*. Cheltenham: Nelson Thornes.
Newby, P. (2010) *Research Methods for Education*. Harlow: Pearson Education.
MacLure, M. (2003) *Discourse in Educational and Social Research*. Maidenhead: Open University Press.

1

WHAT IS LEARNING?

This chapter aims to:

- highlight the importance of practitioners critically engaging with ideas and changing philosophical perspectives that frame their practice
- explore the influence that a number of celebrated philosophers, theorists and practitioners have had on our understanding of learning and how different approaches over the generations have contributed to current practice
- increase awareness of the need for practitioners working with children to have a clear understanding of the terms *learning* and *childhood* and in doing so explore how this can inform their practice.

INTRODUCTION

To critically engage in developing a fuller understanding of learning in the 21st century not only requires knowledge of the historical and cultural influences that have taken us to where we are today but also a recognition that current thinking and practice will change radically in the future. It is, perhaps more than ever before, the case that practitioners working with children need to critically evaluate their own thinking and practice and recognize that what they do is not only bound in time but has its origins in the ideas of a number of key historical thinkers who have laid down the foundations of current practice. Having greater knowledge and understanding of their ideas will assist greatly with the process of critical reflection and evaluation.

This chapter introduces a number of celebrated philosophers and theorists whose ideas, though located in their own times, have influenced the course of our thinking with regard to how children learn. To begin, however, we must try and conceptualize what we mean by the term *learning* in preparation for a fuller analysis of this concept in Chapter 2. We start with a rather challenging proposition offered by Howe (1999, p. 2) some two decades ago that, 'The fact that the single term "learning" refers to a variety of mental events makes it impossible to have a single precise definition of learning'.

WHAT DO WE MEAN BY LEARNING?

It is important at the outset to emphasize that learning is not simply the act of acquiring new information and knowledge within the classroom. The concept of learning is far more complex, and readers will be invited throughout this text to consider learning not only in terms of its complexity but also in terms of the multitude of views that exist in regard to what the term actually means. Jarvis (2005, pp. 2–3), for example, has emphasized the complexity of this term as follows:

> ... when we pause and try to define learning in depth, we cannot help but be struck by the awesome breadth and complexity of the concept ... Does learning take place within an individual or is it an interpersonal process? Should we think of it as a set of cognitive mechanisms or rather as an emotional, social and motivational experience ... What should be the focus of learning, facts or skills?

It can be suggested that a key difficulty in defining learning is that much of the research in this area has been undertaken within the field of psychology, which, as Jarvis (2005, p. 3) points out:

> ... is not a unified body of knowledge and understanding but instead depends on a number of alternative theoretical perspectives or paradigms. Each psychological paradigm has the potential to offer a different vision of the nature of the learner ...

Students attempting to explore the nature of learning can, therefore, be left with more questions than answers about this very complex and challenging construct. However, this is not a bad thing.

In approaching our understanding of learning a useful starting point can be found in the work of Smith et al. (2003, p. 34) who have defined learning in the following way:

> Learning refers to the influence of specific environmental information on behaviour. Within a wide range of variation, the way an animal behaves depends on what it learns from the environment. Thus, individuals of a species may differ considerably in their learnt behaviour patterns.

It is of particular note that Smith et al. use the words 'environmental' and 'species' in their definition. Also of note is the fact that they use the terms 'behaviour' and 'behaviour patterns'. They also appear to liken humans to animals in their use of the term 'species'.

Employing these terms to refer to humans, and to learning, is very much in keeping with the *Behaviourist* tradition discussed later in Chapter 2 in that it places particular emphasis upon the notion that changes in behaviour are central to how we understand and define learning. More importantly, perhaps, Smith et al.'s definition directs us towards the notion proposed by the *Behaviourists* that learning can be adequately explained purely in terms of stimuli and responses, reinforcement and observable behaviours.

In an attempt to offer greater clarity regarding what we mean by the term learning, Fontana (1995, p. 145) has suggested that we give consideration to the notion of 'descriptions' of learning. In doing so, he offers an important distinction between the Behaviourist tradition (more directly, the notion of *Operant Conditioning*) and the Cognitive tradition (more directly, the notion of *Instrumental Conceptualism*):

> This somewhat intimidating title (Instrumental Conceptualism) is used by Bruner to define one of the most coherent and consistent cognitive descriptions of learning and still one of the most useful for teachers … Learning … is not something that happens to individuals, as in the operant conditioning model, but something which they themselves make happen by the manner in which they handle incoming information and put it to use.

This distinction is vital and introduces us to the notion that learning in children is an active process. Having greater clarity in our understanding and descriptions of learning, therefore, is very important, and particularly in relation to how we understand those underlying cognitive processes that drive behaviour. Unlike *Behaviourist* theories, *Constructivist* theories of learning such as those of Piaget and Vygotsky (discussed in Chapter 2) view learning in terms of the child constructing meaning through experiences gained from interacting with their environments. In particular, they see learning as an active, dynamic process in which the child generates new understanding through linking their existing knowledge to new incoming information.

We now turn our attention to childhood when the foundations of learning are laid down, and when most individuals experience the majority of their formal education. However, whilst the term *childhood* appears at face value to be one that is popularly agreed and understood, it nevertheless poses major difficulties for those trying to define it. These difficulties have been acknowledged for generations, as witnessed, for example, by the French philosopher Jean-Jacques Rousseau who some two centuries ago proposed that, 'Childhood is unknown. Starting from the false idea one has of it, the further one goes, the more one loses one's way…' (Rousseau, 1911).

WHAT DO WE MEAN BY CHILDHOOD?

Definitions of childhood abound. Jenks (1996, p. 6), for example, has described childhood as a, '… community that at some time has everybody as its member'.

Less than 10 years before, Article 1 of the 1989 Convention on the Rights of the Child had stated that, 'A child means every human being below the age of eighteen years unless under the law applicable to the child, majority is attained earlier' (UNCRC, 1989, p. 314). A decade later James and Prout (1997, p. 245) suggested that, 'In everyday life age is used as a dividing line to legally exclude children from all kinds of "adult" spaces', whilst Buckingham (2000, p. 6) offered the following:

> The meaning of 'childhood' is subject to a constant process of struggle and negotiation, both in public discourse (for example, in the media, in the academy or in social policy) and in interpersonal relationships, among peers and in the family.

Others, such as Boyden (1997, p. 190) have viewed childhood as a stage and suggest that children are '… demarcated from adults by biological or psychological factors rather than social characteristics'. This notion of stages can be clearly located in the work of the theorist Jean Piaget (discussed later in Chapter 2), but viewing childhood as a stage brings problems and suggests, for example, that in doing so we may consciously or otherwise define this time in the lives of individuals in terms of dependency and lack of maturity, or, as Archard (1993, p. 30) has proposed, a '… state of incompetence relative to adulthood'. Any idea of childhood as a state of incompetence relative to adulthood, however, requires closer examination. One particular problem with this lies in the fact that we may, mistakenly, lower our expectations of children's abilities, and more importantly, their potential. Children develop differently and at vastly different rates, with some even demonstrating very sophisticated thinking and mature behaviours well beyond their age. Advocates of the notion of stages such as James and Prout (1997, p. 10) view childhood as biologically based and, therefore, '… essentially an evolutionary model', whereby, '… the child developing into an adult represents a progression from simplicity to complexity of thought, from irrationality to rational behaviour'.

It is certainly clear that the nature of childhood is changing dramatically with increased accessibility to Information and Communications Technology (ICT) and the media, and a substantial growth in materialism. Having established a starting position with regard to the complex nature of *childhood* as well as that of *learning* we now turn to the ideas of key thinkers who have influenced practice over the generations and who continue to do so. In particular, we focus predominantly upon a number of figures whose contributions to our understanding of learning have led to a much greater appreciation of those most important features of cognition and social and emotional development. We now begin three centuries ago with one of the major thinkers of his time whose ideas continue to inform practice in the 21st century.

Exercise

Consider the benefits to teachers and Early Years practitioners of having a clearer under-standing of the concepts of *learning* and *childhood*. Why might this be especially important in the 21st century?

KEY PHILOSOPHICAL AND THEORETICAL INFLUENCES IN OUR UNDERSTANDING AND PRACTICE WITHIN THE FIELD OF LEARNING

Early Influences

John Locke (1632–1704)

Born into a world characterized by superstition, ignorance and religious intolerance, John Locke is considered to be one of our most enlightened thinkers. Locke believed that our knowledge and understanding of the world is achieved through sensory experience. In taking such a view Locke can be described as belonging to those philosophers who have come to be known as the *Empiricists*. Central to *Empiricism* was the idea of 'empirical thinking', which lies at the very heart of the 'sciences' and in which we observe, gather and quantify data. Locke took the view that individuals should apply reason to their interpretations of the world in which they live and the events that they encounter and should resist accepting what they were told by authorities without question. In many respects he was reacting to the beliefs of the time, many of which were grounded in superstition and fear. Locke believed that when we are born we begin our lives as if we were a 'blank slate' (often referred to in the literature as Tabula Rasa), and it is upon this blank slate that our life experiences, gained through our senses, are written. Locke saw this process as being at the very core of learning and the manner in which all individuals acquired knowledge. Locke believed that our knowledge of the world and how we understand our world is achieved through sensory experience.

During the years between the first and second World Wars, *Empiricism* or the notion that we come to understand our experiences through observation and subsequent analysis of our behaviours, which result from our responses to external sensory stimuli, grew. This view developed particularly within the discipline of Psychology and contributed greatly to what became known as the *Behaviourist* tradition (see Chapter 2). In effect, Empiricism offered psychology, and in particular *Behaviourism*, a methodology at the heart of which was the observation, recording and measurement of behaviours (Gross, 1992; Smith et al., 2003). It is important to note that the Empiricist view is different from the Nativist view, which asserts that we inherit abilities.

Locke saw the primary purpose of education as being that of instilling within children a real and important understanding of the need for virtue, a consideration that currently lies at the heart of much of the thinking around social reform in the UK. Locke was also far ahead of his time in that he saw that learning should be enjoyable and that children benefit from being encouraged to learn how to learn. He also recognized the important role that language played in learning. Indeed, it can be said with confidence that Locke set out many of the basic foundations upon which our current understanding of learning has been built. Indeed, others such as Pestalozzi, Froebel, Dewey and Montessori who followed Locke shared much of his thinking.

We now turn to the work of another influential philosopher who, in challenging the thinking of his time, saw the importance of acknowledging the individuality of children and the potential they bring with them when they are born. In doing so, he not only advanced our understanding of learning but introduced us to new ways of conceptualizing childhood as that most important of times when individuals grow and develop socially and emotionally.

Jean-Jacques Rousseau (1712–1778)

Despite being born generations ago, Rousseau's ideas still hold credence today. The dominant thinking of the time in which Rousseau lived was that we are born with 'original sin' and a primary function of education was to purge children of this sin and the associated guilt that went with it. In contrast, however, Rousseau believed that we are all born 'good' and that we inherit much of what makes up our individual potential. Nevertheless, he recognized that society also played an important role in influencing children as they develop. In particular, he recognized the potential harm that aspects of society could have on children in terms of perverting their thinking and behaviours.

Rousseau set out his ideas on education in his celebrated book *Emile* (1911) in which he introduces us to the life of a young boy named Emile as he progresses from infancy through to adulthood. At the time of writing *Emile* it was popularly believed that children were born with internal drives, needs and impulses, which if not addressed could lead to 'wickedness'. For Rousseau, a central feature of education, and especially the role of a child's tutor was to channel these drives, needs and impulses in a positive and purposeful way. He believed that the process of formal education should endeavour to follow the natural growth of the child as opposed to demands made by society. Rousseau viewed the role of the tutor, therefore, as extremely important and central to the process of developing positive and effective learning environments, particularly where the child is being introduced to new learning. It was through this process that Rousseau believed children came to know and understand the world within which they live. More specifically, he believed that through this process children internalize greater understandings of such vital constructs as, respect for themselves and others, right and wrong, consequences of their actions, honesty and dishonesty, and humility and empathy. For Rousseau, the core function of education was, *'l'art de former des hommes'* (the art of forming men) and he viewed education as the mechanism through which children should not only be given information, but a means by which they could come to benefit society through, for example, learning how to positively and purposefully relate to one another.

Although writing some three hundred years ago, Rousseau recognized how children and young people pass through stages and in doing so recognized that learning is developmental. For Rousseau, the first stage that children went through was from birth to 12 when children were predominantly influenced by impulses and by their emotions. The second stage was up to the age of 16 when, Rousseau believed, reason took over and began to replace actions led by emotions and impulses. Following this second stage, the young person then moves into adulthood. It should be recognized that Rousseau's emphasis upon the innate development of human nature formed the philosophical basis for the views of future thinkers and practitioners, perhaps most notably, those of Pestalozzi.

We now turn to the work of one of the great giants of learning, many of whose ideas remain with us today to such an extent that they are experiencing a significant revival. Whilst most of Froebel's work pertained to early childhood, he nevertheless contributed significantly, as did Rousseau, to our understanding of how early learning prepares us for later development and eventually adulthood.

Friedrich Froebel (1782–1852)

It can be said with confidence that Froebel has had an enormous influence upon the practice of teachers and Early Years practitioners over the centuries and continues to do so, even today. Indeed, Miller and Pound (2011, p. 64) recently commented:

> Froebelians continue to influence official documents in a behind-the-scenes way ... from the Hadow report (1933) onwards, through to Plowden (Central Advisory Council for Education, 1967); *Starting with Quality* (DES, 1990); *Curriculum Guidance for the Foundation Stage* (DfEE, 2000); *Birth to Three Matters* (DfES, 2002); *The Early Years Foundation Stage* (CCSF, 2008).

Miller and Pound (2011, p. 64) have drawn further attention to the recent emergence of Froebel training, which they report as follows:

> ... the Froebel Certificates have recently been re-established at Roehampton University and are developing in Edinburgh ... the next generation of Froebelians is emerging, trained, in the practical apprenticeship way, in reflective practice through in-service training.

Practitioners owe much to Froebel's emphasis upon the importance of play and its role in education as well as social and emotional development. Whilst all practitioners now recognize the value of play this was not always the case, and certainly was not the case when Froebel was developing his philosophy of education and his beliefs around the value of play. Froebel felt strongly that young children could express themselves through play and the extent of his contribution to our understanding of play is today widely recognized. Tizard and Hughes (1984, p. 4), for example, commented as follows:

> The value of learning through play was first put forward by the German educationalist Friedrich Froebel … The kindergarten and nursery school movement which developed from his writings freed young children from the tyranny of sitting in rows chanting and writing ABC.

In essence, Froebel saw play as being central to children's learning and development. Because of his strongly held views about the importance of play he created a range of special educational *materials* that could be employed by practitioners working with young children. These *materials* or *gifts*, as Froebel called them, included, for example, a range of shaped objects such as squared blocks and spheres, which could be used with the purpose of stimulating thinking and learning. Froebel also believed that being active was central to children's learning and development and because of this he developed a number of what he referred to as *occupations*. In addition, Froebel recognized the important role that music could play in the learning of young children and, in particular, the value of children singing whilst they were playing.

Froebel has left us with not just an important way of thinking about education but also a legacy of how to work, in practice, with children. In many respects Froebel set the scene for those who followed to explore further, and in depth, the inner lives of children and, importantly, those emotional, creative and cognitive aspects that underpin learning and inform education and schooling. One such follower whose ideas, like those of Froebel, continue to influence practice today is Rudolf Steiner.

Rudolf Steiner (1861–1925)

The influence that Rudolf Steiner has had on our understanding of learning and teaching has been substantial. This said, there are those who hold a less than favourable view of him and his work has caused, and continues to cause, controversy amongst some practitioners. He has even been referred to as, 'a maverick Austrian scientist' (Edwards, 2002, p. 2). Currently, there are more than a thousand Steiner schools, and over two thousand Early Years establishments around the world. Despite the original philosophy remaining constant, however, many of these schools have developed in different ways.

A central feature of the Steiner-Waldorf tradition is the belief that young children learn by imitation. Steiner founded his first school in the city of Stuttgart after being invited to do so by a leading industrialist, Waldorf Astoria, who at the time was the owner of a very large cigarette factory. The purpose of the school was to educate the children of the workers in the factory hence the legacy by which Steiner schools came also to be known as *Steiner-Waldorf* schools. A central feature of the Steiner-Waldorf tradition is the belief that young children learn by imitation. Miller and Pound (2011, p. 88) describe this perception held by Steiner-Waldorf practitioners thus, '… and whatever is happening around the child becomes part of that child as she absorbs not only the outer actions of the adults, but the inner attitudes too'. The nature of the relationship between the practitioner and the child is of the utmost importance and central to the learning of the child. Miller and Pound (2011, p. 92) have commented as follows:

> Steiner practitioners observe that young children are nurtured by the security of rhythm and repetition – within which their inherent skills and abilities can flourish … Having well thought through and repeated routines build habits that are useful (properly washed hands), respectful (creating a peaceful mood at the table) and comforting ('this is how we always do it here').

Steiner saw the function of education as that of responding to the changing needs of children and by this he not only meant their physical needs but also their intellectual needs and, perhaps most notably, their emotional needs. Underpinning the Steiner philosophy are the following key points. In the first years of a child's education up to the age of seven significant emphasis is placed upon the importance of play, drawing and art, and the natural world of the children, with important links made between science and art. Before the age of seven children are not formally taught reading, the reasoning being that children will come to read naturally if they have developed socially and emotionally. This is also the case with mathematics, with children being introduced to formal mathematics at a later stage than children in state schools. The Steiner philosophy also advocates that children are taught to write before being taught to read.

Children in Steiner-Waldorf schools are encouraged to sing every day and also to learn to play musical instruments. In addition, children are introduced to the practice of creating their own lesson books in which they are encouraged to write and illustrate. Assessment of children takes place mainly through the teacher's observation, with a particular focus being given to the children's social and emotional development. Where possible each child keeps the same teacher throughout their primary schooling until they are due to transfer to the post-primary stage. The thinking behind this is that children come to value the importance of relationships, and, in addition, gain from the knowledge that the teacher has of their social and emotional development.

A further characteristic of Steiner schools is that teachers employ a 'narrative' approach to learning. In doing so, they place significant emphasis on listening, with the children being encouraged to internally represent characters. In this way they develop their imagination. Once introduced to material by way of a story the children may then be encouraged and supported in revisiting the content on the next day and retelling it. Here, the aim is to improve spoken language and, perhaps more interestingly, memory. As this process of listening and recalling are worked through children are then supported in writing down their stories.

Observation plays an enormous part in the practice of teachers in Steiner-Waldorf schools. Nicol (2010, pp. 85–6) has indicated some of the key principles that inform the practice of the kindergarten teacher working in Steiner-Waldorf schools who:

> … understands that learning and development is of course a continuous process, and may wait patiently to watch these unfold … uses insight rather than measurement: the question is: 'Who are you?' rather than 'What can you do?' … respects and refrains from hurrying the child's natural speed of development … meditates on the child, holds the child in his/her thoughts (a process termed as 'inner work') … is aware of and engaged in his or her own self-development.

It is worth considering some of these key principles within the context of current practice in primary schools and Early Years settings. Steiner-Waldorf schools are currently undergoing something of an expansion in the UK. In a recent article (2012) in the UK daily newspaper *The Guardian*, the journalist Jeevan Vasagar reported that:

> In England, Steiner education is on the brink of a significant expansion. At present, the academy in Herefordshire is the only one to receive state funding out of 34 Steiner schools in the UK. In September, it will be joined by a state-funded 'free school' in Frome, Somerset. Two more Steiner schools – in Leeds and Exeter – are applying for state funding under the free schools programme.

We now turn to the work of the McMillan sisters who were instrumental in addressing some of the major social injustices of their time. In looking at the ideas of these two sisters it is worth reflecting upon the view that much-needed social reform is still required to ensure that children are not growing up in poverty, that children are not facing neglect and abuse and that they all have access to learning opportunities that will allow them to properly develop their potential and abilities.

Rachel (1859–1917) and Margaret (1860–1931) McMillan

To properly understand the contribution that Rachel and Margaret McMillan have made to our understanding of learning requires that we also understand the social world within which they lived and worked. London at this time was a city of marked contrasts between the rich and poor. It was a time of much-needed social reform and like many other industrialized cities of the time was characterized not only by extreme wealth and privilege but also by extreme poverty, poor sanitation, high mortality rates in childhood, appalling housing, and some of the worst slums in Europe. Between 1831 and 1866 around 150,000 individuals died of cholera. Londoners living during the 1840s could have expected a life span of 30 to 40 years, whilst by 1911 they could, on average, expect to live until they were in their fifties (Hall, 1998, p. 695). It has been estimated (Horn, 1997) that between 1900 and 1950 there existed within London around 30,000 homeless children who lived on the streets. These children were typically, undernourished, uneducated and unsupervised. It was not until 1899, 10 years after Rachel had moved to London to be with her sister and the first murders of the infamous Jack the Ripper had been reported, that school attendance was made compulsory.

After a sustained campaign the sisters were successful in their quest to have free school meals for children introduced, which followed the passing of the Provision of School Meals Act in 1906. It is interesting that this is now a topic under discussion by many local authorities in the UK. The sisters were also highly influential in having the government introduce medical inspections for children in schools, with the first clinic opening its doors in 1908. Rachel and Margaret were particularly outspoken in their insistence that the first years of a child's life were of the utmost importance and, true to their belief, they founded what was to become the *Nursery Movement*. As part of their determination to alter for the better the lives of children, they emphasized the benefits of open-air learning. In many respects this was in response to the overcrowded and filthy living conditions experienced by the thousands of children growing up and being educated in cities.

In 1904 Margaret published *Education through the Imagination*, and in her later years played an influential role in the training of teachers. She went on to found the Rachel McMillan College in 1930 for this purpose and as a means of improving the training of those wishing to work with young children in her nurseries. Like Margaret, Rachel believed that involving children in nurseries with caring for animals and plants was an important means of developing within them the important values of caring not only for themselves but also for others.

We now turn to the work of more modern philosophers and theorists who have directly influenced practice today and how we view learning in the 21st century. One such theorist is the Russian born physiologist Ivan Pavlov, who in 1904 was awarded the Nobel Prize for his work on the underlying mechanisms in the digestive system in mammals.

Exercise

Identify the contributions that early philosophers have made to our understanding of how children learn and consider whether aspects of their thinking continue to have any relevance for practitioners in the 21st century.

Modern Influences

Ivan Pavlov (1849–1936)

No student of learning can escape the name of Ivan Pavlov. A Russian physiologist born in 1849, Pavlov was the eldest of 11 children, six of whom had died during childhood. It is of particular note that despite being a physiologist Pavlov indirectly gave to the field of learning one of its most basic cornerstones, his work on conditioned reflexes, which led to *Classical Conditioning*, and which has been a major influence in the field of psychology and especially learning.

Although Pavlov is not commonly viewed as a philosopher or theorist in the field of education, his ideas and experimental observations have, nonetheless, provided us with a number of key insights into how individuals learn. Indeed, it would be fair to say that all teachers and Early Years practitioners employ, wittingly or otherwise, in their everyday practice principles initially determined by Pavlov. The principles on which he developed his thinking around learning remain relevant today and are much in use by practitioners working with children. In many respects his contribution to our understanding of learning has been considerable. Pavlov's work is discussed more fully in the following chapter.

At around the same time that Pavlov was developing his thinking in the area of conditioning a young American was developing his ideas on education and, particularly, schooling; these ideas were to influence the practice of countless teachers across the Western world. His name was John Dewey.

John Dewey (1859–1952)

Dewey's views on learning and education continue to influence thinking today though they remain highly controversial. The extent of the controversies surrounding Dewey's ideas can be seen in the following two quotations offered by the British philosopher Richard Pring (2007, p. 3):

> … when I came to Oxford in 1989, I was seated at dinner next to Lord Keith Joseph, who had been Secretary of State for Education under Prime Minister Margaret Thatcher. He accused me of being responsible for all the problems in our schools – because I had introduced teachers to John Dewey.

Here, he quotes the American philosopher Nel Noddings (2005) as follows:

> …not only has he [Dewey]: been hailed as the savior of American education by those who welcome greater involvement of students in their own planning and activity [but also] he has been called 'worse than Hitler' by some who felt that he infected schools with epistemological and moral relativism and substituted socialization for true education. (p. 3)

Dewey is frequently associated with the concept of *Child-Centred Education*. However, it is a common misconception that Dewey advocated the notion of free and pupil-led education. In fact, Dewey saw structure as being important in learning. He did, however, also view the experiences of children as being central to their education and schooling. Dewey argued that children required direction and support with their learning in order to develop their potential and gain the maximum benefit from their learning experiences. Dewey persisted in his view that educators should take full account of the individuality and uniqueness of each child and though this emphasis upon individuality appears obvious now, at the time that Dewey was formulating his views this was far from the reality experienced by many children. In fact, Dewey believed that the individuality and uniqueness of individuals were both genetic and experiential.

Dewey held the view that children need to engage with the curriculum offered in schools in individualized and different ways, and he believed that school curricula should allow for, and embrace, such differences. Related to this was Dewey's belief that education had a wider purpose, that of preparing young people for becoming effective members of their communities and the wider societies in which they lived. To this end, Dewey viewed education and democracy as being intrinsically linked.

At the heart of Dewey's philosophy of education lay his beliefs, derived in large part from his 'Laboratory School', which he had opened in the city of Chicago in 1896 and which admitted children from nursery stage through to their twelfth grade. It was in this school that Dewey had subjected his own ideas about education and learning to scrutiny. The philosopher Richard Pring (2007, p. 16) has commented as follows:

> … behind Dewey's experimental school was a particular view of the normal young learner: someone who is curious and interested, but whose curiosity and interests had been sapped by modes of learning which took no account of that *interest* in learning …

At the centre of Dewey's philosophy of education also lay two further important ideas. Firstly, that schools were communities and should be viewed accordingly, and, secondly, adults involved in teaching children and young people cannot change those experiences that children and young people have already had. Educators, he argued, should involve themselves with the present and with the future, for it is in these two areas that they can have purposeful and meaningful influence. This, of course, is not to say that educators should disregard children's past experiences. In fact they can, Dewey believed, learn from these and take from their own learning of children's experiences ways in which they can work to promote positive change in their pupils. Pring (2007, pp. 15–17) has offered an overview of Dewey's views as follows:

First, the school should be an extension of the home and the community ... Second ... the school should value manual and practical activity ... Third, the interests of young people were to be treated as of importance in their own right, not simply as something that can be harnessed to the aims of the teacher for the purpose of motivating them to do things that they are not really interested in ... Fourth ... Their [school subjects] value lies in their useful-ness... Fifth, a young person whose interests are taken seriously and whose teacher seeks to develop those interests ... will be disciplined by the pursuit of those interests – making the regime of externally imposed discipline irrelevant.

Taking Dewey's views into account then it can be argued that young children's past experiences significantly affect how they experience events in the future and how they learn. Dewey proposed that it is what each individual draws from their experience that is important. Individuals experience events in different ways; what is of benefit for one individual may not be of benefit for another.

We now turn to one of the recognized giants in the field of learning, and especially the learning and social development of young children. Considered to be a key figure even today, elements of her thinking and practice can be observed almost everywhere.

Maria Montessori (1870–1952)

The contribution that Maria Montessori has made to our understanding of learning and child development is universally recognized. Maria was especially interested in understanding the needs of children with learning difficulties and, indeed, she had considerable success with many such children who, at the time, were fre-quently dismissed as being uneducable. Many of her original ideas on learning and child development remain with us today and her influence is everywhere. In fact, Miller and Pound (2011) have drawn attention to the fact that advocates of the Montessori principles have recently worked in tandem with the Office for Standards in Education (Ofsted) in the UK and with local authorities to encourage understanding and the use of approaches based upon Montessori principles as a means of improving educational experiences of young children today. Indeed, it is recognized that these principles have led to effective practice:

In 2008, 88% of Montessori nurseries were considered by Ofsted to be 'outstanding' or 'good'. Concerns remain that local authorities have the power to oversee EYFS (Early Years Foundation Stage) provision and to monitor its quality when assessing nurseries' eligibility for state funding for 3- and 4-year-olds' places. Interpretations of the EYFS can vary from one local authority to another and ... can easily ignore the particular nature of Montessori education. (Miller and Pound, 2011, p. 81)

Maria Montessori is recognized particularly as being a major and influential fig-ure in the field of early education. Maria saw learning not so much as a task but a

journey and she viewed development in young children as being guided by directives that are already within the child's nature (Gray and MacBlain, 2012).
Montessori teachers, therefore, place great emphasis upon the environment in
which children are learning and view themselves as guardians of these environments. By changing the environment Montessori teachers enable the children in
their care to develop at their own individual and natural pace. Because of this,
creativity is given time and space to flourish and thus supports the learning of the
children. She also saw music as an important aspect of children's development.

Montessori introduced us to the idea of the *Casa dei Bambini*, or *Children's House*
in which teachers created environments that stimulated the children and where
they were free to learn and to develop their learning naturally and in an individualized manner. Indeed, Montessori went as far as designing special furniture for
these *Children's Houses*. She also strongly advocated the importance of children
learning through their senses and believed that central to the process of education
was the need for children to take greater responsibility for their own learning.

At the core of the Montessori Method is the idea of 'Planes', or Stages, that children pass through as they learn. It is whilst moving through the first 'plane' that
children experience significant change in their physical, and social and emotional
development. During this first stage the infant takes their first steps, uses their first
words, and begins to engage socially with those around them. By the time they are
ready to progress to the next Plane or Stage they are running, jumping, climbing
and having conversations with others. In effect, they are employing quite complex
and sophisticated language. They are also starting to comprehend the feelings of
others and can adapt their own behaviours and actions to respond to the feelings
of others. They are also learning to make friendships and adapt to meet the complexities of those social interactions they encounter outside of their family. It is also
during the first Plane that children develop their abilities with memory and with
expressive and receptive language. Montessori identified 11 'sensitive' periods
within the first stage or Plane: Movement; Language; Small Objects; Order; Music;
Grace and Courtesy; Refinement of the Senses; Writing Fascination; Reading; Spatial
Relationships; and Mathematics (see Gray and MacBlain, 2012, pp. 152–5 for further discussion of these).

Despite the gains practitioners have made from the ideas put forward and prac-
tised by Maria Montessori, there are also those who have raised some criticisms.
For example, the author John Holt (see later in this chapter) commented in his celebrated text, *How Children Learn* (1967, p. 243) as follows:

> Maria Montessori and her followers did not approve of children fantasizing … Of course
> some Montessori people disagree with this … To whatever extent the Montessori schools
> may still think and act this way, I think they are much mistaken.

Many of the ideas of Montessori and her predecessors stand in marked contrast to those of the next celebrated educationalist whose views on learning, though representative of some areas of the popular psychology of his time were, and still are, deeply controversial. Though controversial, however, they have influenced the thinking and practice of many teachers and parents who have wished for a 'freer' education and 'less repressive' schooling for children.

Alexander Sutherland Neill (1883–1973)

A.S. Neill is perhaps best known for his radical views on the teaching and learning of children and for setting up his quite unique school, Summerhill. Neill's work came about at a time of tremendous social change during the post-war years and especially the 'sixties' when many aspects of the establishment were being challenged by young people. It was one of those periods in history when new ideas and new thinking were to be found everywhere.

Neill's ideas on education and learning can be located within the field of *Psychodynamics* and the sometimes controversial legacies of Freud and *Psychoanalysis*, which enjoyed a high degree of popularity at the time. Indeed, much of the thinking at this time in relation to child development was directly influenced by the legacy of Freud's philosophy. Miller and Pound (2011, p. 22) have commented on how the legacy of ideas offered by Psychoanalysts, '… are embedded in the culture of the industrially developed world, including in relation to the development and care of children'.

The influence of psychoanalysis upon Neill's thinking and philosophy of education can be seen in the following excerpt from his now celebrated book *Summerhill*:

> Freud showed that every neurosis is founded on sex repression. I said, 'I'll have a school in which there will be no sex repression'. Freud said that the unconscious was infinitely more important and more powerful than the conscious. I said, 'In my school we won't censure, punish, moralize. We will allow every child to live according to his deep impulses'. (1968, p. 20)

Neill offered the following view of children's development, '… a child is innately wise and realistic. If left to himself without adult suggestion of any kind, he will develop as far as he is capable of developing …' (1968, p. 20) and in regard to the experience of children at his own school Summerhill, which he ran according to his own philosophy of education and learning he wrote:

> Summerhill is a place in which people who have the innate ability and wish to be scholars will be scholars; while those who are only fit to sweep the streets will sweep the streets. But we have not produced a street cleaner so far … lessons are optional … Children can go to them or stay away from them – for years if they want to. (1968, p. 20)

Whilst Neill's views on education are of great interest, many of these, nevertheless, remain controversial. It is an interesting fact that his school remains open today.

Having explored the ideas of Neill whose philosophy of education lies very much within the psychodynamic field of psychology, we now turn to a major figure whose ideas lie firmly within the *Behaviourist* tradition in psychology. Indeed, he is considered to be one of the founding fathers of *Behaviourism*.

Burrhus Frederic Skinner (1904–1990)

B.F. Skinner was an American psychologist whose name is associated with that tradition in psychology known as *Behaviourism,* and he is especially recognized for developing the concept of *Operant Conditioning,* which will be discussed more fully in the following chapter. Behaviourism as a branch of psychology was gaining recognition amongst academics and thinkers at the time and offering important challenges to the then popular field of psychodynamics and the work of Sigmund Freud, amongst others.

Skinner's work, which owed much to his two predecessors Edward Thorndike and John Watson, sought to investigate, through empirical thinking and experimentation, the nature of behaviour, and more particularly learning. Though not a philosopher in the true sense, it is without argument that our understanding of learning owes a great debt to the work of B.F. Skinner. Like the work of Pavlov, it is certainly the case that many practitioners today, wittingly or otherwise, employ many of the ideas and principles first put forward by Skinner. This is especially the case where practitioners engage in behaviour modification and seek to alter and shape the behaviours of the children under their care. Though firmly rooted within the Behaviourist tradition, it should be recognized that Skinner, like many of his followers and most notably perhaps Jerome Bruner, believed that individuals are not passive learners but are in fact active learners. Skinner's ideas are discussed more fully in Chapter 2.

Whilst Skinner's work formed the basis for much thinking in the area of learning, others focused more upon the formal structures of institutions in which learning took place and where education could be challenged against sociological and political constructs. We now turn to the work of two major contributors, John Holt and Ivan Illich who, like their predecessors, challenged much of the established thinking of their time.

John Holt (1923–1985)

John Holt exercised considerable influence upon many practitioners during the 'sixties' when he published his two widely-read and controversial books, *How*

Children Fail (1964) and *How Children Learn* (1967). It must be remembered that this was a time of enormous change, with an almost unprecedented growth in confidence amongst the emerging youth of the time and a sustained increase in spending power amongst children coupled with an accelerating sense of the perceived need to challenge the establishment. In many respects this was a time of experimentation, characterized by a willingness to challenge the established ideas that had underpinned the education of so many generations beforehand. It must also be remembered that when Holt wrote his popular book *How Children Fail* the world was still reverberating from World War II, which had ended only 20 years earlier. Indeed, many teachers within the profession had seen active military service between 1939 and 1945.

To many at the time, Holt articulated views that had been widely held, but rarely expressed, with regard to why so many children failed to realize any true benefits from their schooling. In *How Children Learn* (1967, p. viii), for example, Holt suggested that:

> Only a few children in school ever become good at learning in the way we try to make them learn. Most of them get humiliated, frightened, and discouraged. They use their minds, not to learn, but to get out of doing the things we tell them to do – to make them learn.

Holt also suggested that a key reason for children failing to learn at school was fear. This, he suggested, was in large part due to children giving incorrect responses when asked questions by their teachers and being teased by their classmates. This will come as no surprise to older readers of this book. It must be remembered that at this time corporal punishment was widespread in schools and seen as perfectly acceptable by many. The renowned philosopher and theologian C.S. Lewis, who is perhaps more popularly known for writing the *Chronicles of Narnia*, for example, spoke about his own schooling in very negative terms. Lewis' biographer A.N. Wilson (1991, p. 23) in commenting on this aspect of Lewis' education wrote as follows:

> C.S. Lewis remained obsessed by Wynyard [Lewis' preparatory school] for the rest of his life. Although he spent only eighteen months as a pupil there, he devoted nearly a tenth of his autobiography to describing it, in the most lurid terms, as a 'concentration camp'.

Holt also suggested that many children fail at school because they feel they are lacking in different ways. Such a proposition raises important issues about children's self-esteem, and whilst Holt's views may have been relevant in the sixties it is worth considering if this remains the case today and if so, why. Holt was also critical of the learning that many children were exposed to in schools, suggesting that they were made to learn material that held little interest for them. At the time, schools placed considerable importance upon formal learning. Children typically sat in rows in their classrooms and dialogue between students was considered by few teachers to be a necessary or even important element in children's learning. Holt appeared regularly on television and gained celebrity status through his writings and popularized notions of how children learn and the factors that cause them to fail. He was also instrumental in acting as a catalyst for parents choosing to educate their children at home. In 1981 he published a further book entitled, *Teach Your Own*, which, again, was controversial and which became a key resource for parents educating their children at home.

Ivan Illich (1926–2002)

Illich was born in Vienna, the son of a civil engineer. In 1941, when just a teenager, he was forced by the Nazis to leave his school because of Jewish ancestry on his mother's side. Ten years later Illich entered the priesthood, but left subsequently, in 1969. Two influential books, *The Celebration of Awareness* (1971) and *Deschooling Society* (1973) led to his ideas and thinking being in much demand. It must be remembered that Illich, like John Holt, was writing at a time of enormous social and political change. The 'swinging sixties' had given a strong voice to young people, especially after the events of 1968 when, in May of that year, a million individuals marched in a demonstration in Paris following an uprising by student activists. At this time the USA was also engaged in a drawn-out conflict in Vietnam, which was the first war ever to be televised.

Illich is recognized for his critical appraisals of many aspects of the social, political and economic world within which he lived. He was, for example, very critical of the part played by institutions in Western societies and their apparent negative impact. Here, it is useful to consider Illich's critical stance with respect to institutions in the light of the current unfolding crises across the modern world that are being driven, in part, by banking institutions, the effects of which run very deep and affect not only business and enterprise but also families, individuals and schools, as well as the vast array of support systems that support these.

Illich was also critical of professionals and expressed particular concern with regard to how large corporations might come to exercise considerable influence over what type of learning should take place in schools. He even went as far as proposing that institutions and professionals could be instrumental in the process of dehumanizing individuals. He argued, for example, that substantial parts of our lives are driven by institutions which lower individuals' self-confidence and self-esteem and adversely affect their abilities and their potential to take initiative and engage in solution-focused thinking and problem solving. It is worth reflecting, at this point, upon the arguments that are being levelled against recent developments in the UK in regard to government directives on the need to change the curricula in schools.

Illich argued that a particular aspect of developing societies is how they increase the number of institutions. In his book *Disabling Professions* (1977) Illich voiced his criticisms of professionals and 'experts'. For example, he proposed that health care systems such as Primary Care Trusts in the UK and Care Services for families with children with a learning disability can, in fact, mask the real problems that adversely affect individuals, communities and the wider society because they are perceived to be dealing with the problem. Illich also felt that in modern societies individuals are increasingly drawn into living their lives in institutionalized ways, a process that starts early when children begin their learning in large educational institutions. Illich was especially critical of the growth of experts in modern societies whom he felt, inadvertently or otherwise, exercise control over what individuals know and should know.

We now turn to the work of a contemporary American philosopher whose ideas are gaining momentum amongst a growing number of practitioners and who is challenging not only our perceptions of such key areas as the role of the family and the parenting of young children but also how we think of teaching as a caring profession.

Nel Noddings (1929–)

It can be suggested that Nel Noddings has brought a refreshing and, in many respects, alternative focus to our understanding of learning and child development in the 21st century. Noddings has addressed the issue of ethics and its relation to 'care' and has given greater consideration in her writing to the importance of relationships than many of her contemporaries or predecessors. In particular, she has explored the notion of care in relation to education, and how children learn within their families and communities, as well as in more formal settings such as schools. Noddings sees the home as being at the very core of children's education and has called for much greater recognition of the importance of the home in children's education and development. Such a view raises some important questions with regard to the nature of parenting and the challenges faced by many families at present.

Noddings (2005, p. 1) has drawn a distinction between two types of caring found amongst teachers and commented as follows:

> It is sometimes said that 'all teachers care.' It is because they care that people go into teaching. However, this is not universally true; we all have known teachers who are cruel and uncaring, and these people should not be in teaching at all. But even for the majority who do 'care' in the virtue sense – that is, they profess to care and work hard at their teaching – there are many

who do not adopt the relational sense of caring. They 'care' in the sense that they conscientiously pursue certain goals for their students, and they often work hard at coercing students to achieve those goals. These teachers must be credited with caring in the virtue sense of the word. However, these same teachers may be unable to establish relations of care and trust ... The relational sense of caring forces us to look at the relation.

Noddings has also highlighted the challenges faced by many teachers and schools in actually caring for their pupils and has suggested that in some instances the conditions encountered by teachers and their pupils are so bad that they militate against the formation of caring relations. She suggests that this may be due to a variety of causes such as pressures from standardized testing, large class sizes and the nature and content of the curriculum.

Noddings also suggests that there are those within the field of education who find it difficult to accept her proposed view of relational caring because of the legacy in education that teachers feel they know best. She suggests, however, that because the world within which children now grow up is so complicated that it is not acceptable anymore to view teachers as knowing best. She puts the case, thus:

> ... we cannot be sure (beyond a small but vitally important set of basic skills and concepts) what everyone needs to know. Every student will need much knowledge beyond the basic but what John needs may differ greatly from what Ann needs. Caring teachers listen to John and Ann and help them to acquire the knowledge and attitudes needed to achieve their goals, not those of a pre-established curriculum. (2005, p. 3)

Understanding what each child needs to know beyond 'the basic' is, of course, a fundamental part of any teacher's role. This said, it is also important to consider the extensive range of abilities, background and individual academic, social and emotional needs that children bring with them when they enter school and move through primary into post-primary education. Society is changing at a rate, which is perhaps faster than has been the case in the past and this is having a marked effect upon how teachers work with children (MacBlain and Purdy, 2011). More specifically, teachers now have to take much greater account of the learning needs of individual children than ever before, in large part, because of their increased accountability.

Exercise

Identify key issues that have been raised by more modern philosophers and theorists and consider how relevant these are to education in the 21st century.

 **Summary**

It is certain that future generations will think differently about learning and how children are taught, and new philosophies and theories will emerge through the experiences and thinking of individuals who are yet to be born. For these reasons it is essential that all practitioners working in the fields of teaching and learning keep an open mind and understand that philosophers and theorists can and do offer us a means by which we can more carefully examine our own thinking and practice as well as that of others. More particularly, practitioners working with children need to critically engage with all elements of their practice as well as the thinking and philosophies that inform policy and decision makers.

RECOMMENDED READING

Beckley, P. (2012) *Learning in Early Childhood*. London: Sage.
Gray, C. and MacBlain, S.F. (2012) *Learning Theories in Childhood*. London: Sage.

REFERENCES

Archard, D. (1993) *Children: Rights and Childhood*. London: Routledge.

Boyden, J. (1997) Childhood and the policy makers: a comparative perspective on the globalization of childhood. In A. James and A. Prout (eds) *Constructing and Reconstructing Childhood* (2nd edn). London: Falmer Press.

Buckingham, D. (2000) *After the Death of Childhood: Growing Up in the Age of Electronic Media*. Cambridge: Polity.

DeBotton, A. (2000) *The Consolations of Philosophy*. London: Hamish Hamilton.

Edwards, C. (2002) Three approaches from Europe: Waldorf, Montessori, and Reggio Emilia, *Early Childhood, Research and Practice*, 4 (1).

Fontana, D. (1995) *Psychology for Teachers* (3rd ed). Basingstoke: Macmillan Press.

Gray, C. and MacBlain, S.F. (2012) *Learning Theories in Childhood*. London: Sage.

Gross, R. (1992) *Psychology: The Science of Mind and Behaviour*. London: Hodder & Stoughton.

Gutek, G. (1997) *Philosophical and Ideological Perspectives on Education*. London: Allyn and Bacon.

Hall, P. (1998) *Cities in Civilization*. London: Weidenfeld & Nicolson.

Holt, J. (1964) *How Children Fail*. Harmondsworth: Penguin.

Holt, J. (1967) *How Children Learn*. Harmondsworth: Penguin.

Horn, P. (1997) *The Victorian Town Child*. Stroud: Sutton.

Howe, M.J. (1999) *A Teacher's Guide to the Psychology of Learning* (2nd edn). Oxford: Blackwell.

Illich, P. (1977) *Disabling Professions*. New York: Marion Boyers.

James, A. and Prout, A. (1997) Re-presenting childhood: time and transition in the study of childhood. In A. James and A. Prout, *Constructing and Reconstructing Childhood* (2nd edn). London: Falmer Press.

Jarvis, M. (2005) *The Psychology of Effective Learning and Teaching*. Cheltenham: Nelson Thornes Ltd.

Jenks, C. (1996) *Childhood*. London: Routledge.

Locke, J. *Some Thoughts Concerning Education*, Vol. XXXVII, Part 1, p. 148. The Harvard Classics. New York: P.F. Collier & Son, 1909–14; Bartleby.com, 2001 http://.www.bartleby.com/37/1/ [27.06.2012].

MacBlain, S.F. and Purdy, N. (2011) Confidence or confusion: how well are today's Newly Qualified Teachers prepared to meet the additional needs of children in schools? *Teacher Development*, 15 (3): 381–94.

MacLure, M. (2003) *Discourse in Educational and Social Research*. Maidenhead: Open University Press.

Miller, L. and Pound, L. (2011) *Theories and Approaches to Learning in the Early Years*. London: Sage.

Neill, A.S. (1968) *Summerhill*. Harmondsworth: Pelican Books.

Nicol, J. (2010) *Bringing the Steiner Waldorf Approach to Your Early Years Practice*. London: Routledge.

Noddings, N. (2005) Caring in education. In *The encyclopedia of informal education*, Available at: http://infed.org/mobi/caring-in-education/

Pring, R. (2007) *John Dewey: A Philosopher of Education for Our Time*? London: Continuum International Publishing Group.

Rousseau, J.J. (1911) *Emile.* London: J.M. Dent.

Smith, K.S., Cowie, H. and Blades, M. (2003) *Understanding Children's Development.*(4th edn). Oxford: Blackwell.

The United Nations Convention on the Rights of the Child (UNCRC) (1989) Official text and unofficial summary. In *Agenda for Children Children's Rights Development Unit*. 313–29.

Tizard, B. and Hughes, M. (1984) *Young Children Learning: Learning and Thinking at Home and at School*. London: Fontana.

Vasagar, J. (2012) 'A different class: the expansion of Steiner schools', *The Guardian*, 25, May.

Wilson, A.N. (1991) *C. S. Lewis: A Biography*. London: Flamingo.

2 LEARNING THEORIES IN ACTION

This chapter aims to:

- familiarize readers with key concepts underpinning the work of the *Behaviourists* and their contribution to our understanding of learning
- explore the contributions made by three major theorists, *Piaget, Vygotsky* and *Bruner* in confronting *Behaviourism* and adding to our understanding of learning and cognitive development in young children
- highlight similarities and differences between these learning theories and provide practical examples to illustrate their relevance to practitioners today.

INTRODUCTION

Some years ago, Bigge and Shermis (2004, p. 5) made the following rather worrying assertion:

> … teachers who do not make use of a systematic body of theory in their day-to-day decisions are behaving blindly; little evidence of long-range rationale, purpose, or plan is observable in their teaching. Thus, teachers without a strong theoretical orientation inescapably make little more than busy-work assignments. True, some teachers operate in this way and use only a hodge-podge of methods without theoretical orientation. However, this muddled kind of teaching undoubtedly is responsible for many of the current adverse criticisms of public education.

This chapter addresses the importance of theoretical orientation in respect to learning and explores the attempts made by a number of key theorists to explain the origins of learning, and thereby inform the practice of teachers and other professionals working with children. The chapter commences with the work of the *Behaviourists*, in particular, *Pavlov, Watson* and *Skinner*. The chapter then examines the work of the Swiss psychologist *Jean Piaget*, before exploring the ideas of the Russian psychologist *Lev Vygotsky* and the American *Jerome Bruner*. The chapter builds upon the previous one, which explored our understanding of learning through the works and ideas of major philosophers and theorists throughout the last three centuries and gives a greater focus to how theories that seek to explain learning can inform the practice of teachers and Early Years practitioners, as well as other professionals working with children. The chapter begins with an examination of the key concepts of *Behaviourism* and the important contributions made by the early works of *Edward Thorndike* and *John B. Watson*.

BEHAVIOURISM

Key Concepts of Behaviourism

The thinking that underpins *Behavourism* is premised on the view that associations develop between stimuli and responses and that these can be considered to account for learning. Take, for example, those occasions when children hear the school bell ring (stimulus) and immediately begin to shuffle and pack their bags away (response). Drawing upon the original notion of *Empiricism*, which originated in the work of John Locke (see Chapter 1), Behaviourists initially proposed that the behaviours of individuals could be observed and examined in a systematic manner and with little if any consideration being given to the individual's personal thinking or their perceptions of the world around them.

Any exploration of Behaviourism needs to begin with the original work of the Russian physiologist Ivan Pavlov (see Chapter 1) who observed how dogs in his laboratory salivated (a natural response to seeing or smelling food) at times when food was not present, but, interestingly, also salivated when stimuli other than food were introduced to them. From this observation, he developed his theory of *Conditioned Reflexes*, which formed a starting point for later theorists examining the nature of learning. Pavlov's theory eventually became known as *Classical Conditioning* and offered the disciplines of Psychology and Education a verifiable and testable means against which attempts at understanding learning could be examined and subjected to scrutiny. Gray and MacBlain (2012, p. 30) have described some of Pavlov's early experiments and observations as follows:

> During his experiments, he noticed that the dogs drooled when a laboratory assistant entered the room. Observing the dogs' behaviour over time, Pavlov concluded that the dogs started drooling in the expectation that they would be fed. Even when there was no food brought for the dogs, the mere sight of the laboratory assistants was enough to make the dogs drool. Pavlov termed this 'associated learning', meaning the dogs had built up an association between the laboratory assistant and food. Fascinated by this form of learning, Pavlov found that he could train the dogs to drool to the sound of a bell.

Now, consider the case of a child who observes her mother scream at the sight of a garden spider. When the child next sees a garden spider herself she also cries out in a startled way. She has, in fact, formed an association between fear and garden spiders and may come to generalize her fear to all spiders and in time may forget what the original cause of the association was when she first observed her mother's initial cry of fear. Associations occur all of the time during children's lives and can be observed by teachers and Early Years practitioners on a daily basis. Pavlov proposed that once associations are learned they become very difficult to erase. Although his work has been criticized for being, essentially, confined to laboratory settings, it, nevertheless, offers a robust explanation for some forms of learning. In subsequent years his original ideas were taken further by such notable figures as Edward Thorndike (1874–1949), John B. Watson (1878–1958) and, perhaps most importantly, Burrhus F. Skinner (1904–1990).

Thorndike

Thorndike is considered to be a pioneer in active learning, which put simply, means that children should be encouraged to learn by themselves as opposed to being instructed by others, most particularly teachers. Though not a scientist and considered by most to be a teacher educator, Thorndike nevertheless acknowledged the principles that informed Classical Conditioning. He believed that most learning occurred through trial and error and he asserted that if outcomes of learning activities were positive then connections were formed which led to the repetition of behaviours. Thorndike developed an experiment in which he attempted to examine the laws that he considered to underpin learning. Thorndike put a hungry cat in a box designed in such a way as to let the cat see a fish outside of the box. He observed that the cat tried to escape from the box in order to eat the fish. However, on each occasion that the cat escaped from the box, he was returned to it. To begin with, the cat's attempts when escaping were of a trial and error type. As time progressed, however, the cat became quicker at escaping because it was making a connection between its ability to escape and a lever on the box, which when pressed, opened the door. Thorndike saw the process of learning within the cat as moving initially from random acts to deliberate attempts to use its paw to push the lever – he referred to this as the *Law of Effect*. In contrast, Thorndike proposed that acts that result in negative behaviours and that produce undesirable or non-pleasurable results become weaker and eventually disappear. Such a view is, however, overly simplistic and was subsequently challenged for not being able to be generalized to other situations. Take, for example, those children in schools who persistently misbehave. When given punishment, such as detentions and time out away from their peers, their unacceptable behaviours do not necessarily weaken and disappear. In addition, Thorndike's *Law of Effect* did not offer explanations for such factors as, motivation, attitude and intentionality.

Watson

Like his successors Watson was greatly influenced by the work of Pavlov and began applying the principles of *Classical Conditioning* to children. In 1913 he established the school of *Behaviourism*, which was based on the premise that all behaviours are acquired through the process of conditioning. In effect, Watson was really the first academic to extend Pavlov's original ideas, which were essentially based on observations of animals, to humans. It should be noted that much of the work originally undertaken by Watson, which was mainly in laboratory settings, would today appear unethical. For example, in an attempt to understand if it was possible to induce reactions of fear in children Watson undertook an experiment in 1920, which has been well documented in the field of psychology and is known as 'The Case of Little Albert' (Beck et al., 2009).

The case of Little Albert

When Albert was nine months old Watson devised an activity to test Albert's reactions to a number of objects, which included facial masks, a rat, a hammer, some cotton wool and a dog. He observed that Albert's only fear was when a loud sharp noise was produced by hitting the hammer on a steel bar. Two months later when Albert was 11 months of age Watson introduced Albert to a white rat and in order to induce fear Watson crept behind Albert as he observed the rat and slammed the hammer against the steel bar. He repeated this action until Albert cried when shown the white rat. Albert's fear then became generalized to the extent that when shown other objects that were also white such as cotton wool and even a Santa Claus mask with white hair he became fearful and cried as he had done with the rat.

Following his experiments with Albert, together with similar experiments involving children, Watson (1928, p. 82) made the following much quoted declaration:

> Give me a dozen healthy infants, well-formed, and my own specified world to bring them up in and I'll guarantee to take any one at random and train him to become any type of specialist I might select – doctor, lawyer, artist, merchant-chief and, yes, even beggar-man and thief, regardless of his talents, penchants, tendencies, abilities, vocations and the race of his ancestors.

There is little doubt that *Classical Conditioning* theory goes quite some way in explaining learning. Indeed, the reader will see similarities in Watson's ideas and those expressed some centuries earlier by the philosopher John Locke (see Chapter 1), who saw the newly born child as a blank slate on which could be written all of the child's life experiences. It can be proposed that Watson and Locke conceptualized learning as a passive process rather than an active one.

Few would disagree that Watson's ideas exerted considerable influence within the field of education. In the years that followed his experimental work, and even well into the sixties and early seventies, many teachers overly concerned themselves with, essentially, gaining correct answers to questions as opposed to a more active pedagogy where they concerned themselves with developing their pupils' understanding and their ability to question and reflect. Indeed, many older readers of this text will recall their school days when they sat endlessly in silence waiting to be asked questions and being directed to give only the correct answers. We now turn to the work of B.F. Skinner who took the ideas of Pavlov, Thorndike and Watson much further and refined these into what most psychologists would agree was a sophisticated and verifiable view of learning.

Skinner

Like Watson, Skinner undertook much of his work within laboratory settings where he experimented with animals, most often rats. He was especially interested in exploring the effects of reinforcement upon the behaviour of these animals, and applied the results of his observations to human behaviour as a way of understanding how humans behave. More particularly, he recognized that reinforcement that is positive strengthens the behaviours of individuals. Examples of positive reinforcement between a teacher and a child, for example, might include the teacher's smiles or verbal praise. A further common feature frequently seen in many classrooms is the placing of stars on a star chart when a pupil has successfully completed a task or demonstrated a desired behaviour. Examples of negative reinforcement, on the other hand, can also be observed in classrooms where teachers may use 'time out' for a child who is presenting with unacceptable behaviours. Teachers employ, almost on a daily basis, positive reinforcement to increase desired behaviours and negative reinforcement to discourage and even extinguish undesirable behaviours.

Importantly, Skinner also observed how the frequency with which reinforcement followed behavioural responses was an important factor in increasing behaviours. In response to these observations he proposed four schedules of reinforcement, which have informed the work of many psychologists and educators tasked with looking at how to change the behaviours of children presenting with problems in school. Gray and MacBlain (2012, p. 37) have illustrated these in Table 2. 1.

Table 2.1   Reinforcement schedules and likely outcomes

Reinforcement	Pattern of praise	Likelihood of repetition
1. Continuous	Praise given at each utterance	Low/moderate
2. Fixed ratio	Praise fixed, e.g. 4th/6th time	Low/moderate
3. Fixed interval	Praise given if 'please' is said within a fixed time period, e.g. 10 mins	Low/moderate
4. Intermittent/ variable	Praise follows no set pattern, 3rd/8th/11th	Moderate/high

Gray and MacBlain (2012, p. 38) have further commented in regard to the relevance of Skinner's original ideas within schools as follows:

> Popular approaches include the token economy and Applied Behavioural Analysis (ABA). Many schools employ an inducement scheme in the form of tokens to reward school attendance, good time keeping, neatness and good work. Pupils can exchange the tokens for prizes such as cinema tickets. As the pupil's behaviour improves, rewards are slowly replaced by verbal praise and eventually good grades.

In taking the ideas of Pavlov, Thorndike and Watson much further, Skinner developed an extremely useful and relevant concept known as *Operant Conditioning.* He based this concept on his proposition that learning was not wholly a passive process as had been considered by the early Behaviourists studying in the field of *Classical Conditioning* but rather an active process. In contrast to Classical Conditioning, Operant Conditioning holds that it is the learner and not the object that triggers changes in behaviour. With Operant Conditioning, which is also often referred to as *Instrumental Conditioning,* learning takes place when behaviours are either rewarded or punished and when, in effect, associations are formed between behaviours and the consequences of those behaviours. Take the example of Darren below.

The case of Darren

Darren is four years of age and every Saturday morning goes to the supermarket with his mother. As he approaches the checkout at the end of the morning's shopping he starts asking for sweets. On every occasion his mother says 'no' and as he gets closer to the checkout his requests for sweets increase and his mother's response of 'no' gets louder. By the time they are at the checkout Darren has begun to cry and the loudness of his crying increases – his mother then gives in and says, rather angrily 'OK'! She gives him some sweets and his crying stops. This pattern of behaviour is repeated every week. Darren has been rewarded, but which behaviours have been reinforced?

A further contribution that Skinner has made to our understanding of learning came through his observations that behaviour could be 'shaped' and then sustained by its consequences. He proposed, for example, that pleasant responses, as in the case of Darren getting his sweets at the checkout, strengthened behaviours, and unpleasant responses weakened behaviours, with the result that they tended to diminish. Put simply, Skinner proposed that, with learning, positive reinforcement strengthens behaviour whilst negative reinforcement diminishes it. One popular approach used within education that is underpinned by the work of the Behaviourists is Applied Behavioural Analysis (ABA).

Applied Behavioural Analysis (ABA)

ABA was developed by Lovaas in 1987. ABA focuses on areas of social significance with a key aim being to systematically reward and reinforce appropriate forms of behaviour. It has been considered to be especially effective in the treatment of children with autism (Keenan et al., 2000).

Behaviourism in action

The principles of Behaviourism can be evidenced daily in classrooms and Early Years settings though, mostly, this is done at an unconscious level. Teachers and Early Years practitioners offer stimuli to children and reinforce their behaviours without really being aware of what they are doing. Indeed, Bigge and Shermis (2004, p. 113) have suggested that whilst Skinner viewed the primary function of teachers as being that of transmitting culture, he also argued that, '… the first task of teachers is to shape proper responses, to get children to pronounce and write responses properly…' and their principal task, '… as consisting of bringing proper behavior under many sorts of stimulus control'. Bigge and Shermis cite the example of spelling, indicating that for Skinner the teaching of spelling to children was, in effect, a '… process of shaping complex forms of behavior'. Indeed, Skinner, like many Behaviourists, saw the computer as being one of the best means of learning for children, in that they could follow carefully designed programmes, with each stage of learning being reinforced through appropriate rewards and with small steps built in to the instructional programme.

Relevance and influence

Though many teachers and Early Years practitioners will be familiar with the term Behaviourism few will have a clear understanding of the actual concepts that underpin it, and yet most teachers and practitioners will be aware of such television programmes as, *Nanny 911*, *Super Nanny*, *The House of Tiny Terrors* and *Jo Frost*, all of which are predicated on principles of Behaviourism. In addition, most teachers and practitioners will use 'Star Charts' and 'Smiley Face' stickers to reward desired behaviours in children, and they may also use 'Time Out' or the 'Naughty Chair' when they wish to discourage particular behaviours. Throughout the fifties, sixties and seventies Behaviourism, which had embraced Pavlov's original work in the area of Classical Conditioning and that of Skinner in the area of Operant Conditioning, dominated thinking and practice in education and teaching.

Attempts at moving away from this theoretical approach can be observed in the ideas and work of A.S. Neill (see Chapter 1), who drew upon the *Psychodynamic* legacy arising from the original work of Freud and his followers, but more particularly in the work of the French psychologist, Jean Piaget. At the time, children's learning was characterized by an emphasis upon learning facts for examinations. Whilst Neil challenged the emotional aspects of this way of learning and highlighted the possible detrimental effects it could have on personality development, Piaget challenged it on the grounds that it did not actually address children's thinking. At the same time others, such as John Holt and Ivan Illich (see Chapter 1), besides challenging the thinking of their time, in particular the conservative nature of the establishment and its emphasis upon traditionalism, were also widening the debate surrounding the function of schools and the nature of the learning experiences on offer to children. The 'chalk and talk' methods of teaching children who typically sat in silence in rows memorizing information were rapidly losing favour. Children in schools began to sit in groups facing each other, often with their backs to the teacher, and the emphasis was swiftly moving away from what you learn to how you learn.

> **Exercise**
>
> Consider to what extent you believe Behaviourism can still inform the practice of teachers and our understanding of children's thinking today.

COGNITIVE CONSTRUCTIVISM

Key concepts in Piaget's theory of learning

Cognitive Constructivism is founded on the ideas of Jean Piaget and proposes that teachers/practitioners can predict what children can and cannot understand at certain stages of development and how their cognitive development progresses as they grow. Piaget proposed that young children, when presented with new information, may not immediately comprehend it if they have not already constructed their own personal understanding and knowledge through experience with their environments, which facilitates the creation and building of internal mental representations within their brains, or 'Schemas'. Nutbrown (2006, p. 7) has suggested that schemas are:

> ... a way of labelling children's consistent patterns of action ... They provide another way of looking at children, by giving focus to observational details which might otherwise become a list of disconnected events without much indication of learning or possible action to follow. Identifying a child's activities in terms of different schemas is only the first part in the process; the next step is to use detailed observations of children to decide how best to extend their learning.

Drawing upon the work of James Mark Baldwin (1861–1934), one of the original pioneer psychologists working in the area of cognitive development in young children, Piaget adopted two of Baldwin's terms *Accommodation* and *Assimilation* to account for two systems through which schemas evolve. *Assimilation* is where new information becomes absorbed within the schema without any particular manipulation of that information and *Accommodation* where the schema itself develops in order to facilitate this new acquisition of information. Hayes (1994, pp. 143–4) has drawn an important distinction between *Schemata* and *Concepts* as follows:

> ... the schema, like the cognitive map, is essentially about action – schemata act as a guide for planning and doing things. Concepts ... are essentially to do with classifying objects and phenomena into groups or types ... For Piaget, it is action that produces thinking: the child performs operations – actions with consequences – on its environment, and so obtains the information which is assimilated or accommodated into the schema. So the schema is simultaneously how the child uses its experience to guide its behaviour, and how it makes sense of the outcome when it has performed the behaviour.

Piaget argued that knowledge and meaning are actively constructed by children through interacting with their environments. This was a significant departure from Behaviourism, which saw children as being in a more passive state and as recipients of information. Piaget's ideas were favourably received and grew in popularity amongst teachers and educationalists. He chose to move away from the emphasis that Behaviourists had given to conducting experiments with children within laboratory settings and chose instead to observe, and actively and purposefully listen to children as they engaged in activities within natural settings. Piaget believed that cognitive development followed; a series of stages, within which are other sub-stages, and that these are 'invariant'; in other words, children must pass through each stage in turn before progressing to the next. His stages are as follows:

The Sensorimotor Stage (0–2 years)

Piaget termed the first stage of cognitive growth the *Sensorimotor Stage* when infants learn through their senses by, for example, sucking grasping and observing. He proposed that newly born infants are not capable of 'thinking', but rather engage in these reflexive activities of sucking and grasping, which are innate.

The Preoperational Stage (2–7 years)

During this stage the young child's thinking continues to develop with a particular feature of this stage being language, which greatly facilitates the development of schemas through Assimilation and Accommodation. This stage has two further sub-stages, the *Preconceptual Phase* (2–4 years) and the *Intuitive Stage* (4–7 years). During the former young children engage increasingly in imaginative and symbolic play with a growing use of words and symbols to represent, for example, objects or people. Imitation of the behaviours of others can also be increasingly observed during this stage. Indeed, Piaget viewed play as an essential and wholly important aspect in the cognitive development of young children. However, he also acknowledged that thinking during this stage was limited by a range of factors, for example, egocentrism, rigidity in thinking and transductive thinking.

The first of these, e*gocentricism*, attempts to conceptualize young children's apparent inability to view the world from the perspective of others. Take the example of Jane who is two years of age and playing the game 'Hide and Seek'. When she covers her eyes she thinks that the other children are unable to see her. Piaget believed that Egocentricism pervaded all of the thinking of children at this age and could explain why young children ascribe feelings to objects around them. With the second of these, *rigidity in thinking*, Piaget believed that young children at this age had not yet developed to a level of thinking whereby they could reverse sequences and adapt meaningfully and purposefully to changes in appearance.

Example

Martin's father has been left to look after him while Martin's mother goes shopping. He decides to make some lunch and cooks four sausages, some beans and some potatoes. When he has cooked the meal he sits Martin in his highchair with a little bowl and then gives himself two sausages and puts two sausages in Martin's bowl. Martin also likes sausages. On reflection Martin's dad thinks to himself, actually I'm quite hungry, I'll take back one of Martin's sausages for myself. He reaches over and takes a sausage from Martin's

(Continued)

(Continued)

bowl at which point Martin goes into spasms of anger because his sausage has been taken away from him. Martin's dad, however, who is a psychology graduate, quickly draws upon his knowledge of Piaget's theory and rapidly cuts the remaining sausage in Martin's bowl into four smaller pieces. Martin looks at his bowl, which now has lots of sausages in it and immediately stops crying and begins eating – he is happy once again because he 'thinks' he has 'lots of sausages'.

In the case of *transductive reasoning* this can be observed where young children make inferences about relationships when, in fact there are none. Take Martin in the above example whose mother is pregnant with his sister-to-be. He observes his mother to have a very large tummy and when he sees other people in the street who are merely very overweight he quizzes his mother if they are also going to have a baby. This type of 'thinking' starts to disappear at around the age of four. However, 'thinking' in the latter stage of the Preoperational Stage appears to remain intuitive, that is, it is based on such observables as shape, size and colour, as opposed to being logical.

Intuitive Stage (4–7 years)

At this stage, Piaget believed, children are developing in their capacity to stand back and view the 'whole' as opposed to 'the details'. He talked of this process as 'decentring', but felt that children's 'thinking' remained limited in that they had not yet developed the capacity to remove their attention from the detail and transfer it to the whole and then back again. For example, a child at this stage observing an adult pouring the same amount of water from a short fat glass to a long slim glass will claim that there is more water in the taller glass. This type of thinking was referred to by Piaget as 'conservation' and he believed that the capacity to conserve marked the end of the Preoperational Stage and the start of the next stage, that of *Concrete Operations*.

Concrete Operational Stage (7–11 years)

The key difference between the Preoperational Stage and the Concrete Operational Stage is that in the latter children have now developed the capacity to apply logic as a means of problem solving. Piaget believed that logic, characterized by operational rules, evolves gradually as the child constructs newer more complicated skills and organizes these into increasingly complex semantic structures. Thinking then becomes more flexible, though it is still constrained by the child's need to have concrete objects to represent this more sophisticated 'thinking'. Piaget used the term *Horizontal Decalage* to account for those inconsistencies in development that he observed in children. This term can be understood as inconsistent performance on tasks that require similar mental operations.

Formal operational stage (11–15 years)

It is during this stage that Piaget believed children's thinking is at its highest level. At this stage thinking is more symbolic and more flexible. For example, children understand that symbols such as the letters 'X' or 'Y' can solve problems in mathematics such as 'If $X + Y = Z$ then what does Y equal if X is 5 and Z is 15?'. Piaget also suggested that at this stage thinking is no longer limited by the experience of the child, or reality. Children, he proposed, can begin to think about the future. He also suggested that during this stage thinking is more logical and children can be observed to engage in deductive reasoning. Children, he argued, can begin to test hypotheses and be more objective and reflective in their thinking. According to Sutherland (1992), however, Piaget failed to fully describe this last stage of development and it was left to neo-Piagetians such as Peel (1971) and Flavell (1963, 1977) to extend his work in this area.

Constructivism in action

Piaget argued that teaching should be appropriate to the age of the child, though he later modified his views in acknowledgement of the fact that children develop cognitively at different rates and some are ready to take on more advanced learning at a younger age than others. Not only was he interested in how children acquire the correct answers to problems, he was also interested in why they failed to acquire the correct answers. In particular, he concerned himself with the notion of 'readiness' and the assertion that children, instead of being accelerated in their learning, should be observed to be at certain 'stages' of 'readiness' before being progressed to more demanding intellectual tasks.

Piaget believed that teachers ought to engage children in tasks that are stimulating and that are appropriate to their stage of development, as opposed to attempting to accelerate their learning. Whilst this view gained a great deal of acceptance at the time it also generated much debate, and even criticism, from many quarters and especially those who saw children's cognitive development as being very uneven across the general population. Those who embraced the ideas of Piaget, and especially Early Years practitioners, were very drawn to the similarities that existed between his ideas and those of Friedrich Froebel, Maria Montessori and John Dewey, discussed in the previous chapter, and especially the notion that young children learn best when engaged in practical activities and where the role of the teacher/practitioner is to nurture the child's emotional and social development by removing any barriers that might militate against this within their learning environments. Like Dewey, Piaget saw the role of the teacher/practitioner very much in terms of it being child-centred and dependent to a greater extent upon the environment. The child was to be viewed very much in terms of engaging in discovery and this, they both believed, lay at the very heart of learning. It is not surprising then that Early Years practitioners of the time particularly embraced Piaget's ideas of 'readiness' and 'child-centredness' (Sutherland, 1992).

Relevance and influence

In contrast to the Behaviourists, Piaget led the way in attempting to explore and account for those internal processes that underpinned learning and that explained thinking. In addition, he gave to researchers in the field of psychology and education new ways of researching very early child development, most notably perhaps, observation and an emphasis upon child-centredness and children's language. For Piaget, it was the 'whole' child that should be at the centre of experimentation and not just the observable behaviours. In proposing a model of how children think he also offered researchers, and practitioners, new ways of understanding child development.

Piaget, however, has been criticized on the grounds that he viewed cognitive development as being marked by different stages, which is very much in contrast to the thinking of Vygotsky and Bruner, discussed later. In his later years Piaget (1970) came to modify this view, as he did other aspects of his theory, to reflect a 'spiral' process of intellectual development in children, illustrating an expanding and upward process in which children engage in reconstructing existing knowledge. This said, he never really accounted for why children are actually driven to move from one stage to another.

The methods employed by Piaget to investigate how children learn have been also heavily criticized in that he tended to observe his own children, sample sizes were small and the language used in his experimental situations was at times too complex for the children (Meadows, 1993) with the result that he may have underestimated the intellectual abilities of those children he observed and upon whom he based his ideas. Donaldson (1978) was especially critical of the type of questions that Piaget used in his experiments with children, suggesting that they were often phrased in such a manner as to catch children out rather than help them. Piaget was also accused of generalizing his observations which were gained from white, middle-class children of educated parents. We now turn to the work of another major theorist whose influence informs and drives much thinking and practice today, Lev Vygotsky.

Exercise

What can the original ideas presented by Piaget offer Early Years practitioners and primary teachers today?

SOCIAL CONSTRUCTIVISM

Key concepts in Vygotsky's theory

The popularity of Vygotsky's ideas grew considerably in the 1980s. Born in Russia, it is important to note that Vygotsky developed his thinking within what was then a strongly communist and Marxist state. Moreover, when his work was translated into English it frequently contained inaccuracies. Vygotsky proposed that all learning is founded upon experiential learning and that much of this learning happens before the child commences schooling. Whitebread (2012, p. 127) has described the central features of Vygotsky's theory as follows:

> ... all learning begins in the social context, which supports children in the processes whereby they construct their own understandings ... all learning exists first at the 'inter-mental' level in the form of spoken language, and then at the 'intramental' level (i.e. within the child's mind, in the form of internal language, or thought) ... This has been termed the 'social constructivist' approach to learning.

Students new to the ideas of Vygotsky will quickly come across references to the *Zone of Proximal Development* (ZPD), a term that has perhaps become overly representative of his work to the exclusion of much of his thinking. Though central to his work, it should be recognized that this term only ever appeared on a few of the literally thousands of pages produced by Vygotsky. The concept of ZPD was defined by Vygotsky (1978, p. 86) as:

> ... those functions which have yet to mature but are in the process of maturing ...'buds' or 'flowers' of development rather than 'fruits' of development. The actual development level characterizes the cognitive development retrospectively while the ZPD characterizes it prospectively.

Now let us turn more specifically to the notion of *Social Constructivism*, which places particular emphasis upon the importance of culture and context in understanding the worlds in which we live and the ways in which we construct our knowledge based on our understanding. Here, culture refers simply to those social patterns of behaviour and beliefs that are passed on through the generations. In passing on culture from one generation to the next humans use cultural tools such as fairy stories, nursery rhymes, art and so on. These have, of course, become much more sophisticated in recent decades with the accelerated use of television, ICT and social websites. Vygotsky believed that these cultural tools played an important part in thinking. The importance of these tools has been emphasized more recently by Pea (1993, p. 52) who commented as follows:

> ... these tools literally carry intelligence in them, in that they represent some individual's or some community's decision that the means thus offered would be reified, made stable as quasi permanent, for the use of others.

More particularly, it is now recognized that these tools exert considerable influence on our perception of events and people around us, and even in the way in which we experience the world. A further, and perhaps the most important cultural tool that Vygotsky saw as mediating learning, was language. Vygotsky believed that by talking and listening to others, children develop and extend their own understanding. Indeed, the importance he attached to language can be seen in his own words (Vygotsky, 1987, quoted in Holzman, 2006, p. 115):

> The structure of speech is not simply the mirror image of the structure of thought. It cannot, therefore, be placed on thought like clothes off a rack. Speech does not merely serve as the expression of developed thought. Thought is restructured as it is transformed into speech. It is not expressed but completed in the word. Therefore, precisely because of the contrasting directions of movements, the development of the internal and external aspects of speech forms a new unity.

Vygotsky viewed language as the means of transmitting meaning. As children use language they engage with those around them through their interpretation of what they hear and say and in this way they enter a process whereby they contribute to their communities and to the wider society. It is the reciprocal nature of these interactions that lies at the core of Vygotsky's Social Constructivism.

Despite devoting much of his life to understanding learning and thinking, it is of note that Vygotsky did not focus in any particular way upon age-related learning and never properly established a theory of child development. Recently, Schaffer (2004, p. 201) in commenting about this indicated that:

> The only statement he made about age was to suggest that children up to 2 years are influenced primarily by biological forces and that the socio-cultural influences which form the focus of his writings do not come into play until after that age – an assertion clearly not supported by more recent work.

In fact, Vygotsky was less interested in individualized learning within the child and more interested in the cultural context of the child. This is hardly surprising, given the fact that he was living and working within a Marxist state, which, it can be argued, chose to reduce individualism in favour of collective thinking dominated by central government. Vygotsky viewed the development of children less as an individual process and more as the sum of those relationships they developed with others around them. He argued, for example, that any attempt at understanding children's development needed to have at its very core the social and cultural contexts within which children grow and develop. Children, he suggested, do not grow up in isolation but rather as part of social matrices, which are created through the dynamic and interconnected relationships they have with others around them (Corsaro, 1992). His thinking on the subject of child development has been well encapsulated in the following, offered by Wertsch (1981, p. 164):

> In the process of development, children begin to use the same forms of behaviour in relation to themselves and others initially used in relation to them. Children master the social forms of behaviour and transfer these forms to themselves … it is through others that we develop into ourselves and … this is true not only with regard to the individual but with regard to the history of every function.

Vygotsky proposed that when children are born they already have the foundations for cognitive development, which included such elements as, attention, memory and visual recognition, all of which enable the development of higher order processing. In effect, he argued that children develop their thinking so that they can engage, for example, in solving problems, applying reasoning and applying recall in memory (Rose et al., 2003). Vygotsky also proposed that children are born with an innate ability that allows them to learn through guidance from others, for example, their parents, older siblings and teachers. In this way, he suggested that the cultural norms of societies and more immediate communities are passed on to the children from outside and become internalized and 'fixed' through experience. In other words, external agents, in particular parents and teachers, mediate the child's learning by providing a bridge from the child's innate abilities to the internalization of thinking and learning. Vygotsky (1978, p. 57) commented as follows:

> Every function in the child's cultural development appears twice: first, on the social level, and later on the individual level; first, between people (interpsychological), and then inside the child (intrapsychological). This applies equally to voluntary attention, to logical memory, and to the formation of concepts. All the higher functions originate as actual relations between human individuals.

Vygotsky also drew an important distinction between lower and higher order thinking, and maintained that the former involved such biological functions as memory and attention whilst the latter involved intentionality, problem solving and logical reasoning. He argued that the social activity experienced by children can be seen as the bridge across which the child moves from lower order to higher order thinking. It should be noted here that in terms of this 'bridging' Vygotsky showed a particular interest in the learning and thinking of children whom we would now refer to as having special educational needs and/or disabilities, and the key importance of adults acting as mediators of learning to these children through the experiences they created for them. This may be one reason as to why his theoretical ideas have been embraced by so many practitioners working with children who present with learning difficulties.

Central to Vygotsky's theory lie four stages, which Gray and MacBlain (2012, p. 75) have described as follows:

1 **Primitive stage**: Children under 2 years of age use vocal activity as a means of emotional expression and for social engagement. Non-verbal gesturing is not unusual during this stage as behaviour becomes increasingly purposeful and goal-directed. At the primitive stage, thought and language are separate. Pointing and staring are not uncommon during this stage and are easily interpreted by a sensitive caretaker who uses language to reinforce non-linguistic communications ...

2 **Practical intelligence**: During this stage, the child's language uses syntactic (rules of speech) and logical forms. These forms of speech are linked to the child's practical problem solving activities ...

3 **External symbolic stage**: Thinking aloud is common during this stage with language used to help with internal problem solving. The transition between external social speech and internal private speech is marked by egocentric speech – also termed thinking aloud. Thinking aloud enables the child to self-regulate and plan their activities ...

4 **Internalization of symbolic tools**: Between 7 and 8 years of age, children internalize thinking and egocentric speech begins to disappear. Problem solving continues to be guided by speech but the voice is internal (thinking). This stage leads to greater cognitive independence, flexibility and freedom. Thought continues to be framed by internalized individual, cultural and societal norms.

It must be emphasized that Vygotsky's concept of stages is very different to that of Piaget. Vygotsky was not proposing a fixed-stage approach but rather what Gray and MacBlain (2012, pp. 75–6) have further described as follows:

Unlike Piaget, Vygotsky did not advocate a staged unidirectional approach to development ... he believed that development is progressive and tends to follow an incremental pathway ... he acknowledged that a child may move backwards or forwards between stages ... as their thoughts mature. Problem novelty or difficulty can cause a child to regress to an earlier stage, whereas experience will progress development.

Social Constructivism in action

Let us focus upon play, perhaps one of the most important foundations for learning. Vygotsky saw play as being extremely important in children's learning and proposed that it is through play that young children develop their understanding of relationships with those around them. One typically observes young children frequently modelling the behaviours of adults as well as cartoon and 'hero' characters they observe on television. Indeed, Vygotsky viewed play as 'self-education' – not as an activity that children merely repeat but as an active process often characterized by mimicking those around them, and, very importantly, independence. Through play the child develops many aspects such as their ability to play alone, to be autonomous and to take risks. Confidence grows and children increasingly take greater control of their play with the emergence of self-made rules as well as showing increasing acceptance of the rules of others. Fantasy is an important aspect of children's play when they are young and Vygotsky saw the role of play in children, which is largely spontaneous and self-initiated, as being part of a self-regulation process. He suggested that, in fact, young children create their own ZPD through setting personal levels of challenge and at the same time their own sense of control (Whitebread, 2012). In this way, their activities are appropriate for their stage of development.

Relevance and influence

A particular area of relevance that has increasingly influenced thinking and practice in education is that of *Dynamic Assessment* (see Chapter 6 and Feuerstein), which has at its core the notion of social constructivism. Here, teachers and Early Years practitioners can be seen to play a crucial role in the lives of children by the way in which they make assessments and subsequent judgements about children's cognitive functioning. Frederickson and Cline (2002, pp. 252–3), however, have emphasized important distinctions relevant to the practice of those working with children, in particular attempts at measuring and making judgements about ability as follows:

'Static' tests such as IQ tests evaluate what a child has learned in the past – their zone of actual development … It is seen as more useful to assess what Vygotsky called the zone of proximal development … For this purpose 'dynamic' measures are required … static tests … establish current levels of performance but usually tell us little about the processes that underlie that competence (Campione, 1989). They ignore functions that have not yet matured …

Consider the following example:

Example

Jamie is now in his forties but recalls the time when at the age of seven he was assessed at primary school by a psychologist who asked him to work through a number of tests. Following this assessment, Jamie's parents were given a report by the psychologist in which it was reported that Jamie had a Verbal IQ of 75 and a Non-verbal IQ of 98 (average range: 85 to 115). Six months after the assessment Jamie moved schools and the report written by his old school to his new school stated that, '... *the results of a recent test by a psychologist indicated that Jamie was of low general ability and would be best suited to working in a lower set*'. Following his move to his new school, however, Jamie blossomed and found that his new teacher spent a great deal of time with him, explaining problems to him, teaching him new strategies for approaching tasks, giving him lots of opportunities to gain in self-confidence, and most particularly developing his vocabulary and general language abilities and encouraging him to read widely. Jamie grew to love reading and gained considerably in confidence. He went on to win a place at the local grammar school before attending university.

In Jamie's case he underwent a 'static' assessment, which took place on a particular day, in a particular place and at a particular age and which attempted to measure his abilities as opposed to his potential or what he was capable of, given the appropriate support. What happened later when Jamie moved schools was that his new teachers began to work with him believing that he was far more capable than had been reported by his previous school. His teachers gave him new strategies to develop his learning, taught him new ways to approach and think about problems, and worked very hard to increase his vocabulary and his general language and to raise his self-esteem. His teachers also encouraged group-based activities where the children worked in groups to solve problems, learn from each other and construct new understandings. In other words, they worked to realize his potential as opposed to maintaining him at a particular level because they had been told he was of 'below average' ability.

The latter school's philosophy of learning was very much in keeping with that of Vygotsky who emphasized the important role that adults play in shaping the environments in which children can develop their intellectual functioning and extend their thinking through language. In effect, Jamie's new teachers were actively and purposefully structuring the classroom and school environments in small steps, or what has now become known as *Scaffolding* (see following section on Bruner) to progress Jamie's thinking. In this way they were supporting Jamie to move increasingly towards becoming a more independent learner. In doing so, they fully recognized the importance of language and actively sought to develop this in Jamie from the moment he entered the school. They did this through a range of devices, in particular listening carefully to Jamie, asking focused and purposeful questions, whilst recognizing that their questioning had a real and valuable purpose, that of developing Jamie's language and thinking. They also recognized that as teachers they were not always the person in the classroom with the knowledge and that Jamie could learn effectively and purposefully from his peers.

Exercise

Consider occasions when teachers or Early Years practitioners might assess children's intellectual functioning and then record the outcomes of their assessment in terms of making judgements about a child's abilities. To what extent should teachers and Early Years practitioners include their own efforts and practice as part of the assessment and recognize that had they done things differently the child might have demonstrated greater ability?

INSTRUMENTAL CONCEPTUALISM

Bruner and learning

Central to Bruner's theory of learning is the notion of *Instrumental Conceptualism*, which has three key elements: acquiring new information, which could also include the reworking of already stored information; the transformation and manipulation of knowledge; and the checking of what Bruner referred to as the 'pertinence' and 'adequacy' of knowledge. Bruner based this view of learning on two fundamental assertions, namely that an individual's knowledge of the world is based on their constructed models of reality and that these models are initially adopted from the individual's own culture, which they then adapt for their own use.

   Bruner's purpose in developing his theoretical perspective in the area of learning was, in some respects, driven by a need to challenge the thinking of his time, which had been dominated by the traditions of Psychodynamics and Behaviourism, originating in the works of Sigmund Freud and Carl Jung, and Pavlov, Thorndike, Watson and Skinner. Addressing this apparent need of Bruner to challenge contemporary thinking Smidt (2011, p. 10) recently commented:

> What made Bruner unusual and special in terms of Western psychologists at the time was his recognition that meaning is not determined by the biological needs we inherit, nor is it determined by individual thought: rather, it comes about through an active search for meaning within the context of a culture.

Bruner also sought to challenge the apparent consensus in regard to policy and decision making in the field of education. Smidt (2011, p. 85) has further commented that, 'Bruner said that we should treat education for what it is, and for him what it was was political'. Indeed, the purpose to which Bruner applied himself was eloquently expressed some three decades ago by the author's professor (Brown, 1977: 74):

> Bruner's thesis was that the study of children in problem-solving situations had concentrated too much upon the nature of the tasks and the stimuli presented to the child, and too little upon the dynamic qualities the child brought to the tasks in order to solve them.

Bruner did not see learning as something that just simply happens to children but rather a process in which children are, and should be, active participants. This idea is central to his thinking on learning and marks him out as separate from the Behaviourists, who, as we saw, viewed learning in terms of stimuli and responses, and reinforcement. The key difference is that Bruner was more concerned with what happens 'inside' the child in terms of their cognitive processing or thinking, in other words, between a stimulus being emitted and the child making a response. Moreover, Bruner was especially interested in the strategies that children use when engaged in learning and particularly when their learning involved problem-solving activities, which underpin and lead to the formation of concepts. Behaviourists, on the other hand, concerned themselves more with how children reacted to stimuli.

Bruner was concerned with the way in which stimuli are represented by symbols and words and how these representations connect with existing concepts and facilitate generalization. Representation of stimuli through, for example, words and symbols was, according to Bruner, of a much higher order, and the inferences that children make through words and symbols are key to their learning. He referred to this as the *Symbolic* mode. Indeed, central to Bruner's theory is the notion that individuals represent their worlds through three *modes*, which he referred to as, the *Enactive* mode, the *Iconic* mode and the *Symbolic* mode. The first of these is to do with actions whilst the second is to do with images and pictures. The third or *Symbolic* mode, as we have seen, is concerned with words and symbols. The three modes do not follow in succession, as Piaget had proposed with his stages but, rather, are integrated with one another.

With the Enactive mode a baby's view of an object, for example, becomes linked with their physical movements. Consider, for example, an infant in a cot who is given a rattle by his mother. When the child shakes the rattle it makes a noise and as it does so the child is alerted to the noise. On each occasion when the child is given the rattle by his mother he will shake it and as this happens over time the child's physical movements become gradually encoded within his memory store through what some practitioners refer to as a 'kinesthetic memory'.

During this process the child's movements are linked to his sight of the object. The concept of a rattle then becomes internally represented as a compilation of visual image, noise and movement. Bruner suggested that the Enactive mode is limited. For example, in this case the child cannot make links to other rattles and his concept of 'rattle' remains located with the particular rattle that the child is focusing upon.

With the Iconic mode Bruner proposed that children internally represent objects as images. In doing this, children can progress their thinking considerably. By being able to create and store images, children can then extend their thinking to objects which are not immediately present in their environment. Again, however, Bruner has proposed that this mode has its limitations. Images that are held by the child are restricted to observable features of the image, for example, the colour, the smell, the texture and so on. Though the child can internally represent images of objects and images of people around them such as their father and mother and brothers and sisters, the Iconic mode does not allow them to internally represent concepts of, for example, kindness, happiness and fun. They will require language to represent these concepts and it is this that lies at the heart of the Symbolic mode. Brown (1977, p. 75) offers the following distinction between icons, or images, which lie at the core of the Iconic mode and symbols, which are the centre of the Symbolic mode:

> A photograph or a model of a cow would be an icon in that it would represent the animal in a very real and obvious way. The symbols C-O-W have no such characteristics. They only signify the existence of the animal by consensus of those who use the word. By eliminating the idiosyncrasies or special characteristics (for it will have to represent a cow) the symbol enables us to work with a general concept unrestrained by particulars.

In exploring Bruner's views of the function of language in children, Smidt (2011, p. 66) has commented:

> Bruner reminds us that, 'Children learn to use language initially … to get what they want, to play games, to stay connected with those on whom they are dependent. In doing so, they find the constraints that prevail in the culture around them embodied in their parents' restrictions and conventions' (Bruner 1983: 103).

As children's abilities with language develop, they can, for example, remove themselves from situations through their thinking. For example, they can engage with their friends and chat about people and situations somewhere else. They can also chat about previous experiences as well as those they might hope to encounter in the future. They can increasingly engage in problem solving, critical reflection and evaluation, which are key processes in the development of higher order thinking skills. This process is one in which Early Years practitioners and teachers of younger children in primary schools actively engage in their attempts to develop children's thinking skills. Take the following example:

Example

Gilly is working in a group of five with her friends, Caroline, Harriet, Kathy and Mike. Their teacher has posed a problem to the class to work on in groups. Each group is provided with one piece of A4 paper and a heavy textbook. The teacher challenges each group to balance the book upon the paper. The children get excited and quickly rush to get on with the task. Most of the groups are then observed by the teacher to be making random attempts at solving the problem. The teacher is particularly interested in the strategies the children employ and especially their use of language. She listens to Gilly's group as they start to work on the task:

Harriet: *This is stupid, it's not possible. We can't do this.*

Mike: *Yeah, it's stupid no one could do this, I give up.*

Harriet: *Yeah, it's stupid.*

Gilly: *Wait, supposing we change the shape of the paper.*

Kathy: *I see, yes. I know, let's try it. Yes, fold the paper like in a zigzag shape, you know, like this.*

Gilly: *Yeah, I see. Turn the paper on its side in a zigzag and then we can balance the book on top. That makes the paper much stronger.*

Caroline: *That's right. That will do it.*

Mike: *Wow! That really works.*

At this point the group has succeeded and by folding the paper in zigzag, or concertina shape they have been easily able to balance the heavy book.

This example is a good illustration of the Symbolic mode and how it allows for, and can develop, more sophisticated thinking. By starting her sentence with, '*Wait, supposing we ...*' Gilly has introduced a hypothesis and has started to engage in hypothetical reasoning, which is of a much higher order than Harriet and Mike's thinking, which is purely an emotional reaction to the problem posed by the task. Gilly's hypothesis is being tested not just by her physical attempts at manipulating the two objects – the paper and the book – but also by her peers' reactions and verbal feedback, for example, Kathy's agreed response to Gilly's suggestion that they alter the shape of the paper and then extending her thinking to suggest a zigzag shape. Here, Kathy is offering positive confirmation of Gilly's hypothesis and taking the thinking of the group further. It is through such carefully managed situations that teachers and Early Years practitioners can develop not only children's language but their thinking. In doing so, they extend their children's cognitive capacity and functioning, both of which lie at the heart of learning. The context within which children learn, therefore, and the experiences that are presented to them by their teachers are crucial and facilitate important progress in, for example, the development of vocabulary, logical reasoning, deduction, and so on.

Entwined within the emergence of language is the acquisition of literacy. Bruner believed that in order for children to access literacy they must be able to recognize not only the written symbols that make up words but also their sounds. Indeed, Bruner went as far as proposing that the internal cognitive structures of children who engage more with reading and writing will, typically, be different to those of children who generally engage more with less language-oriented activities such as drawing and construction activities (Brown, 1977). He also proposed that this latter type of child typically differed from those children who tended to engage much more with their peers and with adults through talk. His rationale for this was that, whilst most young children engage in basic verbal interaction with those around them, this does not, as in the case of those children who engage a lot in speaking and listening, necessarily have a significant impact upon their developing capacity to internally represent thinking. However, when young children actively and purposefully engage with the process of making written symbols which represent their own speech and language as well as that of others, then an important transformative process happens. By representing thinking in the form of written symbols, for example words and mathematical symbols, the child can engage in analysis of those ideas they have realized through the written form of their symbols. One is drawn to considering the importance of very young children making marks with crayons and coloured pens as many young children love to do.

More recently, Bruner's ideas turned to the importance of narrative, which Smidt (2011, p. 92) has drawn attention to as follows:

> For the past two decades Bruner has been systematically developing what some call a narrative view of culture and mind and has argued that reality is itself narratively constructed.

In regard to narrative, Smidt (2011, p. 99) has offered the following:

> The reason children become narrators is because they explore the expectations they have developed about how the world should be. They develop these expectations through their experiences and their interactions and the ways in which they look for patterns and regularities in the world.

Indeed, Bruner saw narrative in terms of 'reasoning', and suggested that, '... *reality is narratively constructed*' (Smidt, 2011, p. 13).

Instrumental Conceptualism in action

Readers will observe similarities between Bruner and elements of other theorists already discussed. One such similarity is that of *Scaffolding*, which in many ways equates with much of Vygotsky's thinking. Vygotsky originally proposed how learning was a social activity whereby children's learning and thinking were progressed through interacting with those around them such as their parents and teachers. Bruner, however, took this notion further and developed his ideas on Scaffolding, which he saw as being everywhere in the lives of children. For example, young children can be observed learning with their grandparents who go about structuring activities for them. This occurs mostly at a subconscious level, but is important in extending and progressing the learning of children.

Relevance and influence

Bruner has had an enormous influence upon the way in which we try to understand learning and on practice in schools. Nowadays, student teachers learn about Scaffolding when undertaking training and are expected to employ this as a means of working with the pupils they teach. A particular benefit of Scaffolding is that it is not a rigid process, but instead very flexible. Grandparents or teachers may actively work to break tasks down into smaller more manageable parts and model to the child how the tasks or problems can be solved, or teachers may put children together in groups to solve a problem and find that the weaker children are learning from the more able through, for example, observing, imitating and using language. It is now generally recognized that this process of working with children to progress their learning can be very motivating for many children.

Another important feature of Bruner's work is the emphasis he placed upon *Discovery Learning*. This form of learning has been viewed by its advocates as an important means by which the internalization of meaning can be strengthened along with the conceptualization of new information into already existing knowledge. Smidt (2011: 10) has commented as follows:

> For Bruner, meaning has always been at the heart of any investigation into mind and cognition. When we talk of meaning we are talking about making sense of something, of understanding or comprehending it.

A number of criticisms have been levelled at Discovery Learning, in particular the notion that children may acquire misconceptions, which go unnoticed by their teachers or that Discovery Learning, whilst suiting some learning styles more than others, may militate against those children who prefer to work in a more didactic fashion. In addition, there are those parents and schools who would perceive this way of learning as a poor use of their children's time, preferring instead to engage the children in a more formal pursuit of knowledge. This may increasingly be the case in the UK as schools respond more to the pressure of achieving targets linked to success in examinations.

STRENGTHS AND WEAKNESSES OF EACH THEORY AND THEIR RELEVANCE TODAY

Each theoretical approach in this chapter has contributed enormously to our understanding of how children learn. Whilst they are very different they are also, in many respects, similar, and students engaged in learning about learning will find it impossible to disregard any one theory in respect of another or to believe that one theory offers all of the answers. Critical readers will engage with the ideas of the Behaviourists and at the same time reflect upon what they can offer in addition to our understanding of such key issues as cognitive development, maturation and motivation, culture and the changing nature of childhood, and the neurological functioning of the brain.

Whilst Piaget emphasized the importance of the environment and gave little emphasis to the role of the teacher, Vygotsky and Bruner saw the role of the teacher as being hugely important, in particular, the role they play in progressing thinking and learning. Unlike Piaget, Vygostky and Bruner also placed much greater emphasis upon culture as being central to the cognitive development of children. It must be remembered that Piaget's work came at a time when our understanding of learning had been dominated by Behaviourism.

Exercises

- What aspects of the above theorists have you experienced when observing practitioners working with children?
- What are the similarities and differences between the above theorists?
- How do each of the above theorists account for learning in children with special educational needs?
- What aspects of each of the above theorists' ideas do you consider most relevant for teachers in the 21st century?

Summary

This chapter sought to familiarize readers with the key concepts of Classical and Operant Conditioning, which lie at the heart of Behaviourism and the contributions made by some of the major contributors in this area of learning theory. The theories of Piaget, Vygotsky and Bruner were also examined, with the advantages and disadvantages of each being highlighted as well as their relevance for practitioners today.

It almost goes without saying that teachers and Early Years practitioners are guided by the theoretical perspectives of these major figures and much of their practice has arisen as a result of decisions made by those who went before them and who continue to influence practice today. Having a deeper and more systematic understanding of these theories and how they inform and contrast with each other requires sustained critical engagement on the part of practitioners. Such critical engagement, however, though often challenging and a little daunting will, ultimately, lead to improved practice and informed understanding as to why we do things in the way we do and why we think about learning as we do. The following chapter now builds upon the ideas expressed by these major theorists and focuses upon the nature of thinking and learning in very young children.

RECOMMENDED READING

Athey, C. (1990) *Extending Thought in Young Children: A Parent–Teacher Partnership*. London Paul Chapman Publishing.

Gray, C. and MacBlain, S.F. (2012) *Learning Theories in Childhood*. London: Sage.

Nutbrown, C. (2006) *Threads of Thinking: Young Children Learning and the Role of Early Education*. London: Sage.

REFERENCES

Beck, H.P., Levinson, S., and Irons, G. (2009) Finding Little Albert: a journey to John B. Watson's infant laboratory, *American Psychologist*, 64(7): 605–14.

Bigge, M.L. and Shermis, S.S. (2004) *Learning Theories for Teachers* (6th edn). Boston: Pearson.

Brown, G. (1977) *Child Development*. Shepton Mallet: Open Books.

Campione, J.C. (1989) Assisted assessment: a taxonomy of approaches and an outline of strengths and weaknesses, *Journal of Learning Disabilities*, 22(3): 151–65.

Corsaro, W.A. (1992) Interpretative reproduction in children's peer cultures, *Social Psychology Quarterly*, 55 (2): 160–77.

Donaldson, M. (1978) *Children's Minds*. Glasgow: Collins, Fontana.

Flavell, J.H. (1963) *The Developmental Psychology of Jean Piaget*. New York: Van Nostrand.

Flavell, J.H. (1977) *Cognitive Development*. Englewood Cliffs, NJ: Prentice Hall.

Frederickson, N. and Cline, T. (2002) *Special Educational Needs, Inclusion and Diversity*. Maidenhead: Open University Press.

Gray, C. and MacBlain, S.F. (2012) *Learning Theories in Childhood*. London: Sage.

Hayes, N. (1994) *Foundations of Psychology*. London: Routledge.

Holzman, L. (2006) Activating postmodernism, *Theory and Psychology*, 16(1): 109–23.

Keenan, M., Kerr, K.J. and Dillenburger, K. (2000) The way ahead. In M. Keenan, K.J. Kerr and K. Dillenburger (eds) *Parents' Education as Autism Therapists: Applied Behaviour Analysis in Context*. London: Jessica Kingsley.

Meadows, S. (1993) *The Child as Thinker: The Development and Acquisition of Cognition in Childhood*. London: Routledge.

Nutbrown, C. (2006) *Threads of Thinking: Young Children Learning and the Role of Early Education*. London: Sage.

Pea, R.D. (1993) Practices of distributed intelligence and designs for education. In G. Salomon (ed.) *Distributed Cognitions*. New York: Cambridge University Press, pp. 47–87.

Peel, E.A. (1971) *The Nature of Adolescent Judgment*. London: Staples Press.

Piaget, J. (1970) *Science of Education and the Psychology of the Child*. New York: Orion.

Rose, S.A., Feldman, J.F. and Jankowski, J.J. (2003) The building blocks of cognition. *The Journal of Pediatrics*, 143(4): 54–61.

Schaffer, H.R. (2004) *Introducing Child Psychology*. Oxford: Blackwell.

Smidt, S. (2011) *Introducing Bruner: A Guide for Practitioners and Students in Early Years Education*. London: Routledge.

Sutherland, P. (1992) *Cognitive Development Today: Piaget and his Critics*. London: Paul Chapman.

Vygotsky, L.S. (1978) *Mind in Society: The Development of Higher Psychological Processes*. Cambridge, MA: Harvard University Press.

Vygotsky, L.S. (1987–1998) *The Collected Works of L.S. Vygotsky. Volume I: Problems of General Psychology. Volume II: The Fundamentals of Defectology. Volume III: Problems of the Theory and History of Psychology. Volume IV: The History of Development of Higher Mental Functions. Volume V: Child Psychology*. (Editor of the English translation: R.W. Rieber.) New York: Plenum Press.

Watson, J.D. (1928) *Psychological Care of Infant and Child*. New York: Norton Company, Inc.

Wertsch, J.V. (ed.) (1981) *The Concept of Activity in Soviet Psychology*. Armonk, NY: M.E. Sharpe.

Whitebread, D. (2012) *Developmental Psychology and Early Childhood Education*. London: Sage.

3

THINKING AND LEARNING IN
THE EARLY YEARS

This chapter aims to:

- examine learning and early brain development
- explore how young learners develop
- examine the relationship between learning and play
- emphasize the importance of language in learning
- highlight early interventions and recent Early Years initiatives in the UK.

INTRODUCTION

It is really only in the past decades that we have begun to more fully understand the nature of thinking and learning in young children. As theorists and philosophers have added to our understanding of child development, so have researchers and practitioners also contributed to the accumulation of knowledge, in particular the learning behaviours of children in informal and formal educational settings (Beckley, 2012; Moyles et al., 2011). New methods of exploring learning have increasingly been taken on board as researchers engage in seeking to understand how children think and how their thinking links to learning. In fact, it would be accepted by most researchers and practitioners working in the field of education that our understanding of how children think and learn has increased dramatically within the last three or four decades. This has led, in many cases, to significant changes in practice and in how childhood is perceived and understood. Whilst significant advances have been made in our understanding, it is, nevertheless, important to recognize that much debate continues as to how children think, how they learn and, perhaps most controversially of all, how they are taught.

This chapter begins by focusing on the part that the brain plays in learning during the early years. The importance of play and how it underpins learning, especially in the early years is then explored before the chapter examines key aspects that are central to developing young learners. Then a number of recent initiatives in the UK in the field of Early Years education are explored before looking at our emerging understanding of the importance of understanding learning and thinking in relation to problem solving.

LEARNING AND EARLY BRAIN DEVELOPMENT

It is surprising how few books written on the subjects of learning and teaching contain any substantial references to the brain and yet this is the organ within all individuals that controls, regulates and drives learning. It is also surprising how few practitioners involved in the teaching of children have any real understanding of how the workings of the brain contribute to learning.

Central to our appreciation of early brain development is our need to understand the important role that neurons play, for it is through these that information passes in the form of electrical impulses. Estimations of the number of neurons in the brain are agreed to be in the region of many billions. It is during the development of the foetus prior to birth that neurons are formed and go on to form different parts of the brain. In doing so, they react and establish responses to different chemicals. This process begins with the more primitive areas of the brain such as the brainstem where the autonomic functions necessary for bodily development lie.

At birth these functions have become relatively well developed and, because of this, newly born infants have the capacity to take in nourishment such as their mother's milk by sucking, breathing and sleeping, hearing and generally experiencing sensations around them such as touch. Following birth it is now the turn of the 'more advanced' areas of the brain to develop, for instance the cerebral cortex, which deals with higher order functioning such as the development of language, thinking, emotions, and so on. Of particular note is the fact that it is during the period following birth and during the early years that most brain development takes place. It is also important to note that the different areas of the brain develop their own functions and do so through chemical agents such as hormones and neurotransmitters.

Following birth, infants continue their learning at an accelerating pace, which involves the strengthening of connections between neurons. Neurons do not make direct contact with each other but, instead, have tiny spaces or gaps, which are known as *synapses* and it is across these that the impulses travel. As this occurs chemicals are released, which are known as transmitter substances. When a transmitter substance crosses to another neuron then it is destroyed. Hardy and Heyes (1994, pp. 262–3) have commented as follows:

All messages in the nervous system are carried in the form of nerve impulses, but their interpretation depends upon which part of the brain receives the message: in one part an impulse
might be interpreted as a spot of light, in another as a sound … Many of the so-called 'nerve
gases' produced for warfare work by preventing the destruction of the transmitter molecules;
death results from the continual excitation of many neurons which causes prolonged con-
traction of all of the muscles of the body.

Synapses are, however, developed at quite an extraordinary rate following birth
and during the early years of development, so it is no wonder that researchers and
practitioners have recognized the importance of stimulating learning in these first
months and years. Indeed, it is generally agreed that the cerebral cortex of an infant
may construct well over a million synapses every second. Whilst many of these
synapses become established many do not and are abandoned by the infant. This
process continues throughout the lives of individuals though by adolescence some
50 per cent of synapses have been shed. Indeed, it has become increasingly recognized that the brain works on the principle of use it or lose it, with connections
between neurons being lost if not used. In this way the connections between neurons that are used become more durable. However, as infants grow they also shed
connections that are not being used and it is as this process develops that the child
constructs stronger pathways, which in a sense, results in the brain becoming
organized.

With advances in our understanding of the structure and functioning of the
brain, particularly in the field of neuroscience, we are coming to better appreciate
how the development of brains in young children interfaces with their environments and how this complex and necessary interaction affects and impacts upon
learning and thinking. The importance of the genetic make-up that a child inherits,
therefore, and the experiences the child has in their environments is now much better understood than even a decade ago. We know, for example, that the quality of
the relationships that children have with their primary caregivers is very important
when considering early brain development.

It is during those first years and even prior to birth that important connections
are made and strengthened. The more that young children engage in activities such
as play, movement, language, and so on, the stronger these connections will
become. For this reason, the experiences they have take on significant importance.
Take, for example, the case of a very young child during the pre-school years who
is read to every night after being put to bed and spoken to in a soft, affirming and
loving way. This child will form connections within their brain that are very different to the child who is allowed to stay up late and watch television and who com-
municates with their parents mainly in monosyllabic terms and shouting. Equally,
if the first child is given lots of opportunities to engage in physical play and exercise

then he will develop stronger sensorimotor connections than the second child who may spend many hours watching television and sitting on a chair.

As we have seen in the previous chapter, theorists have for some time recognized the importance of young children interacting meaningfully and purposefully with their environment and its being central to their learning and cognitive development. The more that young children interact with their environments in this way then the stronger the connections in the brain will be and the more secure the foundations will be for future learning. This is especially the case in regard to language development. Once again, let us take the earlier example of the first child whose parents employed richer vocabulary when talking with him and when explaining facts, their own wishes and desires, and so on. This child will develop much stronger, and qualitatively different, semantic networks than the second child whose parents offered little in the way of vocabulary extension.

A further process that is a feature of brain development is 'myelination'. This is where a 'fatty' substance known as myelin acts as an insulator and allows for the transmission of impulses across synapses. The experiences, and degree of stimulation, that infants and very young children have in these first vital years can affect the development of myelination and, therefore, future learning. By the time children have reached the age whereby they can attend preschool their brains are almost fully grown in size.

It is an interesting feature of brain development that infants and young children can adapt successfully to their environments. Readers might imagine the ways in which infants born into extremely cold or extremely hot environments quickly and naturally adapt. This said, it needs to be recognized that, whatever the environment, all infants and young children need stimulation and enriching experiences. It also needs to be recognized that all newly born infants and young children need to be loved and cared for, as it is through the love and care they receive that they also develop those aspects of their brains that will, in turn, contribute to their capacity to live balanced and emotionally fulfilled lives.

A further interesting and very important aspect of brain development in infants and young children is that of memory. As experiences are encountered by children and then repeated over time, the sensory neural pathways that are created within the brain contribute to the building of memories. Take, for example, a very young child who is lifted and tickled by his father when he returns home from work. Gradually the child will build a memory of that event whereby he learns that when his father picks him up he may well tickle him and that the experience of being picked up will be a pleasant one. Equally, if the experience of being lifted by his father leads to pain then the child also internalizes the interactions with his father as being essentially unpleasant ones. It is in such ways that the brain serves to help infants and young children adapt to their environment and to those around them, and in doing so they come to construct an understanding of the world within which they live. Recently, Claxton, author of the report *An Intelligent Look at Emotional Intelligence* (ATL, 2005, p. 20), commissioned by the Association of Teachers and Lecturers, spoke of very young children as having an 'emotional apprenticeship' whereby they observe how those around them manage their emotions. Claxton drew an important connection between these observations and learning as follows:

> When uncertain how to respond emotionally to a new person or event, babies and toddlers take their cue from the facial expression and tone of voice of the people they trust – parents obviously, but also, very effectively, older brothers and sisters. Whether deliberately or inadvertently, family members act as powerful role models that steer the child's emotional development. Studies of children in the Second World War showed that it was not the events they witnessed that affected their development; it was the way the adults around them reacted to those events. Being around an adult who continually 'loses it' is bad for a child's own emotional development.

DEVELOPING THE YOUNG LEARNER

Central to the development and management of children's learning in their early years is the nature of the environments in which they learn. Of equal importance is the active and meaningful participation of children in what they do and the extent to which children are encouraged to become involved with problem-based activities, not only on an individual basis but also with their peers and other adults. Also of importance is the need for adults working with young children to engage in critical reflection in a purposeful and meaningful way. It is worth taking time at this point to consider what is meant by critical reflection. Daudelin (1996: 39), quoted in Zwozdiak-Myers (2007, pp. 160–1) has offered a helpful starting point:

> ... reflection is the process of stepping back from an experience to ponder, carefully and persistently, its meaning to the self through the development of inferences: learning is the creation of meaning from past or current events that serves as a guide for future behaviour.

This definition is useful as it places particular emphasis upon a number of key constructs that can act as signposts in directing us towards understanding those elements that can be observed to underpin best practice when working with young children, namely: *'stepping back'*, *'carefully and persistently'*, *'meaning'*, *'inferences'* and *'behaviour'*. These words and phrases not only offer practitioners a means by which they can examine and evaluate their own practice, in particular their own behaviours, but they also provide the means by which practitioners can reflect with purpose on their own management of the environments they create for children. In addition they provide practitioners with the means by which they can observe, interpret and understand the actual behaviours of the children with whom they are working.

Exercise

Recall an account of a sequence of behaviours you have observed in young children. Take time to identify the words and phrases you might have used to describe the behaviours, and then consider what specific information these words and phrases would actually communicate to others.

When one observes effective practitioners working with young children it becomes quickly apparent that the conversations they have when talking about the children are characterized by a strong sense of purpose about what they are asking of the children, about the nature of the learning environments they are creating, and about the tasks they are giving to the children. Conversations are also characterized by their objective nature and there is little evidence of overly descriptive accounts when discussing learning. Instead, discussions are focused and typically evidence-based. These types of conversations suggest a deeper and more systematic understanding of the nature of those emotional, social and cognitive factors that reflect the individual learning needs of each child.

Effective practitioners also take time to engage purposefully in careful and meaningful observation. In doing so, they critically reflect upon the inferences they find themselves making about the behaviours of children and they make time to listen carefully to what parents are saying, or not saying, about their children. They 'carefully and persistently' focus upon patterns of behaviour in children, especially those specific micro behaviours that can be observed when children are playing and working by themselves and with others. Careful and purposeful observation and correct interpretation of behaviours can tell practitioners a great deal about how their children learn, their stages of cognitive development, their language development, social learning, and so on. Observing, for example, how often a child initiates verbal interactions during structured and unstructured play and the ease with which a child engages in verbal interaction with others can provide significant amounts of very useful information.

It is worth exploring a little further the importance of practitioners engaging in purposeful and meaningful observation of children's behaviours and the way they listen to children. This has been recognized for some time. Dowling (2005, p. 30), for example, has commented as follows, 'The task of really getting inside children's minds and understanding them can only properly be achieved through observing their actions and conversing with them', whilst Penny Lancaster (2006, p. 69) has suggested that:

> Listening to young children fits a rights-based approach in relating to children. It … advocates a move away from viewing young children as passive recipients of adults' decisions, where choices and decisions need to be made on their behalf.

Lancaster (2006, p. 72) suggests that in order to respect the voice of children practitioners need to have, '… understood how they [the children] have made sense of their experiences'. This point is crucial and emphasizes the importance of Early Years practitioners and teachers in primary schools giving time, not only to active and purposeful observation but also active listening within different contexts and really hearing what children are saying. In doing so, it is important to give children 'thinking' space to process information at a level appropriate to their own level of development and in their own time. This is especially important where adults are talking and listening to a child. To not do so might, in some cases, result in important aspects of a child's emotional, social and cognitive development being missed and children learning to be passive agents in what are essentially adult dominated relationships. In extreme cases where children may be experiencing emotional trauma in their lives they may even fail to have their trauma and home situations recognized. In the deeply sad and disturbing recent case of the young child Victoria Climbié, who was physically abused and then died, Penny Lancaster has noted:

> Victoria Climbié needed someone to listen to her life experiences, her concerns, her feelings and her perspective of her situation, but no one did. Her rights were overlooked and the care she received was steered by adult demand. (2006, p. 65)

Equally important to observing and listening to young children is the need for Early Years practitioners and primary school teachers to develop their observation skills and to take time to reflect and critically analyse their observations, either by themselves or with their peers. Reflective and purposeful observation can not only inform practitioners about children's social, emotional and cognitive development but can also inform them in regard to effective assessment and intervention, and subsequent planning of learning activities. Nutbrown (2006, p. 99) in respect to the importance of observation, has suggested that:

> … observation and assessment are the essential tools of watching and learning with which practitioners can both establish the progress that has already taken place and explore the future.

In commenting on observation in the classroom, as undertaken by Montessori teachers, Feez (2010, p. 24) has noted:

When learning to observe, trainee Montessori teachers sit where they will not disturb, distract or interact with the children in any way. They record everything, including small details others might not recognize as being important. In particular, they record:

- everything that interests each child, no matter how apparently insignificant
- how long a child sustains interest in each activity they choose, whether for seconds, minutes or hours
- how a child moves, especially movement of the hand
- how many times a child repeats the same activity
- how a child interacts with others.

Such an approach to the observation of young children can inform practitioners wishing to develop their own practice.

Now, take the case of Mark.

Example

Mark is in his first year at his local primary school. Mark's teacher feels intuitively that something is not right and she has already expressed concerns to the Special Educational Needs Coordinator (SENCo) and the head teacher. Together with the SENCo she takes time to observe Mark during class activities. Firstly, they both observe Mark working in a group situation with other children where they are tasked with collaborating together to solve a problem. Secondly, they both take time to observe Mark outside in the playground. What they find during both observations surprises them. Because they have chosen to focus mostly on Mark's micro behaviours (those tiny sequences of behaviours that we all do) they come to realize that within the classroom when Mark was working with the other children he did not once initiate any verbal interaction even though the group worked together for nearly an hour. Again, outside in the playground they observed that not once did he initiate any verbal interactions with others. They did observe, however, that he continually ran around the playground going from one group of children to another after only a few minutes and hovering on the edge of each group, but never actually joining in. When they again observed him a week later in the same social situations his behaviours were similar, in that he did not initiate any verbal communication with the other children. Subsequent discussion with the school social worker and assessment by the school's educational psychologist led to the realization that Mark was being severely neglected at home.

It is clear from the above example that Mark is an unhappy child and though he generally presents within class as being a quiet rather unforthcoming child it is not until his teachers actually take time to direct their observations towards his micro behaviours and patterns of behaviour that they fully appreciate that all is not as it should be. Now consider the following:

In considering the development of young learners it is perhaps now, more than ever, important to understand the influence that technology plays. Few young children nowadays fail to have access to televisions, computers, mobile telephones, and so on. Indeed, many readers will be familiar with those concerns, often expressed publicly, about the diet of aggression and violence and sexualized activity now available to young children through the media. Indeed, there is a significant number of children now entering school with poorly developed listening skills, with delayed language development and lack of maturity, and little in the way of even adequate preparedness for formal learning. For these children, the type of formal learning environment being offered by their school is crucial.

Now let us explore further the importance of creating suitable learning environments for young children, and especially those who enter school with poorly developed skills and knowledge or who are beginning their education having just arrived from a different country or culture. It is clear that the culture of Early Years settings and primary schools has undergone significant change in the last decades. There has, for example, been a large increase in the diversity of children's needs, as can be witnessed by the growing number of pupils with a wide range of special educational needs and/or disabilities now being educated in mainstream settings. It was estimated that, in England alone, in the year 2008 there were approximately one and a half million pupils with special educational needs in schools, representing approximately 20 per cent of the school population. In addition, just over half of the 223,600 children (nearly three per cent of the school population) with formal Statements of Special Educational needs had been included within mainstream schools (DCSF, 2008). In regard to linguistic diversity it has been estimated that there are currently some 900,000 pupils in schools in England learning English as an additional language, with estimates of some 200 languages being spoken.

To help us in our attempts to gain a better understanding of the individual needs of children entering formal education and how Early Years settings and primary schools can meet the wide range of diversity it is worth framing our own thinking and analysis within those theoretical constructs referred to earlier in this text. By doing so, we can compare our own perceptions of how we think children should learn, against a 'tried and tested', though admittedly not universally accepted, approach to teaching and learning. Through making such comparisons, readers will not only gain a much deeper understanding of the original ideas of these theorists and philosophers but will also generate within their own thinking new hypotheses and new insights. One notable example, which continues to exert significant influence on practitioners today, is that of Maria Montessori (see Chapter 1).

Montessori originally identified 11 'sensitive' periods during the first stage (or Plane, 0 to 6 years) of development. During the period from birth to around 12 months children are developing their abilities in movement, for example crawling and walking. Exploration of their environments is also a feature of this stage as children move about touching, grasping and holding objects and people. Young children typically move forward from making arbitrary sounds to babble and then to forming and using words and phrases. This is then followed by sentences, indicating understanding of their own ideas and actions to those of others around them. It is also during this first stage that children between the ages of one and four can be observed fixating upon objects and the detail contained within these objects.

This is a crucial feature of children's early learning as they are developing important attention and concentration skills, in addition to their emerging visual skills, which facilitate internal representations within their brain of visual features, for example contours and shapes. This process of fixation and visual representations within the brain also facilitates the process of verbal mediation whereby children attach verbal labels, including random sounds, to these objects. If, in the case of some children coming from dysfunctional families, they have few opportunities to engage with such learning situations then they may well be disadvantaged when they commence formal education. More particularly, they will have failed to move purposefully through this 'sensitive' stage and their development may have been restricted and even distorted in some ways. This has huge implications for how the learning of these children is managed and how the adults charged with managing their learning interpret their behaviours. For example, ought such children to be labelled at a very early age as having special educational needs or should they be viewed as children who require nurturing, greater access to expressive and receptive language, support with developing attention skills and improving concentration, and so on?

Montessori also proposed that with children between the ages of two and four there can be observed a desire for consistency and sameness. Some children at this stage can be observed to become distressed if their environments are altered. Children at this stage also appear to respond positively to routine. Readers might again wish to reflect upon the impact that established routines and consistency both at home and in the classroom have for young children, and especially those children who live in dysfunctional homes characterized by disorganization and lack of stability. Readers might also wish to consider different parenting styles and how some parents are keen to impose clear boundaries within the lives of their children whilst others reject this notion and seek to avoid the imposition of any boundaries. It is also worth considering that parenting styles transcend all sections of society, with particular types of parenting not being restricted to any one 'class' or determined by income.

Montessori believed that between the ages of two and six young children typically demonstrate a natural interest in some aspects of music, for example, rhythm and singing. She also suggested that 'Grace and Courtesy' and 'Refinement of the Senses' can also be observed in young children at this stage. Young children at this stage between the ages of two and six demonstrate strong tendencies towards imitating the behaviours of adults and older siblings. Here, we can once again see the importance that good role modelling by parents and significant others in a child's life can have for them and how this can support future learning and important skills necessary for effective education, such as good listening skills, attentiveness, emotional control and perseverance.

Other elements that Montessori identified during this stage were (see Gray and MacBlain, 2012, p. 154):

- an apparent fascination with writing where the young child at around three to four years of age can be observed trying to copy letters and words or numbers and symbols
- an interest in reading where the young child between three and five years of age can be observed to display interest in the sounds of letters and words
- an interest in spatial relationships between four and six years of age where the young child internally represents relationships between objects and their immediate environments
- a development of basic concepts in mathematical thinking using concrete materials between four and six years of age.

Independence and the ability to care for oneself are key features of Montessori's philosophy. Again, readers might reflect upon the absence of this for some children who come from homes where their parents may be involved in substance abuse, criminality and neglect. Readers might also wish to reflect upon the notion of encouraging independence within children and how many parents feel anxious about allowing their children to play outside away from home and to take risks. Indeed, this is an aspect of parenting that has received much recent attention in the media.

In Montessori nurseries children engage with tasks such as putting on their clothes and tidying up their classrooms. This type of learning supports children's development in regard to contributing in later years to their own communities. This is a rather seductive idea and one imagines the importance of preparing children to be 'good' members of their communities and to develop sound values that will mean that they more fully engage with society and come to view themselves as active participants who develop sound work ethics.

Repetition of tasks is a further feature of the Montessori Method as this is believed to underpin future abstract reasoning. As new concepts are introduced to young children a three-step process is employed by Montessori practitioners, namely, introducing the new concept, understanding it in concrete terms, and then understanding it in abstract terms. Teaching and learning, therefore, become individualized processes for each child, which is also a key feature of the principles underpinning the recently introduced *Statutory Framework for the Early Years Foundation Stage*, in the UK (see below).

Drawing upon Montessori's views about repetition, it is worth considering the purpose of over learning and rehearsal for children with the specific learning difficulties of dyslexia and dyspraxia. For many such children, who present in learning situations as inattentive and lacking in concentration, a primary need is to be given opportunities to engage in over learning and repetition as a means of confronting difficulties with short-term memory, organization and planning. A very important aspect of short-term memory is rehearsal. Many young children who are observed within classroom situations to be failing with aspects of literacy, typically experience difficulties with rehearsal and may well not have properly internalized efficient strategies for reading and writing text. All too often, such children use inefficient strategies when approaching reading and writing tasks. For example, they may guess at words or try to sound out individual letters and words when they have an impoverished understanding of blending and little knowledge about the structural analysis of words.

For many such children their specific difficulties are related primarily to phonological processing. Effective practitioners, therefore, when working with children displaying such specific difficulties employ much over learning which is sequential and cumulative in practice, and most importantly that employs multisensory and kinaesthetic activities. Central to these types of interventions is the acknowledgement by Early Years practitioners and teachers of the importance of movement and coordination, which underpins the multisensory approach.

LEARNING AND PLAY

Play is central to learning. It is through play, for example, that young children learn to cooperate with others and to form and maintain relationships. Through play they develop their language skills, their capacity to think and problem solve, their observational skills and abilities to listen, and so on. In fact, play lies at the very core of children's development, and, as readers will appreciate, carries on throughout adolescence and the entirety of adulthood.

Smith et al. (2003, p. 218) have drawn an important distinction between play and exploration in very young children, located they suggest within the ideas of the Behaviourists and the Piagetians (see Chapter 2) as follows:

> These were often subsumed together in earlier writings, perhaps because of the influence of behaviourism and learning theory. Both exploration and play were awkward for traditional learning theorists, as neither was obviously goal-seeking or under the control of reinforcers. It is also true that with very young children, during sensori-motor development ..., the distinction between exploration and play is difficult to make, as for young infants, all objects are novel. By the preschool years, however, the distinction is clearer.

Smith et al. go on to suggest three types of play: locomotor or physical activity play, which includes exercise play and what is often referred to as rough-and-tumble play; play with objects as well as fantasy play and sociodramatic play; and finally language play (2003, p. 219). Readers will be familiar with these types of play where, with the first of these, young children can be observed in playgroups engaged in physical activity such as running and jumping, often without objects being present. Pellegrini and Smith (1998), cited in Smith (2003, pp. 220–1) have proposed that in physical activity play there are three developmental stages, namely: 'rhythmical stereotypes' such as the kicking of legs and waving of arms that can be observed in infants; 'exercise play' such as running and jumping, involving the child's whole body. This can be observed in preschool settings and overlaps with the type of rough-and-tumble play so frequently observed in primary school playgrounds and at home between young siblings – the third stage.

Smith et al. further propose that the next type of play, fantasy play, can be observed in children as young as 12 months. The earliest pretend play, they suggest, involves children in directing actions towards themselves and depends greatly upon using actual objects such as those found around the home. The ultimate in imaginary play, Smith et al. suggest, is where children have an 'imaginary companion'. They suggest that between a quarter and a half of children between the ages of three and eight (with most giving up this notion by age 10) have some type of 'imaginary companion'. Children with 'imaginary companions' can be often observed engaging in quite sophisticated pretend play with their 'imaginary companions'.

The final type of play suggested by Smith et al., is that of language play. Again, readers will be familiar with the many ways in which young children use words and sounds to make themselves and others laugh and the joy they get from listening to and telling stories that involve noises made by animals, giants, and so on.

Children can also be observed to gain much from listening to rhyming poems, riddles, nursery rhymes, and so on. When children play together in groups such as at each others' birthday parties they can often be observed by their parents to have great fun and fits of giggles when they say 'silly' things to each other.

As children grow older they move towards playing games that have rules and clearly defined structures. This enables them to learn about cooperation, boundaries, relationships, and so on, and offers opportunities for children to move outside of their homes and join local clubs such as cricket and football clubs. Others may join outdoor pursuit clubs and engage in less group-oriented activities, which offer elements of risk as well as opportunities to play together with others and develop friendships.

Of course, the nature of play is changing and younger readers of this text may recall listening to older friends and relatives recounting the good old days when they played outside all day from early morning until the sunset and when they only had pieces of wood, lengths of rope and old pram wheels to play with. Nowadays, the nature of play for many children is very different. Significant numbers of children, for example, spend excessive amounts of time playing indoors on computer games, and this, rather worryingly some would argue, starts from too early an age. Take the case of Ned, aged six years, who gets up most mornings at around 7 o'clock and switches on the television in his bedroom, which he watches until his mother brings him some breakfast cereal at 8 o'clock and urges him to dress himself. As he dresses, he continues to watch television until he leaves the house for school. When he returns from school he plays in his room with his computer games and then comes downstairs for a meal at 6 o'clock for around half an hour when the television remains on as all of the family watch it. After his meal he remains watching television most evenings until around 9 o'clock and at weekends until around 10 o'clock. Clearly, Ned's play is very restricted and he rarely plays out of doors. Learning opportunities that he might engage in such as climbing, running and jumping and cycling are few and far between and these are important activities not only in terms of socializing but also in terms of developing sensory-neural pathways in the brain, which in turn, develop physical attributes such as gross and fine motor coordination, and attention span.

Exercise

Should Early Years practitioners and primary school teachers play a more active role in getting parents to restrict the amount of time children watch television and play on computers when at home, and if so, how might they do this?

THE IMPORTANCE OF LANGUAGE

Most if not all readers will be aware of the function that language plays in learning. Before looking more closely at how spoken language impacts upon learning it is worth exploring the importance of written language, for it is through written language that children are typically asked to demonstrate much of their learning when at school. Arguably, this aspect of language has received little attention by researchers working in the field of language and communication. Some decades ago Brown (1977, p. 119) made the following observations:

> Before the child can write or read he must be able to identify the symbols and the sounds they represent. Evidence suggests that visual recognition may be possible quite early, but that the association of the symbol with a sound, a cross-modal link between vision and auditory discrimination, may take longer. For written language the child must also have a high degree of motor coordination.

There is a further important consideration here in that some researchers, perhaps most notably Bruner (see Chapter 2) have suggested that the cognitive structures of children who are actively encouraged to engage in written activities alongside reading activities will typically be different. Drawing upon the work of Bruner (1975), Brown (1977, p. 119) has again commented as follows:

> He [Bruner] suggested that the mind of a person who spent much of his time in these activities might be 'profoundly different' from that of one who was involved in non-linguistic activities such as drawing or building, and perhaps even different from that of one who mostly talked and listened. He suggested that there may be a minimal use of language in ordinary discourse which has little effect upon an individual's thought patterns, but beyond that level it may transform them. The most important step in this transformation he saw as instigated by the transference from speech into some form of notation such as writing or mathematical symbols. In this form it becomes more powerful. The rules which must be obeyed to construct written sentences may allow some people to analyse the products of their thoughts and to operate with formal operations (Piaget's term) in ways which would not otherwise be possible.

Clearly such a view has important implications for the practice of Early Years practitioners and teachers in primary schools in the UK, many of whom are becoming increasingly concerned by a growing perception in some quarters, even in government, that children ought to be introduced to a more formal pedagogy involving writing and reading at preschool level. Such concerns have been recognized for some years. Miller and Pound (2011, p. 165), for example, have commented as follows:

> External pressures from government guidance or a management hierarchy can lead practitioners to focus on curriculum 'delivery' or 'coverage' as the main focus of their practice. Such

a view would have been anathema to the foundational theorists ... but in England it has become a feature of the Early Years Foundation Stage (EYFS) (DfES, 2008) and the National Curriculum in primary schools, causing uncertainty for many practitioners.

Though the debate continues as to the nature of the pedagogies in Early Years settings and primary schools it is, nonetheless, important to emphasize that stimulating spoken language alongside reading and written language, even in its most basic form such as that of making marks and symbols, must continue to receive serious consideration by practitioners and parents alike.

Exercise

Consider the view that the work of Early Years practitioners should not involve any formal teaching and that children under their supervision should engage totally in learning through play. Consideration could also be given to the lack of formality in many European countries in regard to the education of young children and also other philosophies of education such as that of the Steiner tradition.

It should also be recognized that language is central to the social and emotional development of children and from a very early age infants learn to gain the attention of others around them, to get food, to be played with and cuddled, and so on. Indeed, most infants become competent in their abilities to communicate with others and have their needs met long before they acquire words and phrases. In this regard, we can acknowledge that humans are most probably programmed to acquire language and to develop through stages of this acquisition. For some children growing up in households where language is limited they may come to experience difficulties in expressing their feelings and emotions (see Chapter 7).

It is certainly the case that many children currently entering primary schools in the UK have language delay and poor listening skills. Palmer (2006, p. 105) recently offered the following rather disturbing observation:

Everywhere I went it was the same story: four- and five-year-olds were coming to school with poorer language skills than ever before; they weren't arriving with the repertoire of nursery rhymes and songs little ones always used to know, and children of all ages found it increasingly difficult to sit down and listen to their teacher or to express complex ideas in speech or writing ... I also discovered that this issue was bothering teachers across the developed world.

Palmer's accounts are worrying and suggest a growing malaise amongst many children and sections of the UK population where children are not being supported in many areas of language development. In an attempt to address the importance of language development in young children Cowie (2012, p. 83) has proposed four key areas of language that she suggests young children have to master:

1. *Phonology* refers to the system that governs the particular sounds (or phonemes) used in the language of a child's community in order to convey meaning ...

2. *Semantics* refers to the meanings encoded in language. Phonemes are in themselves meaningless but they are combined to form morphemes, the smallest meaningful units of language. These may be whole words ('cat' in English, 'chat' in French) or grammatical markers, such as '-ed' at the end of a verb to make the past tense.

3. *Syntax* refers to the form and order in which words are combined to make grammatical sentences. The child progresses, for example, from saying 'Ben cup' to saying 'Ben wants that red cup'. The rules that govern such sequences are known as *syntax*.

4. *Pragmatics* is knowledge about how language is used in different contexts. The young child must learn to adapt her language to the situation in which she finds herself ...

It is of course important to recognize that whilst many children have poor experiences of language modelling at home and in their immediate communities other children experience more specific and even neurological difficulties in some of the above four areas identified by Cowie. Children with dyslexia, for example, can be observed to have problems with aspects of their language functioning, as can children with dyspraxia and Asperger's Syndrome (see Chapter 8). For this reason, it is crucial that Early Years practitioners and primary school teachers are informed about the nature of language development and the potential difficulties that face children who enter learning environments with delayed language, or more worryingly perhaps, language disorder, when referral to a Speech and Language therapist will be appropriate.

EARLY INTERVENTION AND RECENT INITIATIVES IN THE UK

The UK is certainly not short of initiatives. In fact, there are some who would argue that education in England over the last few decades has been essentially flooded with initiatives. They are everywhere. Early Years and primary education, especially, have had their share of initiatives, and whilst teachers and Early Years practitioners may have at times welcomed these, they may also, at other times, have felt completely overwhelmed by them. We now look at a number of key initiatives whose origins were not always in the UK but have come to influence practice in the UK. We commence with HighScope, which although originally developed in Michigan in the USA is now used within the UK, as well as throughout the world.

Drawing initially upon the work of Piaget and Dewey, HighScope has also drawn upon other theorists and researchers over the years such as Vygotsky and Bruner (see Chapter 2), and more recently, Goswani (2002) and Snow et al. (1998). In the UK, HighScope has also drawn upon the experiences of practitioners in the USA and is used across many sections of the education system. Indeed, it is used creatively to address, for example, the learning needs of young children with additional needs or those who are considered to be vulnerable. Like other approaches HighScope seeks to support young children in actively building their knowledge and understanding of the world in which they live. Learning, therefore, is an active rather than a passive process. Miller and Pound (2011, p. 103) comment as follows:

> HighScope practitioners are as active and involved as children in the early years setting … The HighScope approach promotes independence, curiosity, decision-making, co-operation, persistence, creativity and problem solving in young children.

Such principles are now fully recognized and accepted by most if not all primary teachers and practitioners working in Early Years settings, who regard these principles as central to their work with children. This said, they also need to be viewed critically against the shifting dynamic of government-imposed change and directives currently in the pipeline for education in the UK, for example, an apparent, and growing, emphasis on the use of formal teaching methods at preschool level.

Exercise

How do the principles of the HighScope approach fit with those policy and decision makers who argue for less creativity in primary and post-primary schools and a return to a more traditional way of teaching and learning where children are much more directed in their learning and rewarded with praise when presenting the desired responses?

Another initiative introduced in the UK which has received a great deal of interest was the *Sure Start* initiative, which was introduced back in 1998 by the then Chancellor of the Exchequer, Gordon Brown. Though aimed particularly at children and families in England, other regions, namely Wales, Scotland and Northern Ireland embraced and adapted this initiative to meet their own needs. Sure Start was initially introduced with the aim of giving those children who needed it the best possible beginning in their lives. Proposed improvements in child care support for families, and early education, as well as important aspects relating to health and well-being, were viewed as central to the approach, with greater attention being given to the development of communities. The funding allocated to this initiative was significant; around £540 million was allocated between 1999 and 2002. It was estimated at the time that some 150,000 children living in deprivation would benefit. The government initially agreed to provide funding for this initiative for 10 years. However, the Chancellor reported in 2003 that the government planned to relocate Sure Start to within local government by 2005, thereby establishing Sure Start centres in all communities.

More recently, the UK government has introduced the *Statutory Framework for the Early Years Foundation Stage*, which became mandatory on 1 September 2012 for all early years providers, that is, maintained and non-maintained schools, independent schools, and all providers on the *Early Years Register*, although there may be some exemptions to this last group. The introduction of this new Framework, which builds upon existing practice is premised on the view that '... every child deserves the best possible start in life and the support that enables them to fulfil their potential' (DfE, 2012, p. 2).

The Early Years Foundation Stage (EYFS) Framework embraces the notion that children today are not only developing quickly but that the life experiences following birth and up to when they commence formal schooling at age five are extremely important and exert a significant impact upon them. Such a view is, of course, not new and has been promoted throughout the centuries by philosophers and theorists (see Chapter 1). What appears to be new, however, is the emphasis that government is placing upon ensuring that all providers must offer children provision that is effective, purposeful and that falls within parameters that are viewed as key to children's social, emotional and educational development. Good parenting is also viewed as a key aspect of development in these first years, as is the need for children to access learning that is of a high quality.

Of note is the fact that Ofsted will have regard to the EYFS in as much as they will undertake inspections of the implementation and application of this new Framework and report on the quality and standards of provision being offered. Following inspections by Ofsted they will publish their reports and may in some instances issue a 'notice to improve' or a 'welfare requirements notice'. Of particular note is the fact that any provider who fails to comply with a 'welfare requirements notice' is committing an offence.

It is now worth exploring this new EYFS Framework in much greater detail as it currently affects the practice of all providers working with young children.

The *Statutory Framework for the Early Years Foundation Stage* proposes four overarching principles, which should be central to practice in Early Years settings:

- every child is a **unique child**, who is constantly learning and can be resilient, capable, confident and self-assured [Readers should refer to the section on developing emotional intelligence in Chapter 7 where the concept of resilience is more fully explored];

- children learn to be strong and independent through **positive relationships**;

- children learn and develop well in **enabling environments**, in which their experiences respond to their individual needs and there is a strong partnership between practitioners and parents and/or carers; and

- **children develop and learn in different ways and at different rates** (DfE, 2012, p. 3).

Now consider the following:

Exercise

Consider how realistic the above principles are for Early Years practitioners working with children from severely disadvantaged and dysfunctional homes. What steps can be taken to ensure that providers adhere to these principles?

The *Statutory Framework for the Early Years Foundation Stage* proposes seven areas in regard to learning and development and how these should inform and shape practice in Early Years settings. These are: communication and language; physical development; personal, social and emotional development; literacy; mathematics; understanding the world; and expressive arts and design. The first three of these are seen as 'Prime' areas, which are viewed as especially crucial, and the next four as 'Specific' areas, which providers must use to support children in developing the first three. The Framework emphasizes the importance of providers taking particular consideration of the individual needs of children as well as their stage of development. Information gained from consideration of these areas should, the Framework proposes, inform the planning of children's experiences. Particular attention must be given to the 'Prime' areas when working with very young children, which the Framework indicates, 'reflect the key skills and capacities all children need to develop and learn effectively, and become ready for school' (DfE, 2012, p. 6). The Framework also gives particular attention to whether children have special educational needs or disabilities which might call for specialist intervention, and in this way links with families to assist them in accessing relevant services from external agencies where this is appropriate.

In addition to the above, the Framework places particular emphasis upon the importance of assessment as follows:

Ongoing assessment (also known as formative assessment) is an integral part of the learning and development process. It involves practitioners observing children to understand their level of achievement, interests and learning styles, and to then shape learning experiences for each child reflecting those observations … (DfE, 2012, p. 10)

Of encouragement to many practitioners in regard to assessment will be the inclusion within the Framework of the clear emphasis that is placed upon the reduction of paperwork:

> Assessment should not entail prolonged breaks from interaction with children, nor require excessive paperwork. Paperwork should be limited to that which is absolutely necessary to promote children's successful learning and development. (DfE, 2012, p. 10)

The Framework also places particular emphasis upon child protection and indicates, for example, that, 'Providers must have and implement a policy, and procedures, to safeguard children' (2012, p. 13). Similarly, the Framework also places emphasis upon the qualifications, training and skill level of providers and their need to engage effectively with induction training for new staff and continuing professional development.

The British Association for Early Childhood Education (2012) has produced a most helpful publication *Development Matters in the Early Years Foundation Stage (EYFS)*, which offers clear guidance to providers and practitioners in an accessible and helpful format. In particular, it offers information regarding the learning of children in all of the 'Prime' and 'Specific' areas from birth to 11 months through to 40 to 60 months, giving providers, practitioners, parents and carers, and other relevant professionals, an indication of what can be expected of children at different ages and stages.

Summary

The importance of understanding thinking and its relationship to learning cannot be emphasized enough. At the very core of this relationship lies the early development of cognitive and neurological functioning. Children born into families where there is much stimulation, care and love will typically enter formal education with greater opportunities to embark upon their learning and schooling, which will lay down the building blocks for future success. Those children who are not, may find that they commence formal education with more poorly developed cognitive and neurological structures, which may well put them at a distinct disadvantage.

This chapter has explored a number of key issues central to this relationship, with particular emphasis being placed upon the role of the teacher and Early Years practitioner and the importance of creating effective and purposeful environments where children can develop their learning and thinking. The importance of play and language has been especially emphasized as these two elements are central to the development of thinking and learning. Recent initiatives in regard to Early Years practice and preparing children for their formal education were explored and offer an introduction to the following chapter, which now explores learning in the family.

RECOMMENDED READING

Department for Education (DfE) (2012) *Statutory Framework for the Early Years Foundation Stage: Setting the Standards for Learning, Development and Care for Children from Birth to Five*. Runcorn: DfE.

Gray, C. and MacBlain, S.F. (2012) *Learning Theories in Childhood*. London: Sage.

Miller, L. and Pound, L. (2011) *Theories and Approaches to Learning in the Early Years*. London: Sage.

REFERENCES

Association of Teachers and Lecturers (ATL) (2005) *An Intelligent Look at Emotional Intelligence*. London: Association of Teachers and Lecturers.

Beckley, P. (2012) *Learning in Early Childhood*. London: Sage.

British Association for Early Childhood Education (2012) *Development Matters in the Early Years Foundation Stage (EYFS)*. London: British Association for Early Childhood Education.

Brown, G. (1977) *Child Development*. Shepton Mallet: Open Books.

Bruner, J.S. (1975) Language as an instrument in thought. In A. Davies (ed.) *Problems of Language and Learning*. London: Heinemann.

Cowie, H. (2012) *From Birth to Sixteen: Children's Health, Social, Emotional and Linguistic Development*. London: Routledge.

Daudelin, M. (1996) Learning from experience through reflection. *Dynamics*, 24(3): 36–48.

Department for Children, Schools and Families (DCSF) (2008) *Special Educational Needs in England*. London: DCSF.

Department for Education and Skills (DfES) (2008) *Statutory Framework for the Early Years Foundation Stage*. Nottingham: DfES Publications.

Department for Education (DfE) (2012) *Statutory Framework for the Early Years Foundation Stage: Setting the Standards for Learning, Development and Care for Children from Birth to Five*. Runcorn: DfE.

Dowling, M. (2005) *Young Children's Personal, Social and Emotional Development*. London: Paul Chapman Publishing.

Goswani, U. (ed.) (2002) *Blackwell Handbook of Child Cognitive Development*. Malden, MA: Blackwell Publishers.

Gray, C. and MacBlain, S.F. (2012) *Learning Theories in Childhood*. London: Sage.

Feez, S. (2010) *Montessori and Early Childhood*. London: Sage.

Hardy, M. and Heyes, S. (1994) *Beginning Psychology: A Comprehensive Introduction to Psychology* (4th edn). Oxford: Oxford University Press.

Lancaster, Y.P. (2006) Listening to young children: respecting the voice of the child. In G. Pugh and B. Duffy (eds) *Contemporary Issues in Early years*. London: Sage.

Miller, L. and Pound, L. (2011) *Theories and Approaches to Learning in the Early Years*. London: Sage.

Moyles, J., Georgeson, J. and Payler, J. (2011) *Beginning Teaching, Beginning Learning: In Early Years and Primary Education*. Maidenhead: Open University Press.

Nutbrown, C. (2006) Watching and listening: the tools of assessment. In G. Pugh and B. Duffy (eds) *Contemporary Issues in the Early Years*. London: Sage.

Palmer, S. (2006) *Toxic Childhood*. London: Orion Books.

Pugh, G. and Duffy, B. (eds) (2006) *Contemporary Issues in the Early Years*. London: Sage.

Smith, K.S., Cowie, H. and Blades, M. (2003) *Understanding Children's Development* (4th edn). Oxford: Blackwell.

Snow, C.E., Burns, S. and Griffin, P. (eds) (1998) *Preventing Reading Difficulties in Young Children*. Washington, DC: National Academy Press.

Zwozdiak-Myers, P. (ed.) (2007) *Childhood and Youth Studies*. London: Learning Matters Ltd.

4 LEARNING IN THE FAMILY

This chapter aims to:

- explore the importance of families and their place in the learning of children
- explore the nature and structure of families today and their impact upon children's learning
- examine cultural interpretations of families with particular reference to the work of Pierre Bourdieu
- explore the concept of attachment and its potential impact upon the learning of children, with particular reference to those children experiencing loss
- examine the importance of play within the family and how this influences and impacts upon learning.

INTRODUCTION

The importance of families and their contribution to children's learning cannot be emphasized enough. Winsdale (2012, p. 20), for example, explains the importance of the relationship between families and learning as follows:

> Families of all kinds … are social institutions within which children routinely accomplish some of the major educational achievements of their lives – learning to speak, to form intimate relationships, to master basic skills of living and to engage with ethical lessons of how to live.

Within families, newborn babies learn not just from their parents but also from older siblings and family friends. Later, as teenagers and then as young adults they will continue to learn within and from their families. Learning, however, is not unidirectional. Older family members also learn from children. Take, for example, the case of the elderly grandmother who is being introduced to the new technologies of computers and websites by her nine-year-old grandson who has developed a high level of proficiency with computers. As the child teaches his grandmother he is also learning from her by observing her responses and by listening to her. In a sense they are constructing understanding together. In the hours and days that follow he may well reflect back upon this time with his grandmother and think about how she behaved and about the type of questions she asked him. He may even relate this experience and his own reflections about his grandmother to others and in doing so will reflect further upon the whole episode.

What is important in this example is the nature of the interactions taking place. Whilst some of the learning that the grandchild experiences is incidental and not specifically directed by his grandmother, there is purpose to what he is doing, and in many respects it is creative, reflective and intuitive. For all young children this will be the case. Though much of the learning experienced in the first years appears on the surface to be random and incidental it will, nevertheless, involve purpose and direction. It is within the family then that children typically first engage in these processes of purpose, direction, intention and reflection.

In a celebrated study of young children's learning at home and at school Tizard and Hughes (1984) tape-recorded the conversations of 30 girls about the age of four from two social class backgrounds (15 in each). These recordings took place both at the children's nursery school and in their homes. The authors identified five factors originating within the child's home that they considered to be especially important for children's learning. The first factor identified by the authors was the vast number of activities that occurred within the home such as hearing and observing telephone conversations, planning and eating of meals during the day, observing visits from friends, relatives, neighbours, and so on. Within the home, outings are discussed, planned and take place to the local shops, supermarkets, church, school, relatives, and so on. It is through such events that children begin to learn about their social worlds, and come to construct their understanding of these worlds, not only at an individual level but also in tandem with those around them. It is also through these activities that the behaviours of others become modelled to them, facilitating and extending social learning. Secondly, Tizard and Hughes observed the extent to which, when at home, '… parent and child share a common life, stretching back into the past and forward into the future' (1984, p. 250). It is this commonality of experience and life events, past and future, that helps facilitate the parents' understanding of their child's intentions. In addition, this commonality also helps the child understand and integrate new experiences into their previous experiences, and in doing so builds their knowledge of the world around them. Indeed, such processes lie at the very core of intellectual development and children's learning.

Thirdly, it was also of interest that Tizard and Hughes identified the fact that at the time of their study only 11 per cent of families in Great Britain had more than two children who were under 16 years of age. In such families, parents, they implied, are more available to their children and, therefore, can spend more time engaging with them and offering quality experiences. Most particularly, they suggested, parents in such families can talk with their children. It can be proposed then that in families with a small number of children or an only child, learning may well be more effective. Such a proposition needs to be treated with caution as clearly this will not be the case with every family. However, it does raise some important issues. Just over a decade ago Buckingham (2000, p. 65), for example, commented as follows:

> Even for those who live in traditional nuclear families, children spend decreasing amounts of time with their parents, and more in institutionalized child-care of some form; and they are also less likely to have siblings available for companionship.

It is likely that the number of children in institutionalized child care will have increased since Buckingham's observation. A fourth factor identified by Tizard and Hughes was as follows:

> … learning is often embedded in contexts of great meaning to the child. Making a shopping list, helping with the baby, writing to Granny, deciding how many cakes are needed for tea, playing card games, are activities that, because of their interest to the child, make it easy for her to learn. This principle is well understood in primary education, but it is much easier to put into effect in the home than in the school. (1984, p. 251)

The nature of the close relationships within the home greatly supports children's language development; the child can, for example, ask many questions and feel they are being actively listened to. Tizard and Hughes described this as the '"curriculum" of the home' and suggested that mothers who were especially close to their children typically had high expectations of them, which then contributed to their formal education adding positively to their children's early foundations of learning through the perceptions and expectations of their teachers. The implications of Tizard and Hughes' findings become more relevant when we consider the number of families where both parents are leaving for work early in the morning and returning home during the early evening.

The fifth factor they identified was the 'close, and often intense' relationships that exist between the child and their mother. Whilst they suggested that this might, in some instances hinder learning, for example, where the child interferes with activities through their demands, they also recognized that closeness to the mother ensured that the child was learning from their mother. They also acknowledged that the 'curriculum' within homes varies from one mother to another, 'It was a matter of great personal concern to most mothers in our study that their child should acquire the skills, knowledge and values that they believed to be important' (1984, p. 252). This, of course, raises some obvious issues in that what might be considered valuable by one mother may not be seen as valuable by another.

FAMILIES OR HOUSEHOLDS: THE CHANGING NATURE OF FAMILIES AND ITS IMPACT UPON LEARNING

Having discussed how children learn in families, we now examine how the impact of change in families can affect the learning of children. Every family is different and families over time change in all manner of ways. In some families change can be a hugely significant and even destructive force, whilst in others change can be slow and gentle. Change in families has, perhaps, become more evident in recent decades as the nature and structure of families has altered in what some would say is a quite radical way. In fact, there are many researchers working within the field of families, children and young people who now prefer to use the term '*household*' as opposed to '*family*'. It has been estimated (MacBlain and MacBlain, 2004), for example, that in 2001 there were 3.1 million children growing up in households with a lone parent. A year later, it was again estimated (National Statistics, 2003) that in the spring of 2002 one-fifth of dependent children growing up in Great Britain were living within lone-parent families. This was twice that of the number of children in lone-parent families in 1981 some twenty years before (Gray and MacBlain, 2012). This number has gradually risen since then, with the number of lone-parent families now being greater than ever before.

Rates of divorce have also been increasing at what some suggest is an alarming rate. Indeed, in 1998 Rowntree (quoted in Brown, 1999, p. 66) alerted us to the fact that, 'If recent trends continue, more than a third of new marriages will end within 20 years and four out of ten will ultimately end in divorce'. Whilst the emotional and social effects of parental separation and divorce upon children and their learning appear obvious, the economic effects are also worthy of particular note. Buckingham (2000, p. 65), for example, has commented:

> Single-parent families are much more likely to live below the poverty line, and to be dependent on state benefits; while lone mothers are less likely to be employed than those in two-parent families. Such families are also disproportionately represented among groups that already suffer from poverty, notably Afro-Caribbeans.

Added to the number of children in lone-parent households who have experienced parental separation and/or divorce is that group of children whose parents choose not to marry or to live together and choose instead to rear their children within a lone-parent household (MacBlain and Purdy, 2011). This may be due to a variety of circumstances, for example, young women and girls who find themselves pregnant and giving birth to children in their school years or during early adulthood. Recently, the newspaper columnist James Chapman, writing in the British newspaper *The Daily Mail* (18 April 2011) commented as follows:

> Some 46 per cent of children are born to unmarried mothers, according to research by the Centre for Social Justice. The think-tank said a child growing up in a one-parent family is 75 per cent more likely to fail at school, 70 per cent more likely to become a drug addict, 50 per cent more likely to have an alcohol problem and 35 per cent more likely to be unemployed as an adult.

Such comments, however, need to be examined in context and given careful analysis.

The size of families is another important factor. Fontana (1995, p. 25) in making reference to the longitudinal study undertaken by Davie et al. (1972) commented on how they:

> … found that, irrespective of social class, children from large families tended to do less well in reading, number work, oral skills and creativity than other children or children with one or two siblings.

Fontana suggests the reasons for poorer performance in children from larger families may be due to parents in large families having less time to devote to each of their children, with the result that each child has fewer opportunities to interact verbally with their parents, a point alluded to by Tizard and Hughes earlier. It was of interest also that Davie et al. found that the child who appeared to experience the most difficulty was the eldest child. Fontana suggests that this may be due to the fact that in larger families the eldest child can often be left to look after themselves as parents need to allocate much greater time to the younger and most recently born children.

Exercise

Consider the difficulties that might face parents with young children who choose to live far away from their own parents and wider family. What might the benefits for these children be and what might constitute significant challenges for them?

CULTURAL INTERPRETATIONS: THE WORK OF PIERRE BOURDIEU

A particular feature of this book is the importance given to relating practice and thinking to philosophy and theory. In attempting to understand the nature of learning within families it is useful to draw upon the work of the French sociologist and philosopher Pierre Bourdieu, who has, in recent years, commanded a growing number of followers who see his ideas as having real currency and relevance to our lives today. Drawing upon the ideas of previous thinkers, Bourdieu has added significantly to our understanding of the complex nature of societies, and more specifically how individuals exist within societies and come to be perceived by those societies of which they are a part. As with others before him, such as John Holt, Ivan Illich and A.S. Neill (see Chapter 1), Bourdieu's growing influence has led many to question aspects of modern societies, the institutionalized structures that exist within them, and how these impact upon the education and learning of children and young people.

Bourdieu has suggested, for example, that cultures found within and amongst the 'upper' classes are, in practice, superior to those found within the 'lower' classes. Individuals from the former, he argues, typically assert that poor attainment, lack of progress, and failure in children from the latter is due to the individuals themselves. Bourdieu also argued that if failure amongst children from the lower or working classes is measured through success in examinations then this is erroneous as failure should be seen as a direct cause of the education system and not the culture that children come from. Readers may wish to reflect here upon the extent to which education in England, in particular, is influenced, and even, some might say, dominated, by independent or 'private' schools and the perceived benefits that children attending independent and fee-paying schools gain over those children who do not.

Bourdieu suggests that education systems reproduce the cultural values of the upper classes who dominate societies and through the imposition of these values they come to be legitimized and popularly accepted. The culture of the upper classes is then seen as desirable by those in the lower or working classes. Bourdieu sees this possession of values held and exercised by the upper classes as 'cultural capital'. Those children who are born into these upper class cultures have, he argues, an inherent advantage in that they are socialized into what is perceived to be the desired culture. This, therefore, affects attainment in the formal education system.

Bourdieu also talks of *Habitus*, which refers to such constructs as life style, expectations, behaviours, and so on. The Habitus of different classes is different and facilitates different decision-making processes, aspirations and expectations. Behaviours, aspirations and expectations that children observe within their Habitus influence not only their behaviours but also their internal representations of how they themselves can interact with society and develop their skills, talents and potential. Bourdieu sees the formal education process as a means of marginalizing individuals from the lower classes and consequently this creates greater space for those from the upper classes. Again, readers may wish to consider the extent to which different sections of society, for example families living in economically deprived areas, might be marginalized from the more 'well-off' who typically follow a well-defined path of achieving good grades at school and attending university before taking up professional careers.

LONE-PARENT FAMILIES AND LEARNING

Many children in lone-parent families grow up in happy circumstances and live fulfilled and purposeful lives, and are carefully and attentively nurtured. Others, however, do not and it is a sad fact that a significant number of children grow up in lone-parent households where finances are problematic, where their primary caregiver may have a number of unsuitable partners and where many of their emotional and social needs fail to be met. Take the case of Maggie below.

Example

Maggie is aged eight years of age and lives with her father and older brother who is 12 years of age. When Maggie was five years old her mother was diagnosed as having cancer, and shortly before Maggie's eighth birthday, her mother died. Maggie then found herself growing up in a family where she observed her father to be highly stressed as he attempted to run the household and ensure that Maggie and her brother received regular meals with school lunch boxes each day, had the necessary clean clothes for school, maintained cleanliness in the home and spent time with each of them when they became distressed at the loss of their mother.

It is clear that Maggie had a great deal to cope with from an early age as the secure structures that had been put in place by her parents had become fractured. In fact, her whole world would have been shattered as she came to realize through the pain of her loss that the world is indeed an unreliable place. There can be little doubt that her school work was adversely affected, and whilst other children absorbed themselves in their learning and play activities, it is likely that Maggie would have spent much time revisiting aspects of her mother's illness and subsequent death during lessons when she ought to have been concentrating and enjoying her learning. Now compare the life experiences of Maggie with those of Martha.

Example

Martha is also aged eight years of age and lives as an only child with her father. When she was two years old her mother and father separated and two years later they divorced. Since the divorce Martha has lived with her father in the family home and she has, in effect, been looked after by a succession of 'nannies' who have been employed by her father who is a highly successful businessman and needs to travel away from home, often abroad, on a regular basis. Her mother who lives some distance away began a relationship with another woman shortly after her divorce and has cohabited with this woman since then. She sees Martha on alternate weekends and during school holidays. Money is plentiful and when Martha was seven years of age her parents agreed that she should be sent to board at an expensive independent school in a different part of the country some two hundred miles away. At her new school Martha is taught in classes of no more than 12 children and she tells her parents that she feels she has settled in well to life in her boarding house where she is one of 30 girls aged 11 to 18.

Again, it is clear that Martha, like Maggie, has experienced the loss of living with both of her parents in the family home, but her loss is of a different nature. At an emotional level she will have had to attempt to understand her parents' separation and then her own separation from her father and her home when she begins to board in her new school. Whilst it is not easy to understand or quantify the difficulties that Maggie and Martha might have experienced in their young lives and the impact upon their learning it is clear that their lives have changed and, especially, the nature of the parenting they receive and their experience of a 'family' home. For Martha, she has also experienced the loss of her 'family' home as she has been sent to board many miles away and only sees her parents occasionally, and rarely together.

Different children respond to their life situations in different ways. Some have much more resilience than others and acquire relevant coping strategies that support them as they grow up. This said, it is also clear that many children have low resilience and poor coping strategies, and for them growing up in a lone-parent household can be a very difficult experience. Equally, for many lone parents rearing children the challenges can be enormous. This has been particularly the case in regard to child care and preschool education in the UK, which many would argue has been inadequate. Mayall (2002, p. 13), for example, has commented as follows:

In the 1970s and 1980s, when other European countries were providing universalist high quality state-run nurseries, British pre-school children were (and still are) the victims of a ramshackle patchwork of poor services. Indeed, as we bitterly noted (Hughes *et al.* 1980: Ch. 5), they could not be called services, but rather an ad hoc system which operated certainly not in the interests of children, nor even of the people who ran them, and certainly not for 'working mothers', who struggled to finance the household in the face of inaccessible, insecure and unaccountable 'provision'.

AFFLUENCE AND DEPRIVATION: THEIR INFLUENCES ON LEARNING

Just over 10 years ago Buckingham (2000) drew our attention to the assertion that an 'underclass' had emerged in Great Britain in which many children are failing to have their needs adequately addressed. Buckingham also drew attention to the fact that in the years between 1979 and 1992 the proportion of children being reared in households with incomes that were less than half of the average British income grew from one in 10 to one in three. He further indicated that there were around one million children growing up in homes that were not fit for human habitation. More recently, Mayall (2002, p. 13) has commented:

> And since child poverty was (and still is) a running sore in the UK, the conditions in which many children lived (and still live) their lives at home and in the neighbourhood were appalling. (Rahman et al. 2000; Hood 2001)

In contrast to this there are significant numbers of children attending independent fee-paying schools who have access to many privileges, including private tuition, opportunities for travel such as educational trips abroad and opportunities to interact at a social level with educated and successful adults. In addition to the life experiences that these children can have many will have had excellent opportunities to develop their language skills, in particular their vocabularies and expressive language skills, often resulting in much higher levels of self-confidence and self-efficacy.

Exercise

Consider the learning experiences that children from different social backgrounds have and attempt to identify those factors that act as barriers to some children from more affluent backgrounds and to those from less affluent backgrounds.

The subject of inequality and how economic deprivation and affluence impact upon children's learning has been the subject of continuous debate for generations. However, it is also worth making comparisons in regard to how children in a modern industrialized society such as the UK function in relation to others. Rather worryingly, Cowie (2012, pp.1–2) recently commented as follows:

The Innocenti Report published by UNICEF (2010) provided evidence that, in comparison with other countries in the developed world, children in the UK scored very poorly in terms of emotional health and well-being. The UNICEF study found that UK children rated their own health as being low, and they also described themselves as the least content in the developed world and as more likely to feel lonely and excluded …

An international study of child well-being in the developed countries (UNICEF, 2007) reported that the UK ranked in the bottom third … Today's young people seem to face severe stresses that were unknown a generation ago.

ATTACHMENT AND ITS INFLUENCE UPON LEARNING

It almost goes without saying that children are born helpless and rely from the very moment of birth upon the adults in their world to provide care and nurturing. Because of their helplessness children are born with a predisposition to form relationships. They are, in effect, born to be social individuals. This is the same throughout all societies and is something that is common to all of us. This predisposition to be a social individual means that our species continues to evolve, with families and communities being central to our existence and our future. But what does it mean to be a social individual? Not only are we born with a need to have food, as in the case of the infant suckling their mother for breast milk, but we are also born with a need to form social and emotional bonds with others. This lies at the very heart of the relationships that we form throughout our lives. In fact, the nature of the relationships we form as infants will for many of us influence not only our behaviours and how we learn but also our personalities for the remainder of our entire lives.

The first relationship that any child has is with its mother who carries the growing child within her and then gives birth. For most children, the adults that the child first comes into contact with after birth are their immediate family members, for example their father, older siblings, relatives such as grandparents, and so on. It is with these significant others that their first social encounters grow and the infant begins their journey of interacting with others, all of whom, ideally, have as their primary intention a need to nurture and care for the growing child and to support them with their early learning. It is also within the family that most children first learn to love and to be loved. The importance of love in the lives of children and its impact upon their social, emotional and cognitive development, and more particularly, their learning has not always been well understood. Sadly, this appears to continue to be the case. Recently, Curran (2012, p. 5) commented as follows:

IT IS EXTRAORDINARY TO ME that in the last 15 years of brain research, all those billions of dollars spent in laboratories has shown to me one single important message. It can best be set out as follows:

- If a child is in an environment where they are *understood* as an individual human being then,

- Their *self-esteem* will be improved, and

- If their self-esteem is good they will gain *self-confidence*, and

- If they are in an environment where their self-esteem is good and they have self-confidence, they will feel *engaged* with that environment.

And what does all that add up to? Well, love as it happens.

But what do we mean by this commonly used word 'love' and how does it apply to young children's learning? A useful starting point in trying to answer such a question can be found in the writings of the renowned psychologist and psychoanalyst Erich Fromm (1975), who despite writing around three decades ago, did in fact offer a comprehensive and appealing account, which can act as a guide for practitioners working with children of all ages.

Fromm suggested that love must contain four elements. He identified these as, *Care, Responsibility, Respect* and *Knowledge*. It is worth looking at these more closely as they may go some way in helping us understand those processes through which children come to not only engage in learning to love themselves and others but also how they shape their interactions and relationships with those around them and hopefully learn to be productive members of their communities (including schools) and society as a whole. For children with limited experience of love in their lives this can be a difficult and even painful road to travel and they can, for example, struggle greatly throughout their time in formal education (MacBlain et al., 2006). These children's lives may be characterized by a lack of care, typified, for example, by poor diet, lack of appropriate clothing, limited time spent supporting them at home with their learning, neglect and abuse, and so on.

Fromm emphasized how care was central to the love a mother has for her child, 'No assurance of her love would strike us as sincere if we saw her lacking in care for the infant, if she neglected to feed it, to bathe it, to give it physical comfort ...' (1975, p. 28), and yet we have to address ourselves to the fact that such assurances do not, for many children, exist, as was the case with the recent highly publicized cases in the UK of Victoria Climbié and Baby P., both of whom lost their lives at the hands of their parents and immediate caregivers. For too many children growing up in the UK there is little care shown to them by their parents, and their early lives can be often characterized by lack of security, inconsistency in daily routines around such features as sleeping and eating, and poor diet, all of which impact adversely upon their learning. Recently, Pearce (2009, p. 59) has articulated the process of care following birth as follows:

> When children are born they are totally dependent on adults to care for and protect them. They are innately endowed with the capacity to call attention to their fundamental needs, but do not

have the capacity to satisfy their needs themselves. They rely on adults to do so … The maintenance of routines is a sense of comfort and reassurance to the child as it facilitates an understanding
of the predictability of events and the behaviour and responsiveness of others.

Alongside care comes responsibility, though Fromm asserted, rather worryingly, that,
'Today responsibility is often meant to denote duty, something imposed from outside' (1975, p. 29). Though he was writing some decades ago this still has relevance
today. For Fromm, responsibility should take the form of acts that are voluntary. They
should, he suggested, be an individual's '… response to the needs, expressed or unex-
pressed, of another human being' (p. 29). Again, it is worth taking time to consider
the differing perceptions that parents have today of what actually constitutes parental 'responsibility' and whether this is a consistent perception across all elements of
society or one that requires fuller understanding. Take, for example, the case of a
parent who sees nothing wrong with leaving her young primary-age child alone at
night when she goes out socializing in the evening with her friends. She may view
this behaviour as wholly responsible as her child has a mobile phone that she can use
to contact her if there is a problem.

The third element identified by Fromm is that of respect and by this he did not
mean '*fear and awe*' but:

> … the ability to see a person as he is, to be aware of his unique individuality. Respect means
> the concern that the other person should grow and unfold as he is. Respect, thus, implies
> the absence of exploitation. I want the loved person to grow and unfold for his own sake,
> and in his own ways, and not for the purpose of serving me. If I love the other person, I feel
> one with him or her, but with him *as he is*, not as I need him to be as an object for my own
> use … Respect exists only on the basis of freedom. (1975, p. 30)

Here it is worth reflecting upon the argument that some young children can be manip-
ulated and exploited by controversial elements of the media such as advertising that
promotes thinness and the acquisition of material goods, and because of this fail to
develop respect for themselves and for others. It is also worth taking time to reflect
upon how some young children might be overly pressurized by parents to perform
better than their peers and to achieve very high levels of academic success. The extent
of the pressure that some children can be placed under by their parents and by schools
was captured extremely well by the popular author Oliver James (2007, p. 280) who in
drawing attention to the pressure that some very young children are placed under by
the growing competitiveness in certain elements of society offered the following:

> A London private nursery school was recently exposed in a newspaper as doing tests on two-
> year-olds to see whether they would be suitable for entry at three. The test was to leave the
> toddler alone in a room with five others; the ones that failed were deemed to be those who
> went after their mother when she left the room.

Fromm gave particular emphasis to the fact that it is not possible to respect another individual without knowing that person and talked of knowledge in the following way:

> There are many layers of knowledge: the knowledge which is an aspect of love … is possible only when I can transcend the concern for myself and see the other person in his own terms. I may know, for instance, that a person is angry, even if he does not show it overtly; but I may know him more deeply than that; then I know that he is anxious, and worried; that he feels lonely, that he feels guilty. Then I know that his anger is only the manifestation of something deeper, and I see him as anxious and embarrassed, that is, as the suffering person, rather than as the angry one … We know ourselves, and yet even with all the efforts we may make, we do not know ourselves. (1975, pp. 30–1)

Fromm offers the following example with regard to knowledge and its relevance to childhood:

> In children we often see this path to knowledge quite overtly. The child takes something apart, breaks it up in order to know it; or it takes an animal apart; cruelly tears off the wings of a butterfly in order to know it, to force its secret. The cruelty itself is motivated by something deeper: the wish to know the secret of things and of life … The other path to knowing 'the secret' is love. (1975, p. 31)

Once again, it is useful to pause and reflect upon what Fromm is saying here and its relevance to those working with children. Consider, for example, the young child in a classroom who is observed by his teachers to be very aggressive and angry almost on a daily basis. He strikes out at others and swears loudly when reproached by adults in the classroom and during break times. To fully understand his 'anger' is not to restrict our thoughts to his behaviours but instead to go beyond that and explore his anger at a deeper level, for it is likely that his real emotional issues will be driven in large part by such debilitating factors as anxiety, shame, embarrassment, loneliness and isolation, and guilt. But, almost certainly, none of these will be recognized or properly understood by the child. It is the adults around him who will need to recognize and understand these factors and not, as is too often the case, be blinded by their own emotional reactions to the child's behaviours.

Recently, James (2012) has introduced us to the notion of 'Love Bombing' – a means by which parents can give their children intense and condensed experiences, in which they feel very loved and very much in control. James has commented as follows:

> When it comes to dealing with disobedient or shy or clingy or aggressive or impatient children, love and control, it seems, really are the answer. What is more, because so many parents are, or have had periods of, living very busy or miserable or complicated lives, most of us need to reconnect with our children from time to time. Love Bombing does the job. (2012, p, 2)

James' notion of 'Love Bombing' and how it can affect the lives, and very importantly how it might positively affect the feelings of children when approaching learning tasks either by themselves or with others is very appealing, and once again underscores the importance of children having love in their lives as well as how this can contribute to better learning. What is also very appealing about 'Love Bombing' is the fact that fathers can also be fully engaged at an emotional level with their children.

It almost goes without saying that children form attachments to fathers as well as mothers. The degree to which this occurs, however, and the circumstances in which children grow up varies enormously. Significant numbers of children do not, for one reason or another encounter a father in their early years (MacBlain and MacBlain, 2004). Others who, for example, have developed early anxieties and fears because of the behaviours of their parents towards them may come to develop strong attachments to only one of their parents or primary caregivers. At one level this can be understood in terms of the child seeking security because the parent or parents may be the sole source of security for the child. This is the case with many children who are neglected or abused by parents during their early years. An obvious explanation for this can be found within that most inherited of drives; the need to survive.

In the 1970s and 1980s Mary Ainsworth, who was a co-researcher of John Bowlby, a key author and researcher in the field of attachment, developed what has become a popularly accepted way of considering and classifying aspects of attachment and attachment disorder in young children. The classifications she developed were: *securely attached, insecurely attached: avoidant* and *insecurely attached: ambivalent*. Main and Solomon (1986) later added a further classification, *disorganized*. With the first of these, the infant child demonstrates a preference for their primary caregiver and when separated from their primary caregiver can be observed to interact with others who are strange to them without any sustained anxiety. In addition, they can be observed to lack sustained anxiety when exploring their environments. With the second, the young infant can be observed to be detached from their primary caregiver following separation. With 'insecurely attached: avoidant' children they can be observed to be overly clingy when separated from their primary caregiver, with sustained anxiety and distress following separation. With the final type the young child can be observed to show little consistency in their response to their primary caregiver following separation. As Pearce (2009, p. 23) has commented:

> Rather, they display bizarre and contradictory behaviours (such as seeking to be close to their caregiver but with their gaze averted, approaching the caregiver only to stop and stare before full physical reunion occurs, and alternately, engaging with and disengaging from their caregiver almost simultaneously).

The positive effects of attachment and the detrimental effects of attachment disorder on children's learning are obvious. However, to suggest that the effects are obvious is also to ignore and, more particularly, fail to understand the complexities that lie at the very core of social and emotional development and especially the importance of trust.

The whole idea of early separation and loss in infancy has been well documented in the literature and has formed the basis for much debate within the field of psychology and more particularly psychodynamics (Freud, 1913; Blos, 1962; Wolfenstein, 1966; Kline, 1972; Black, 1974). It is accepted by many practitioners working in the field of psychology and psychotherapy that the young child's first experience of separation, with resulting feelings of pain, is when the child is physically separated from the mother at birth (Blos, 1962; Bowlby, 1980; Miller, 1987). In the days and weeks that follow birth, the child will increasingly be separated from their mother for short periods of time as the mother attends to other tasks in the home.

Following such periods of separation, the child, typically, is nursed and comforted by their mother, who will attempt to banish any pain she sees in her child. As these periods of separation increase, the child comes to internalize representations of their mother's absence and related behaviours and, in so doing, comes to know that their mother will return even though she is out of sight, and that their life will not be adversely affected by this temporary state of separation. Such learning becomes generalized within the child's broader developmental and life history and forms part of the unique structure of each individual's emotional make-up. If, however, the young child experiences much greater periods of separation from their mother, then the child internalizes this separation in a way that can make them emotionally vulnerable to loss or separation in the future and may, in turn, have adverse effects on the way in which the child later relates to others during adolescence and adulthood, 'leading him to avoid those who may reawaken the feelings of vulnerability, or, aggressively reject those who could evoke them' (Raphael, 1984, p. 403).

Such feelings of loss, resulting from separation, may even affect the degree to which the child can later express emotion:

> … for he may have learned that others will not accept his anxiety and anger or his sadness and despair. Thus he may build for himself a way of living that denies these effects or prohibits their release. (1984, p. 403)

One is drawn to understand more fully this notion of building a 'way of living' as it raises important questions regarding the extent to which children can, at a subconscious level, engage more fully with their lives and as a result of parental bereavement during childhood, for example, their formal learning in school. Let us now consider the following example of Ben and Alice:

Example

Ben is eight years of age and has been brought up with two very caring parents who devote lots of their own time to talking with him. They take time to get to know what motivates him and what makes him anxious or fearful. When Ben is asleep they talk often about how Ben's personality is developing. In this way they are really getting to know Ben and to understand him. They constantly tell him that they love him and demonstrate their love in many ways, not least in the quality time they spend with him, the frequent hugs and cuddles they give him and the consistent way in which they manage his behaviour and their own behaviours when they interact with him. Ben's parents speak to him in soft tones and never raise their voice. They take time to develop Ben's vocabulary and encourage him to ask questions and to use new words to describe things and to explain himself. Ben's parents have many friends who act similarly towards their children and Ben gains in many different ways from having adoring and attentive grandparents who provide firm but sensitive boundaries. Their intentions are always to do the best for Ben.

In contrast, Alice's parents spend little time with her. She is also eight years of age. Like Ben's parents they both work but their spare time when not working is spent engaged in following their own interests, which they do not share with Alice. Alice's father likes to go to the pub most nights to play darts. Alice's mother watches television most nights and at the weekend likes to go dancing with Alice's father at a local club. For as long as Alice can remember she has spent every Friday and Saturday night at her grandparents' house where she sleeps over, returning to her own home in the afternoon when her parents arise after having a lie-in following their late nights. Alice's grandparents are not educated people and spend the evenings watching television. They tend not to talk with Alice other than to ask her about meals, drinks, and so on. When Alice was very young she was described by the Health Visitor and staff at her preschool nursery as an extremely clingy child. When her mother left her at her nursery school in the mornings Alice became distraught, and even when her mother returned to her to calm her down, Alice remained anxious and inconsolable. At primary school Alice is very attention seeking and constantly follows her teacher around. On occasions her teachers have spoken with the head teacher expressing their concerns over her attention-seeking behaviours and her clinginess. Alice's current teacher has expressed particular concerns that Alice is showing signs of over-dependency, which is affecting her social learning. She has described Alice as '*poor at making friendships*' and as '*struggling to take initiative and does not seem to make the links between effort and outcome*'.

It is clear from the above example that Alice has less support and consistency available to her from her family. This has been the case since she was an infant and now that she is moving through her primary school it is becoming apparent that opportunities for learning in her family are limited. This becomes even more obvious when her family experiences are compared with those of Ben who is currently thriving in primary school and has grown into a very active and confident child who is accessing the curriculum without any apparent difficulties. Alice, on the other hand, has struggled with her reading and spelling and finds most areas in mathematics to be confusing. Ben has many friends whereas Alice has very few.

As indicated earlier, whilst the majority of children grow up with two parents there are others who lose contact with one or both parents through separation and divorce. There is another distinct group of children, however, who lose parents following bereavement. This is not an insignificant number. Two decades ago Wells (1988) reported that in England and Wales around 40 to 50 children each day experienced the death of a parent. Some years later the psychologist John Holland (2001) estimated that around three per cent of children at school will have lived through the death of a parent whilst at school. When represented in actual numbers this accounts for a substantial number of children, being about fifteen to twenty thousand children per year. More recently, *The Children and Young People's Mental Health Coalition* (CYPMHC, 2012, p. 4) published a guide for schools in which they indicated that, 'In an average classroom: 10 young people will have witnessed their parents separate; 1 will have experienced the death of a parent…'. A closer look at loss as experienced by many children reveals the complexities and challenges they face and particularly the influence that loss has upon their learning.

Some newly born infants fail to experience the primary caregiving of a mother. Take, for example, the case of the celebrated philosopher Jean-Jacques Rousseau, referred to in Chapter 1, who has contributed so much to our understanding of learning and development in young children. Born in Geneva in 1712, Rousseau's mother died some nine days after giving birth to him. Similarly, the German philosopher Friedrich Froebel, born in 1782, experienced the death of his mother some nine months after his birth. It is of interest that both of these men dedicated much of their lives to writing about early child development and education, possibly a reaction to their own loss of a mother.

Grieving is a universal experience and occurs in all cultures and in all societies. References to the subject are found in abundance in primitive writings as well as in modern literature, in art, and in the writings of philosophers. The universality of grieving takes on a more identifiable and natural coherence when one begins to examine the writings of those philosophers and literati who have, over time, offered insights into their own and others' biographies and emotional states following the death of a parent. Indeed, literature offers us a most useful reference point through which we can learn about the nature and impact that losing a parent can have upon children and their subsequent development and learning. In fact, literary texts abound with references to the nature of bereavement experienced by children. Specific reference points, for example, can be found in the biographies of many notable writers, namely the German authors Herman Hess and Franz Kafka, the Russian author Leo Tolstoy, the French novelist and playwright Albert Camus whose father died before his first birthday, and the Irish author C.S. Lewis who, himself, lost his mother during childhood. The philosopher De Botton (2000, p. 9) has commented:

In their different ways, art and philosophy help us, in Schopenhauer's words, to turn pain into knowledge.

We can now turn firstly to the famous English poet John Keats (1795–1821) and then the more contemporary French philosopher Jean-Paul Sartre, both of whom lost a parent during early childhood. Andrew Motion's recent biography of Keats (Motion, 1997) serves well as a case study as it transcends the boundaries of culture and time, and reveals the patterns of emotional stress, isolation and dislocation, the difficulties with relationships, and the depression in individuals experiencing childhood bereavement.

Born in 1795, Keats lost both his mother and father when still a child. His mother died after a sustained illness in 1810 and by that time he had already lost his father. At 15 years of age Keats had not only lost his mother and father but also his brother and two uncles. In his biography of Keats, Andrew Motion described the young Keats' return to school after the death of his mother as follows:

> While the miserable spring turned into summer, Keats immersed himself even more deeply in his books. The small child became in the eyes of his school-fellows a kind of miniature man: reserved and preoccupied where only a short while before he had been rumbustious and full of jokes. (1997, p. 40)

It becomes clear from Motion's description of the young Keats, that interactions with peers were greatly affected by the death of his mother. Keats appeared to withdraw from the world he had known earlier and to begin creating a new world characterized by melancholy and impoverished relationships with his peers, his surviving family, and the adults he came into contact with. Raphael (1984, p. 82) has commented in relation to bereavement experienced by very young children and the lasting legacy of loss as follows:

> It is at this age that the infant is first inconsolable ... No other person can replace her ... He simply wants her. In this response is the kernel of the difficulty that we face with loss. The cry of the infant's anguish awakens every fiber of our response to hold and comfort him ... Yet our comforting does not ease the pain, at least initially, for he wants only her. Yet it is only with our comforting that the pain will eventually ease and he will be supported to accept his loss, to relinquish the bond.

A further useful reference point has been offered by Daniel Golman in his book *Emotional Intelligence* and assists us in our understandings of the effects on young children of their loss. Drawing upon the work of the neuroscientist Joseph Le Doux, Golman (1996, p. 22) speculates on the existence of '*emotional memories*' which can remain with an individual throughout their lives and which can result in such feelings as anger and confusion and which can, in some circumstances, work to undermine and adversely affect relationships with others, not least those of young children progressing through their school years. The views of Le Doux offer some support for the assertions made previously by Freud and challenges us to explain loss within a biological context:

> Le Doux turns to the role of the amygdala [the main area in the brain where signals triggered by epinephrine and norepinephrine arrive] in childhood to support what has long been a basic tenet of psychoanalytic thought: that the interactions of life's earliest years lay down a set of emotional lessons based on the attunement and upsets in the contacts between infant and caretakers. These emotional lessons are so potent and yet so difficult to understand from the vantage point of adult life because, believes Le Doux, they are stored in the amygdala as rough, wordless blueprints for emotional life. Since these earliest emotional memories are established at a time before infants have words for their experience, when these emotional memories are triggered in later life there is no matching set of articulate thoughts about the response that takes us over. One reason we can be so baffled by our emotional outbursts, then, is that they often date from a time early in our lives when things were bewildering and we did not yet have words for comprehending events. We may have the chaotic feelings, but not the words for the memories that formed them. (Goldman, 1996, p. 22)

The nature of the relationships that young children have with their surviving parent is complex and can have an enormous impact upon their subsequent social and emotional development. The extent of this complexity can be found in the works of the French philosopher Jean-Paul Sartre (1967, p. 13):

> Following her mother's example, my mother preferred duty to pleasure. She did not know my father very well, either before or after their marriage, and she must sometimes have wondered why this stranger had resolved to die in her arms … Personally, I benefited from the situation … On my father's death, Anne-Marie and I woke from a common nightmare: I was cured. But we were the victims of a misunderstanding: she lovingly rejoined a son whom she had never really left; I regained consciousness on the lap of a stranger.

Sartre's reflections and interpretations of the way in which the adults around him dealt with his father's death at the time are very revealing and pose considerable questions. Sartre's mother, for example, appeared to bring an exaggerated sense of 'duty' to her relationships as opposed to 'pleasure', a significant factor that is likely to have influenced the young Jean-Paul's psychological and emotional develop-ment, as well as the manner in which he constructed his own view of the world and the subsequent realities he internalized as his *'blueprints for emotional life'*.

In contrast to the complex nature of Sartre's memories now consider the rather harrowing and disturbing memories offered relatively recently by the writer and poet Diana Gittens (1998, pp. 100–1):

> Over the years I have struggled to understand two early memories of my mother. In the first, I am simply looking at the dark green window blind drawn down beside my parents' bed, yearning to pull the round silky handle that would release it and let the light in. This image always made me feel deeply disturbed and nauseous. In therapy I eventually accessed the rest of the image; it concerned my mother's sexual abuse of me and her subsequent telling me I was disgusting and

calling me names I did not understand. The other memory was of lying on the living room sofa and waking up from a nap with a jolt as my mother jabbed her lighted cigarette on to the back of my hand. She then walked out and returned with a wide grin on her face, asking me, what had I done to myself? She gently dabbed my wound with iodine while telling me I must never, ever play with lighted cigarettes again. I remember feeling utterly confused. I hadn't wanted to do those disgusting things, had I? It wasn't me who burned myself, was it? Or had I? Did I? Surely she had to be right – she was my mother – and yet … Not only did I learn – slowly and painfully – not to trust her, but I also learned I could not trust myself.

Whilst the above account clearly indicates the complexities that can occur within close family relationships, it also challenges us to consider how learning can take place for many children who grow up in vastly different but more distorted and dysfunctional family contexts. This stark and disturbing account of Gittens' early memories underlines the importance of viewing learning as more than just a process that occurs purely to bring about new knowledge and understanding. More particularly, it confronts all of us with the realities of the darker side of human experience and how learning unfolds for many children and young people whose lives are blotted with pain. Unlike in previous decades, the degree to which abuse and neglect takes place is now far more apparent. It is recognized (McKee, 2004), for example, that multiple factors can be involved in neglect and abuse, such as: inadequate parenting, marital problems and discord, financial problems, and substance abuse. MacBlain et al. (2006, p. 187) offer the following:

> Whatever the situation that families and children find themselves in, the impact on children is clear – those who have been abused struggle to properly access the academic curriculum and to learn effectively. Attempts made by teachers to work with children subjected to abuse or neglect can lead to little progress on the part of the child.

Exercises

- Why do some children in lone-parent families appear to adjust much better to the challenges and demands of growing up?
- Why do some children growing up in low income, dysfunctional families present at their schools as being more confident and outgoing than many of their peers?

THE IMPORTANCE OF PLAY WITHIN THE FAMILY

The importance of play within the family cannot be emphasized enough. From birth through adolescence to early adulthood parents play with their children. The type and quality of this play, however, varies enormously. For some children their experiences of play within their families will be purposeful, fun and educational, leading to significant developments in emotional intelligence, self-esteem and self-efficacy. The nature of play, however, has changed dramatically in the past few decades and continues to do so. Many children now spend much more time playing inside their homes than perhaps was the case 20 or 30 years ago. Zwozdiak–Myers (2007: 6) has commented:

> ... there seems little doubt that the default for contemporary children's play is interior whereas for previous generations, particularly in the second half of the twentieth century, it was exterior.

Take the case of Chris in the following example:

Example

Chris is 10 years of age and lives with his father and mother and two sisters. The family is reasonably well off and Chris has his own bedroom. One day when talking with his teacher Chris describes a typical Saturday when he has no school:
'Well I get up late because I like to lie in bed and watch telly, I have my own telly in my room and only I am allowed to watch it. I don't let my sisters into my room. Then I get up for my dinner. My dad always tells me off for lying in bed so long but he doesn't really mind. Then I like to play on my computer and my friend Tom comes round and we do that all afternoon. It's great we really like it. Sometimes we play outside but it's nicer at home.'

Recently, Ginsberg (2007, p. 183) drew attention to the hugely important role that play has in the development and learning of children as follows:

> Play allows children to create and explore a world they can master, conquering their fears while practicing adult roles, sometimes in conjunction with other children or adult caregivers ... play helps children develop new competencies that lead to enhanced confidence and the resiliency they will need to face future challenges. Undirected play allows children to learn how to work in groups, to share, to negotiate, to resolve conflicts, and to learn self-advocacy skills ... Ideally, much of play involves adults, but when play is controlled by adults, children acquiesce to adult rules and concerns and lose some of the benefits play offers them, particularly in developing creativity, leadership, and group skills ... Perhaps above all, play is a simple joy that is a cherished part of childhood.

Ginsberg also drew attention to unseen and often poorly recognized benefits that play can have for those children who may be less verbal than others and who may find mixing with others a challenge:

Less verbal children may be able to express their views, experiences, and even frustrations through play, allowing their parents an opportunity to gain a fuller understanding of their perspective. (Ginsberg, 2007, p. 183)

He also emphasized how play should be viewed as an important part of the academic life of children, as play:

... ensures that the school setting attends to the social and emotional development of children as well as their cognitive development. It has been shown to help children adjust to the school setting and even to enhance children's learning readiness, learning behaviors, and problem-solving skills. Social-emotional learning is best integrated with academic learning; it is concerning if some of the forces that enhance children's ability to learn are elevated at the expense of others. Play and unscheduled time that allow for peer interactions are important components of social-emotional learning. (Ginsberg, 2007, p. 183)

An important consideration, however, is the reduction in time that many children have for play. This can be seen, for example, in situations where children have to give increasing amounts of time to their studies at the expense of being able to play out with their friends. This is especially the case in some other countries outside of the UK where children appear to study for excessively long periods of time. Readers may wish to consider the growing emphasis that is currently being placed upon a return to examinations for children in secondary schools in the UK and how this might lead to a significant reduction in important leisure time as these children become increasingly tasked with allocating time to engaging in the memorization of facts for examinations upon which their futures will depend.

A further potential barrier to play in the UK is that many parents are now fearful of letting their children play outside and away from their homes because of high-profile cases over the years in which children have been abducted. This fear can frequently be found when talking with young mothers. A further issue that has become much more prominent in the last decades is the extent to which children now desire toys that are of a much more sophisticated nature. Given this growing emphasis on technological playthings, and the perceived need by many parents to feel that they should spend more time being with their children, it can be suggested that many parents have become prisoners of their children's demands (Gray and MacBlain, 2012).

THE LANGUAGE OF FAMILIES AND ITS INFLUENCE UPON LEARNING

In drawing attention to the important role families play in regard to language development, Cowie (2012, p. 87) has proposed how:

In Western cultures, parents usually nurture the acquisition of words and sentences through myriad rewarding interactions which result in an enormous expansion of language knowledge and use throughout the first five years. From this perspective, the quality of the relationship between caregiver and child is of critical importance …

A telling and perhaps worrying inclusion in the above statement by Cowie is the use of the word 'usually', denoting an apparent reluctance to include all parents and an acknowledgement that perhaps some children fail to have this nurturing. This said, few readers will not have experienced the joy of listening to the wonderful and comforting sounds made by infants in their first weeks and months of life. Few will also have failed to be moved by the naïve and humorous expressions offered by children when trying to express themselves. Fontana (1995, p. 75) has commented as follows:

The more language a child hears, the quicker their vocabulary develops, but *responsiveness* also plays a part. Infants whose parents talk to them in response to sounds or other behaviours are faster in language development …

A worrying development in recent decades has been the number of children entering primary schools with language delay, often characterized by poor vocabulary and listening skills and inattentiveness to others. This frequently means that teachers are working with some children who are, in a sense, coming from behind others. Take the following two examples:

Example

Bob and Andy have just started at primary school. They are both five years of age and have been looked after by their respective grandparents. Their teacher observes both of them during the first days in their new school. She observes how Bob finds great difficulty sitting still for more than a few minutes and when she starts to talk to the class he persists in getting up and running around the room. When she asks him to sit down with the other children and listen to her he frequently swears at her and runs off. Andy, on the other hand, is observed to sit still and becomes quickly absorbed in what the teacher is saying. When she talks with Andy she finds that his vocabulary is quite advanced and he takes time to listen to her. Bob, however, continually interrupts the teacher when she talks to him and does not wait for her to finish sentences before making demands upon her, which are frequently little to do with what she is asking of him.

Human language is highly sophisticated and contains a number of key characteristics, for example, a range of elementary sounds or phonemes, and morphemes, which, unlike phonemes, are meaningful entities through which information can be transmitted (Brown, 1977, p. 109). In a study undertaken by Ricks (1972), cited in Brown (1977, p. 97) Ricks recorded the cries of a number of babies within a range of situations, for example, when they were hungry, tired, uncomfortable, and so on. His research indicated that parents could identify the types of cries they heard from all of the babies, as well as a foreign baby, suggesting that there exists within individuals a 'universal sound-system', which acts as a means by which newly born infants can communicate not only basic needs but also meanings to their parents. As infants grow and learn to communicate meaning in more and more sophisticated ways they also learn that their requests will be either rewarded and subsequently reinforced or possibly ignored. In some cases, young children who find their requests to be repeatedly ignored, or even punished, may turn to other methods of having their needs met such as shouting or crying or being aggressive.

Exercises

- Consider the view that children growing up in lone-parent families are at a disadvantage when it comes to their learning.
- How have philosophers and theorists contributed to our understanding of learning in families?
- Does poverty continue to affect children's learning in the 21st century?
- Consider how children's learning might be affected by the loss of a parent through, for example, parental separation, divorce and bereavement.
- Consider the nature of play in the 21st century and why play in families is so important.
- What factors lead to language delay in young children and how can families support their children's learning through language?

Summary

The role that families play in the learning of children can never be emphasized enough. Learning begins from inception and carries on throughout adolescence and into adulthood with children learning all of the time from parents. For many children, however, this process is halted prematurely when they experience the bereavement of a parent or where their childhoods are characterized by neglect and even abuse. School often offers the only stability and nurturing for some of these children and a significant challenge for teachers and schools is to be able to manage the learning of such children in a way that allows them to benefit from their schooling and to succeed in adulthood.

This chapter sought to explore the important role that families play in the learning of children and how the type and quality of play and language in families can impact upon learning and social and emotional development. Cultural aspects of families were explored with particular reference to the work of Pierre Bourdieu and how modern technology and materialism impacts upon learning within families. The concepts of love and secure attachment, which some argue are so sadly lacking in many children's lives were explored, with particular emphasis being given to the challenges facing some children growing up in lone-parent families and those children experiencing loss and especially bereavement.

RECOMMENDED READING

Cowie, H. (2012) *From Birth to Sixteen: Children's Health, Social, Emotional and Linguistic Development.* London: Routledge.

Miller, A. (1987) *The Drama of Being a Child.* London: Virago Press.

Pearce, C. (2009) *A Short Introduction to Attachment and Attachment Disorder.* London: Jessica Kingsley.

REFERENCES

Black, D. (1974) What happens to bereaved children? *Therapeutic Education,* 2: 15–20.

Blos, P. (1962) *On Adolescence: A Psychoanalytical Interpretation.* New York: Free Press.

Bowlby, J. (1980) *Attachment and Loss. Vol. 3: Loss, Sadness and Depression.* London: Hogarth.

Brown, E. (1999) *Loss, Change and Grief.* London: David Fulton.

Brown, G. (1977) *Child Development.* Shepton Mallet: Open Books.

Buckingham, D. (2000) *After the Death of Childhood: Growing up in the Age of Electronic Media.* Cambridge: Polity Press.

Cowie, H. (2012) *From Birth to Sixteen: Children's Health, Social, Emotional and Linguistic Development.* London: Routledge.

Curran, A. (2012) Autism and the brain's working: how far have we got?, *Debate,* 144: 5–6. Leicester: The British Psychological Society.

CYPMHC (2012) *Resilience and Results: How to Improve the Emotional and Mental Wellbeing of Children and Young People in Your School.* The Children and Young People's Mental Health Coalition, 25 September.

Davie, R., Butler, N. and Goldstein, H. (1972) *From Birth to Seven.* London: Longman.

De Botton, A. (2000) *The Consolations of Philosophy.* London: Hamish Hamilton.

Fontana, D. (1995) *Psychology for Teachers* (3rd ed) Basingstoke: Macmillan Press.

Freud, S. (1913) *Mourning and Melancholia.* (Pelican Freud Library, Vol. 11.) London: Pelican, 1984.

Fromm, E. (1975) *The Art of Loving.* London: Unwin Books.

Furman, E. (1974) *A Child's Parent Dies: Studies in Childhood Bereavement.* New Haven: Yale University Press.

Ginsberg, K.R. and the Committee on Communications and the Committee on Psychosocial Aspects of Child and Family Health (2007) The Importance of Play in Promoting Healthy Child Development and Maintaining Strong Parent-Child Bonds, *Pediatrics*, 119 (1): 182–191.

Gittens, D. (1998) *The Child in Question*. Basingstoke: Macmillan Press.

Golman, D. (1996) *Emotional Intelligence*. London: Bloomsbury.

Gray, C. and MacBlain, S.F. (2012) *Learning Theories in Childhood*. London: Sage.

Holland, J. (2001) *Understanding Children's Experiences of Parental Bereavement*. London: Jessica Kingsley.

James, O. (2007) *Affluenza*. London: Vermilion.

James, O. (2012) *Love Bombing*. London: Karnac Books.

Kline, P. (1972) *Fact and Fantasy in Freudian Theory*. London: Methuen.

MacBlain, S.F. and MacBlain, M.S. (2004) Addressing the needs of lone-parent pupils, *Academic Exchange Quarterly*, 8 (2): 221–5.

MacBlain, S.F. and Purdy, N. (2011) Confidence or confusion: how prepared are today's NQTs to meet the additional needs of children in schools? *Journal of Teacher Development*, 15 (3): 381–94.

MacBlain, S.F., McKee, B. and MacBlain, M.S (2006) The curriculum: confronting neglect and abuse, *Academic Exchange Quarterly*, 10 (2): 87–191.

Main, M. and Solomon, J. (1986) Discovery of insecure-disorganized/disorientated attachment patterns: procedures, findings and implications for the classification of behaviour. In T.B. Brazelton and M. Yogman (eds) *Affective Development in Infancy*. Norwood, NJ: Ablex.

Mayall, B. (2002) *Towards a Sociology for Childhood: Thinking from Children's Lives*. Maidenhead: Open University Press.

McKee, B. (2004) Child protection in education: training the trainers. Paper presented at European CAPE conference, 10–12 July, Lancaster, UK.

Miller, A. (1987) *The Drama of Being a Child*. London: Virago Press.

Motion, A. (1997) *Keats*. London: Faber and Faber.

National Statistics (2003) *Social Trends*. London: Stationery Office Books.

Pearce, C. (2009) *A Short Introduction to Attachment and Attachment Disorder*. London: Jessica Kingsley.

Raphael, B. (1984) *The Anatomy of Bereavement: A Handbook for the Caring Professions*. London: Hutchinson.

Ricks, D.M. (1972) The beginnings of vocal communication in infants and autistic children. Unpublished M. D. thesis, University of London. Cited by Cromer, R.F. (1974) The development of Language and cognition: the Cognition Hypothesis, in Foss, B. (1974) *New Perspectives in Child Development*. Harmondsworth: Penguin, p. 97.

Sartre, J-P. (1967) *Words*. Harmondsworth: Penguin.

Tennant, C. (1988) Parental loss in childhood. *Archives of General Psychiatry*, 45: 1045–50.

Tizard, B. and Hughes, M. (1984) *Young Children Learning: Learning and Thinking at Home and at School*. London: Fontana.

United Nations Children's Fund (UNICEF) (2007) *Child Poverty in Perspective: An Overview of Child Well-being in Rich Countries*. Florence: UNICEF Innocenti Research Center.

United Nations Children's Fund (UNICEF) (2010) *The Children Left Behind: A League Table of Inequality in Child Well-being in the World's Richest Countries*. Innocenti Report card 9. Florence: UNICEF Innocenti Research Center.

Wells, R. (1988) *Helping Children Cope with Grief*. London: Sheldon.

Winsdale, J. (2012) Positioning among the lines of force in schooling: an issue for psychologists and counselors in schools, *Educational and Child Psychology*, 29 (2): 20–31.

Wolfenstein, M. (1966) How is mourning possible? *Psychoanalytic Study of the Child*, 21: 93–123.

Zwozdiak-Myers, P. (ed.) (2007) *Childhood and Youth Studies*. Exeter: Learning Matters Ltd.

LEARNING AND SCHOOLING

This chapter aims to:

- emphasize the importance of viewing learning and schooling within a temporal and historical context
- examine the function of schools within the 21st century
- explore the nature of learning against current curricula and government influence
- highlight the complex nature of transitions between schools and the importance of understanding the impact that transitions can have on children
- explore social, economic and political influences upon learning
- consider learning and schooling within a rapidly changing global context.

INTRODUCTION

Two decades ago Schostak (1991, p. 11) offered the following distinction between schooling and education:

> Schooling refers to all those processes of control, coercion, and socialization through which the values, attitudes, behaviour and common knowledge of individuals are moulded to produce shared 'realities'. Schools, the institutions of the media, the business world, churches, the political and legal framework and the 'family' can be seen variously as instruments in the processes of schooling. Education, by contrast, provides a critical perspective on the processes of schooling with the object of liberating individual expression and action in the exploration of experience in order to draw out alternative possibilities.

Since Schostak offered the above distinction the world has changed dramatically. Following the destruction of the Twin Towers in New York in 2001 societies across the globe have, for example, become alert to the threat of terrorism and actively engage in educating the young to be more tolerant and more understanding of others. Schools, in particular, have sought to address this and have been increasingly responsive to a growing number of directives from government.

In addition to the perceived threat of terrorism the global economy has also changed dramatically, with the result that much funding that was once available to schools and the education system is now no longer available. For some schools this has meant significant change in the manner in which they can meet the needs of their pupils, in particular those pupils who require additional resources such as Learning Support Assistants working with them in the classroom, support from other professionals such as educational psychologists, school social workers or Information and Communications Technology (ICT). In the UK the degree and pace of change in education, and especially schooling, has accelerated greatly since the election of the Coalition Government in 2010. Following its election significant changes have occurred in the way in which schools are being funded and managed, with some suggesting that this has been a step forward whilst others are arguing that many of the changes introduced by the Coalition Government have been a massive step backwards.

SCHOOLING WITHIN A HISTORICAL CONTEXT

Schooling in the UK as we now know it has changed almost beyond recognition since the time of William Shakespeare and Charles Dickens, and even since the sixties and seventies. Though there are some identifiable similarities there are also even greater differences. What is clear, though, is that the manner in which children are schooled is continuing to change at an accelerating pace and it is inevitable that in the next century the education system in the UK and much of what happens in schools today will have changed dramatically.

Currently, within the UK, new types of schools such as *Free Schools* and *Academies* are emerging and offer reminders of previous generations when schools were run by a range of interest groups such as charities, entrepreneurs and churches. Indeed, the history of schooling in the UK needs to be viewed as at best haphazard and contrived, and at worst disjointed, ill-conceived and non-effective. Understanding the historical context within which changes in education, and more specifically schooling and learning, have occurred allows us to have a greater understanding of why we educate our children in the way we do and why change appears to continue to define the education system in the UK. A useful entry point in making sense of the unfolding historical context of education and how we have arrived at the point that we are at in the UK when we are now introducing Free Schools can be located in the 19th century in what became known as *Ragged Schools*.

In 1818, some two years after the renowned philosopher Friedrich Froebel (see Chapter 1) opened his first school in Frankfurt, Germany, a cobbler living in Portsmouth, England named John Pound started using his shop to educate local children who were poor and destitute. Pound introduced the children to such activities as cooking and mending shoes and also taught reading and writing together with religious education and nature. About the same time, Thomas Cranfield who had spent time as a soldier was also running a number of Ragged Schools in the city of London, which again catered for poor and destitute children. In fact there was a considerable growth in Ragged Schools at this time. Drawing upon the work of Montague (1904) and Eagar (1953), Smith (2001, p. 3) has offered some insights into the extent to which this type of school was expanding in the 19th century:

> For example there were around 200 teachers in 1844, over 1600 in 1851 (Montague 1904: 169). By 1867 it was reported that the 226 Sunday Ragged Schools, the 204 Day Schools and the 207 Evening Schools had an average attendance of 26,000 children. (Eagar 1953: 123)

It was also about this time in 1828 that the celebrated educator and modernizer Thomas Arnold was appointed as headmaster to the famous Rugby School, which is popularly associated with the novel *Tom Brown's Schooldays*. Rugby School was amongst those that catered for children of the more privileged upper classes. Though catering for the children of the more privileged classes, many of the practices that were part of everyday life at the school would now be considered wholly unacceptable. In addition, the curriculum offered to the pupils was vastly different to that offered today. In fact, it was Arnold who changed much of what took place in the school, and in doing so he created a model which has greatly influenced education and schooling throughout the UK over the last two centuries. In many respects, Arnold's ideas were ahead of his time in that he modernized the curriculum. For example, he included modern foreign languages and also introduced mathematics and history, which we now take for granted as necessary parts of children's learning in schools. Arnold also set about establishing the Prefect system, which continues to be common to most schools in the UK today. Unlike the Prefect system today Arnold used this system as a primary means of maintaining order and discipline in his school with the older boys being accorded authority over the younger boys in their role as prefects.

In 1870 the Elementary Education Act, commonly referred to as *Forster's Act* was passed in England. This Act set out the foundations for elementary education for children aged from five to 12. Ten years later in 1880 education became compulsory for all children up to the age of 12. The passing of Forster's Act came at a time when many enlightened thinkers and industrial entrepreneurs were openly expressing the view that educating the young would bring greater prosperity to the country. In 1902 a further Education Act known as *Balfour's Act* gave control of education to Local Education Authorities. With this Act came a significant growth in post-primary schools as well as financial support for voluntary elementary schools which came under the control of the Church of England and the Roman Catholic Church. It is worth considering, at this point, the current decline in the role of Local Authorities that is taking place under the Coalition Government in England and the huge increase in schools opting out of Local Authority control in order to acquire the status of Academy and gain more autonomy.

In 1918, the *Fisher Act* made education compulsory for children from five to 14 and passed responsibility for secondary education to the state. At this time, however, many children could remain at their elementary schools until the age of 14, as opposed to attending one of the many new secondary schools that were opening. Then, in 1944 the *Butler Act* brought into being the raising of the school leaving age to 15 as well as formalizing the divide between primary and secondary schools at the age of 11. A particular feature of this Act was to create a system whereby children after the age of 11 could attend a Grammar, Technical or Secondary Modern School depending upon their performance in a formal examination taken at the age of 11 known as the '*Eleven Plus*'. Two decades later, in 1965, the then Labour government in England released *Circular 10/65*, which called upon Local Education Authorities to implement a process whereby they would start converting secondary schools into the new *Comprehensive System*. Thus began the process of doing away with the then existing system of Grammar and Secondary Modern Schools as well as the Eleven Plus examination. At the time this was hugely controversial, with many opposing the closure of Grammar Schools whilst others advocated their closure, embracing the new Comprehensive System in which children would be educated together in the same school. For many teachers who had worked in Grammar Schools and who found themselves having to teach in Comprehensive Schools, the changes were too much and they simply could not cope. A significant number left the profession.

The controversy over the closure of Grammar Schools has persisted, even today, with some areas in England still maintaining Grammar Schools. It must be remembered that alongside the introduction of the Comprehensive System there existed the 'private' or Independent Sector which included such schools as Rugby School mentioned earlier. As in the case of Grammar Schools, there have also been those who have advocated the closure of Independent Schools, which, they argue, typically benefit from charitable status, are elitist, and cater largely for the privileged few. Others, however, strongly embrace Independent Schools because of their traditions and because they are viewed as setting exemplary high standards. This debate has gained recent momentum with the publication of a report by the Office for Standards in Education (Ofsted) (2013), *The Most Able Students: Are They Doing as Well as They should in Our Non-selective Secondary Schools?* (see Chapter 9), which has emphasized a distinction between how well more able children are progressing in non-selective state maintained schools, as compared with those in selective schools such as Independent Schools (see Chapter 9).

Later, in 1996, the passing of a new Education Act, which followed on the back of the 1981 Education Act (see Introduction) placed much greater emphasis upon the relationship between children's environments and in particular the level and type of support offered to children with learning difficulties, 'A child has special educational needs if they have a learning difficulty which calls for special educational provision to be made for them' (Department for Education and Employment, 1996, Section, 323). Here we can see how the focus was shifting from within-child factors to factors within the child's environment and how these affected children's learning. With an increase in the inclusion of children into the mainstream who had special educational needs and/or disabilities and who would have previously attended Special Schools, however, there came increased challenges for many teachers. Table 5.1 shows a time-line which indicates the extent of government influence in education in the UK and the significant nature of change facing teachers and schools.

Currently, the UK is experiencing major changes in how children are schooled. The changes are driven by new ideas and, some would argue, reconstituted philosophies and self-interest. Whether or not these changes will lead to better education and better learning opportunities for the children of the future remains open to speculation and only time will tell.

The election of the current Coalition Government in the UK saw the passing of the 2011 Education Act. Details of the Act published on the Department for Education's website (DfE, 2013, p. 1) offered the following, indicating that the Act:

> ... includes measures to increase the authority of teachers to discipline pupils and ensure good behaviour ... removes duties on schools and local authorities to give them greater freedom to decide how to fulfil their functions ... The Academies programme will be extended, with Academies for 16 to 19 year olds and alternative provision Academies ... The Act will change school accountability, with more focused Ofsted inspections and wider powers to intervene in under-performing schools. Ofqual, the independent qualifications regulator, will be required to secure that the standards of English qualifications are comparable with qualifications awarded outside the UK ... The Act also makes provision to give effect to pro-posals to increase college freedoms, giving them greater control over their own governance and dissolution arrangements ... [It] will enable the Government to introduce an entitlement to free early years provision for disadvantaged two year olds ... make changes to the enforce-ment powers ... [and] also make provision regarding direct payments for people with special educational needs or subject to learning difficulty assessment.

It is clear that this new legislation is designed to make significant changes in the structure of education and the underlying principles that guide practice in schools in the UK. Only time will tell how these new and significant changes unfold. Once again, this emphasizes the importance of practitioners working with children to understand the nature of those philosophies that underpin popular thinking and perhaps more particularly the thinking of policy and decision makers who exert

Table 5.1   Timeline of relevant legislation

1883	**Education Act (*Factory Act*)**
	Two hours compulsory schooling for children introduced. Many children then educated within factories or in Church Schools or Dame Schools where children were taught basic literacy and numeracy by well-meaning women.
1870	**Education Act (*Forster's Act*)**
	The state takes responsibility for education and provides elementary education for children aged five to 13. Schools came under the control of local authorities.
1876	**Education Act (*Sandon's Act*)**
	Placed a duty upon parents to make sure their children attended school and brought into being school Attendance Committees.
1880	**Education Act (*Mundella Act*)**
	Attendance at school for children aged five to 10 years made compulsory and for those aged up to 14 unless officially exempted, for example, in order to take up employment.
1902	**Education Act (*Balfour's Act*)**
	Local Authorities replaced School Boards in taking responsibility for the employment of teachers and allocation of places to schools.
1918	**Education Act**
	School-leaving age raised to 14 years.
1944	**Education Act (*Butler's Act*)**
1951	**General Certificate of Education (GCE) – 'O' and 'A' levels introduced**
1963	Newsom Report (*Half Our Future*)
1965	Circular 10/65 (*The Organization of Secondary Education*)
1967	Plowden Report (*Children and their Primary Schools*)
1970	**Education Act (*Handicapped Children Act*)**
1973	**Education Act (*ROSLA*)**
	School-leaving age raised to 16 years.
1978	Warnock Report (*Special Educational Needs*)
1981	**Education Act**
1985	The Swann Report (*Education for All*)
1985	White Paper (*Better Schools*)
1987	DES Consultation Document (*The National Curriculum*)
1987	Circular 11/87
	(*Sex Education at School*)
1988	**Education Act (*Education Reform Act*)**
	National Curriculum introduced, making education the same for children in all schools funded by the state. English, Science and Mathematics became compulsory. GCSEs introduced as a replacement to GCE O' and 'A' Levels and the Certificate of Secondary Education (CSE) examination originally introduced in the sixties for children not taking GCE 'O' Levels.
1992	**Education Act (*Education Schools Act*)**
1996	**Education Act**
	Schools placed under a legal duty to use best endeavors to meet the special educational needs of children. Local authorities placed under a legal duty to undertake statutory assessments of children where schools could not meet their individual needs.
2008	**Education and Skills Act**
	Places a duty on all young people in England to participate in education or training up to age 18. By 2013 it will be compulsory for young people to take part in education or training up to the age of 17 years with the age being increased to 18 years in 2015.
2009	**Apprenticeships, Skills, Children and Learning Act**
2010	**Children, Schools and Families Act**
2011	**Education Act**

considerable influence and authority over the course of education and ultimately children's learning.

THE FUNCTION OF SCHOOLS

Talk to anyone about schools and they will have strong opinions, and it won't be too long before they are recounting their own personal experiences of school days, good or bad. Anecdotes about school days abound and everyone appears to be an authority on the subject. Try to offer your own views to others on how schools might be better organized, and how children should be taught, and you run the risk of not only being challenged and contradicted but also subjected to a range of alternatives probably at great expense to your time. Thankfully, much has changed in the last decades as our understanding of the nature of child development and learning has improved. In a wonderful autobiographical account of his childhood the celebrated author Frank McCourt (1997, p. 84) recounts aspects of his own schooling, which though taking place in Ireland some 50 years ago will offer some familiarities for the older readers of this text who will be able to relate to how some, if not most, schools functioned at the time of their childhood. The education experienced by the author of this current text was in many respects very similar:

> There are seven masters in Leamy's National School and they all have leather straps, canes, blackthorn sticks. They hit you with the sticks on the shoulders, the back, the legs, and, especially, the hands. If they hit you on the hands it's called a slap. They hit you if you're late, if you have a leaky nib on your pen, if you laugh, if you talk, and if you don't know things. They hit you if you don't know why God made the world, if you don't know the patron saint of Limerick, if you can't recite the Apostles' Creed, if you can't add nineteen to forty-seven, if you can't subtract nineteen from forty-seven, if you don't know the chief towns and products of the thirty-two counties of Ireland, if you can't find Bulgaria on the wall map of the world … They hit you if you can't say your name in Irish, if you can't say the Hail Mary in Irish, if you can't ask for the lavatory pass in Irish … If you ever say anything good about Oliver Cromwell they'll all hit you.

In seeking to explore the function of schools Chitty (2002, p. 2) has offered three broad dimensions: individual fulfilment, preparation for the world of work, and schooling as an 'essential element of social progress and social change'. The first of these can be located in the ideas and philosophies explored in Chapter 1, where most philosophers and theorists (with the exception, perhaps, of A.S. Neill, John Holt and Ivan Illich) recognized the important role that schools in their time played in the individual development of children. The second is more controversial and lies at the heart of many key debates relating to what should be taught in schools and what the actual purpose of schools really is.

This second dimension has acquired greater significance in recent years as austerity measures have begun to affect rates of employment not only in the UK but across the globe. The nature of what is being taught in schools and the rationale for having government-directed curricula is now gaining much greater consideration as jobs are becoming fewer and fewer, and as individuals are having to think more carefully about their skills and knowledge base and how these can be traded on the open employment market. The third dimension is also acquiring much greater attention as society engages in social change at what many consider to be an unprecedented and accelerating rate. One very important consideration with this final dimension, however, has been emphasized by Chitty as follows:

> ... even in a comparatively small country like Britain, there is no one clear overriding view about the kind of society we want to live in. The pessimism of the 1970s gave way to the crude certainties of the 1980s ... In the field of education, we seem singularly uncertain as to how to deal with some of the more enduring elements of the Thatcherite vision of schooling, enshrined particularly in the 1988 Education Reform Act and in the original blueprint for the National Curriculum. (2002, p. 5)

This difficult and uncomfortable relationship between the proposed needs of society and schooling has always existed and will continue to do so as new governments emerge and as the economic and political landscapes change. We only have to reflect upon the emergence of the Nazi Party during the 1930s in Germany and the magnitude of their effect upon schooling, learning and the curriculum, or the direct influence of government in communist countries, to see how this uncomfortable relationship between society and schooling can manifest itself. Some decades ago, in the early 1970s, the celebrated political theorist Duverger (1972, p. 236), in contributing to the existing political debates of the time between Marxism and liberal democracy that shaped much of the thinking of the time, commented as follows:

> The psychological influence of the state begins first with children in the form of education. The primary goal of education is to incorporate new generations into society ... The principal objective of education is to transmit to new generations all the experience of civilization developed by previous generations.

More disconcertingly, however, Duverger also proposed that:

> An education strongly oriented toward material techniques and an immediate professional education, one that does not attach much importance to general education, discourages the development of critical thinking and favors conservatism. But, on the other hand, an education, which – without neglecting technical and professional skills – emphasizes general culture will result in producing less conformity and more originality. (p. 236)

One is again reminded here of the significant impact that the theorist Jerome Bruner (see Chapter 2) has had in regard to how we attempt to understand learning, but more importantly, perhaps, education and schooling. In several respects, Bruner chose to challenge many of the underlying ideas that policy and decision makers expounded in regard to the purpose of schooling and the function of education. Smidt (2011, p. 85) has offered the following sharply acute comment in regard to Bruner's thinking of the time: 'Bruner said that we should treat education for what it is, and for him what it was was political'. It is interesting at this point to consider Bruner's perception of the function of schools, which, he emphasized is part of the process through which culture inducts children. Cultures, he suggested are:

> ... made up of institutions (such as schools, hospitals, universities, libraries, banks, companies, shops, law courts, legal systems and more) where the roles that people can play are determined and where the respect accorded to these roles is worked out. (Smidt, 2011: 85)

Bruner proposed that it is only possible to fully make sense of the function of schools when we consider them within the wider sphere of those aims that society has for its children. Bruner viewed motivation as being key to children's learning and progress in school and suggested that the role played by teachers in motivating children was crucial. More particularly, he believed that teachers should encourage their pupils to actively and purposefully engage with their learning, which would increase their motivation and inner feelings of satisfaction and excitement.

Exercise

Are too many schools failing to keep up with the pace of change and are they failing to prepare children for working in the 21st century?

LEARNING AND CURRICULA

It will be difficult for many teachers and Early Years practitioners currently in practice to recall a time when the National Curriculum did not exist and inspections were not privatized. It may seem surprising that in the years that followed World War II the very idea of a curriculum emanating from central government would have been an anathema. Indeed, Smith (1957, p. 161), cited in Chitty (2002, pp. 48–9), proposed that, 'no freedom that teachers in this country possess is so important as that of determining the curriculum and methods of teaching'.

A central element in the development of curricula over the past decades has been the emphasis upon testing and many would argue that this has become excessive. Chitty (2002, p. 151), for example, has drawn particular attention to the adverse effects that over testing can have upon children. Referring to a survey published in August 2000, *Tested to Destruction? A Survey of Examination Stress in Teenagers*, Chitty cited the following statistics:

> ... by the age of 16, most youngsters will have taken sixty or more external tests and examina-tions ... with the figure rising to around seventy-five for those staying on into the sixth form ... Based on detailed responses from more than 8,000 secondary school students in England and Wales, the report claimed that many teenagers were enduring a variety of stress-related illnesses, had difficulty sleeping and were developing eating disorders such as bulimia and anorexia ... Yet far from heeding the results of this survey the government has recently announced ... that compulsory school tests are to be introduced for those 12-year-olds who failed to reach the required standard in the existing primary school tests taken at 11. (p. 151)

A significant factor in the delivery of the curriculum has been the changes in the inspection regime within schools and Early Years settings. Following political influ-ence, which led to the Education (Schools) Act in 1992, government brought about a reduction in the number of inspectors (HMI) from around 500 to 170 and intro-duced the new Office for Standards in Education (Ofsted).

A new UK government took over the reins in 2010 and is proposing what are, arguably, some of the biggest changes in education for generations. These proposed changes are taking place within the context of major ideological shifts in thinking. Following the recent Green Paper, a new Act of Parliament is being introduced which will open the way for these major changes. Amongst the changes that are proposed are much greater emphasis upon developing knowledge within the core subjects, Science, Mathematics and English; greater use and application of System-atic Synthetic Phonics in the teaching of reading; encouragement of schools to adopt the English Baccalaureate examination and more opportunities within schools for those pupils who may wish to pursue a vocational path; national testing at the ages of 6, 11 and 16; preventing pupils taking many re-sits for GCSE examina-tions and placing examinations at the end of a course; placing much greater emphasis upon written grammar, e.g. spelling and punctuation, when marking examinations and allocating marks and grades; and reforming performance tables to take much greater account of the government's expectations that more pupils will have a bet-ter knowledge and skills base and more accurate levels of literacy with clearly set out minimum standards expected at both primary and secondary level.

It has been suggested that too many teachers remain overly concerned with the delivery of content and fail to engage sufficiently with the processes of reflection and those metacognitive structures that underpin thinking and learning, and of which teachers are themselves a dialectical part (Fisher and Rush, 2008; Fisher, et al., 2010). This being so, significant numbers of children may fail to have their individual needs met, and fail to reach their true potential (Long, et al., 2007). Fisher et al. (2010: 94) have recently commented:

> ... students preparing to enter the teaching profession should have as a major priority the need to devote real time to embracing theoretical views on learning ... To do so would potentially free them from vague and distorted notions of what learning actually is and lead to much greater understanding of the nature and function of knowledge, the purpose of learning, and the manner in which individuals at different stages of their development process information and construct meaning of the world around them, and act rationally to improve their lives through effective learning.

Despite the continuing debates surrounding the theories of teaching and learning and the effectiveness of varying pedagogies, the central debate in the UK remains dominated by overly simplistic and polarized views underlying binary arguments of teaching and learning as being essentially traditional and teacher-led or modern and child-centred (Geens, et al., 2009; Peace and Mufti, 2012).

Exercise

What are the benefits in having a national curriculum? Should schools be free to offer their own curricula?

TRANSITIONS BETWEEN STAGES AND BETWEEN SCHOOLS

Few, if any, readers will fail to recall the day they started school and their subsequent transfer from primary to post-primary education. Some will even recall with vivid memories that most emotional of times when they first left their parents to enter the classroom with their new nursery teacher or playgroup leader. For some, the memories will be joyful whilst for others they may be painful. After all, not everyone gets the same start. Readers may wish to compare their own experiences with those of the author Laurie Lee in his much celebrated autobiographical text, *Cider with Rosie*:

> The morning came, without any warning, when my sisters surrounded me, wrapped me in scarves, tied up my bootlaces, thrust a cap on my head, and stuffed a baked potato in my pocket ... The Infant Room was packed with toys such as I'd never seen before – coloured shapes and rolls of clay, stuffed birds and men to paint. Also a frame of counting beads which our young teacher played like a harp ... (1962, pp. 44–5)

Transition is perhaps best considered as a process rather than an event in the lives of children. Bronfenbrenner (1979, p. 26), quoted in Kennedy et al. (2012, p. 20) has, for example, defined transitions as, 'Whenever a person's position in the ecological environment is altered as a result of change in role, setting or both'. Bronfenbrenner's definition is an interesting and useful one as it places particular emphasis upon the changing 'role' of the child from that of being a family member to that of being a student outside of the family home and within a more formal context typically populated by strangers. In this new more formal environment expectations of the child's role, though similar in many respects to those at home, will also be very different.

It is undoubtedly within the family that most young children are first prepared for entry into formal education, be this nursery school, playgroup or primary school. The culture of families, however, will vary and these cultures will exert significant influence upon children when they commence more formalized learning. The family's influence upon the child's initial transition to formal learning and future learning is immense. Within their families, children acquire varying capacities for meeting and managing new situations. Each child's transition from their family to new formal learning situations will be different and the process they go through in making these very early transitions will be as important as the outcomes they experience (Crafter and Maunder, 2012). It is worth considering again the view held by Bronfenbrenner who saw transitions in terms of a dynamic process that occurs between the individual and the social, cultural and historical context within which they live. This process, he argued, is characterized by its reciprocity, with the individual's own personal and individual attributes actually affecting the nature of the transition.

In drawing upon the wider literature, Jadue-Roa and Whitebread (2012, pp. 32–3) indicated three perspectives that have been developed to facilitate research within the area of early transitions:

> The first relies on the belief that a transition is a critical process that puts the person in risk of harm, because there is a lack of continuity that threatens the emotional and psychological well-being of the child ... the second is concerned with readiness for school and future success in academic activities ... The third approach acknowledges transition as part of the school life of a child. Young children's perspectives, voices and agency are sought, so that by empowering them in their own life experience processes, there is less risk of emotional distress and later negative impact on school success ...

Kennedy et al. (2012, p. 19) with regard to the readiness of children for transitions in their early years, have further commented on the:

> ... increasing interest to policy-makers in the UK, as indicated by the recent plethora of Government-commissioned reports ... the new focus from the DfE on the three prime areas of learning in the Early Years Foundation Stage ... the development of a new website

(www.foundationyears.org.uk) to support parents, carers and practitioners in ensuring children are as ready for school as possible ... the introduction of a new 'progress check' at age 2 years, an assessment by setting-based practitioners, to ensure any issues relating to an individual child's learning and development are identified early.

It is most important for parents and primary caregivers to work in partnership with professionals working in Early Years settings and schools. In doing so, they send strong messages to their children in regard to boundaries, values and expectations. To fail to do so, or to demonstrate to their children conflict with their children's teachers, will invariably result in the child learning that professionals may not share the same values as their parents. This can be problematic. Take the following extract from an interview between a child psychologist and the father and mother of John who is aged eight and who has been referred to the educational psychologist because of his aggression towards others:

Example

Psychologist: *I would like you to tell me a little about how John is at home please.*

Father: *What are you getting at? Do you think we don't look after him properly?*

Psychologist: *No, I don't mean that. I would like to gain a picture of how John is at home as well as at school.*

Mother: *We run a pub so we are very busy. I put him up to bed after tea time and he likes to watch TV before he falls asleep. I make sure he is OK before I go down to serve behind the bar and I go up every half hour or so to check he's OK.*

Psychologist: *One of the concerns the school has is that he swears at his teacher when he gets angry. Does he swear at home?*

Father: *No, he never swears.*

Mother: *He used to but we stopped it and now, his father's right, he doesn't swear now.*

Psychologist: *What made him stop swearing at home?*

Mother: *That's easy. Every time he swore we put a spoonful of mustard in his mouth and he knows that if he swears that's what he will get. We only had to do it a few times.*

The above example demonstrates a marked division between the values of the school and those of the home in the manner in which behaviour is being managed. It is clear that the parents have very different views with regard to 'punishment'. It is also clear that the school and the parents will need to work more closely together to find a common way for managing John's behaviours and demonstrate to John that his parents and teachers are working in partnership with each other. The challenges facing the school in working with John's parents appear obvious. One particular challenge will be the need for the school to 'unlearn' John's unwanted behaviour of swearing and seek to replace this with a different behaviour. John will be resistant to change as he has learned this type of response at home, but, more importantly, this response will have been reinforced and strengthened by the responses of his parents, which appear to lack sensitivity and understanding. In addition, the school will have to set about trying to 'unlearn' the parents' view that making him take a spoon of mustard in his mouth is an appropriate punishment. They may see such a behavioural response to John's swearing as being completely acceptable. If the school insists that they stop doing this and replace putting mustard in John's mouth with another behavioural response, they may go along with the school's directive but may continue to view the school's response as wrong. In such a case, the school may need to meet on a regular basis with the parents, which will take from their own time.

Once considered a necessary part of a child's education, with little consideration being given to the emotional, social and academic effects, it is now recognized that transitions are worthy of more extensive research and closer evaluation. Indeed, Choi (2012, p. 29) has recently emphasized how government departments in the UK have been consistently drawing attention to the need to target the transition between primary and secondary school as a key factor in improving the attendance of a significant number of pupils.

Children in nursery schools or playgroups may move to infant or primary schools, possibly leaving behind friendships and important relationships with key adults who have created the environments that lay down many of the foundations for future development and learning. Later on, the majority will leave behind these new environments where they have shared the same teacher as their friends and been part of a relatively small community in which everyone knows everyone else and move into post-primary education. Crafter and Maunder (2012, p. 14) have drawn attention to how primary schools, have '… shared practices in relation to expected behaviour and responsibilities'. Shared practices, though apparent in post-primary schools, do not always have the sameness as in primary schools where staff tend to meet and talk with each other on a daily basis. Transitions between primary and post-primary education can be extremely challenging for some children (Chedzoy and Burden, 2005). Lyons and Woods (2012), for example, have suggested that approximately 25 per cent of children find the transition to secondary school to be problematic. Now consider the following example:

Example

Jenny is 11 years of age and lives at home with her father and mother. Jenny's father is much older than her mother and both parents are extremely protective of her. She was born prematurely and has an August birthday, which makes her one of the youngest in her year at school. Her grandparents have continually expressed their concerns that her parents are overly protective of Jenny and do too much for her. Jenny is nearing completion of her first year at secondary school having previously attended a small rural primary school. In the weeks preceding transfer to her secondary school she became very anxious. Most of the children in her primary class were going to different schools and only three of her classmates transferred to the same school as Jenny. Throughout her first year at school Jenny has struggled to make friends and tends to spend most of her time with one other girl. Her poor academic progress has given rise to concern amongst her teachers who describe her as an *'overly quiet little girl'* who *'does not readily contribute in class discussion'*.

Lyons and Woods (2012, p. 9) have commented that 'Lack of a strongly supportive peer group leaves children vulnerable during transition'. At this stage, friendships are extremely important, with peers offering emotional and social support and a means by which the young person making the transfer can start to safely construct this new educational world of which they will be a part until their future transition into the early stages of adulthood. In Jenny's case she appears to be feeling vulnerable and may not have developed the maturity and resilience needed to make a transition that encourages her to interact with her peers in a more confident manner. In some respects, it can be argued that she is lacking in self-efficacy and that the transition is not helping her with this. In a recent study, Tobell (2003), cited in Choi (2012, p. 27) undertook a study in which 30 girls in their first year of secondary school were interviewed about their transition. The girls tended towards describing their transition in a less than positive way, suggesting difficulties in having fewer personal relationships with peers and an expectation upon them that they should show 'a sudden increase in responsibility as a young adult'. Clearly, transition from primary to post-primary education can for some children be an unhappy experience, whilst for others it can be a very exciting, rewarding and happy time. Teachers working in both sectors need to continue developing their knowledge and understanding of this important time in the lives of children and how it impacts upon their learning and social and emotional development.

> **Exercise**
>
> How can practitioners gain from researching transitional stages in education? Are schools and Early Years settings currently equipped to do enough to facilitate transitions for young children with a wide range of individual needs?

SOCIAL, ECONOMIC AND POLITICAL INFLUENCES ON LEARNING

The decades that have followed the original 1943 White Paper *Educational Reconstruction* and the subsequent 1944 Education Act have been characterized by much heated political debate, with politicians, some would argue, all too frequently interfering and meddling in education, and even going as far as suggesting the deconstruction and reconstruction of education in the UK. Take, for example, the following extract from an interview with Sir Keith Joseph, Education Secretary during the government of Margaret Thatcher in the 1980s, after leaving office (quoted in Chitty, 2002, p. 29):

> We have a bloody state system I wish we hadn't got. I wish we'd taken a different route in 1870. We got the ruddy state involved. I don't want it. I don't think we know how to do it ... But we are landed with it ... We've got compulsory education, which is a responsibility of hideous importance, and we tyrannise children to do that which they don't want, and we don't produce results.

Earlier, in 1981, Sir Keith, in addressing the Conservative Party Conference spoke of his enthusiasm for a *Voucher System*, which he described as 'a noble idea' whereby parents would have much greater choice; the idea being that parents would be given a voucher for their child's education, or as he indicated in a speech to the Institute of Directors in 1982 (Chitty, 2002, p. 29):

> The voucher, in effect, is a cash facility for all parents, only useable in schools instead of money. It would come from the taxpayer ... it would give all parents, however poor, a choice of schools regardless of how much these schools cost, be they in the private sector or the maintained, that is, the public sector ... A voucher would provide an equal moral treatment for all parents. It would not, of course, provide an equal background for all children, because the home is very important in the education of a child, and homes differ from one another in the combination of love, discipline and encouragement that is given to the child.

Readers may wish to consider the views expressed by Sir Keith Joseph in relation to recent and proposed initiatives by the current government, such as, for example, the introduction of *Free* schools. It is, of course, not possible for schools to function outside of social, economic and political dimensions of influence. The extent to which they can and do function is important because it raises numerous issues that require consideration. Each of these three dimensions exerts its own unique but interrelated factors. In drawing attention to the political influence of the previous Blair government, in particular government directives, refering to American schools, Merz and Swim (2011, p. 305) have, for example, suggested that, 'Most public school principals and teachers wrestle with developing and implementing a vision amongst the imposition of mandates'. Indeed, Cox (2011, p. 3) has argued that in England the culture of primary schooling:

> ... has been sustained, at least in part, by a performance orientation towards education and a target-driven political agenda... Added to this, there has been the overriding expectation, over the past two decades or so, that teachers must comply with policy initiatives.

The result of this, Cox suggests, is overload and over-prescription on the part of teachers. Rather worryingly, she also suggests that the opportunities that teachers have had in the past to use their own professional judgement have become more limited. Arguably, this indirectly affects the learning of their pupils as the teacher's autonomy decreases. There are those who have suggested that quality teachers will leave the profession if this continues.

Recently, in 2012, Daniel Boffrey, the Policy Editor of the national UK newspaper *The Observer* felt able to write as follows:

> Morale among state school teachers is at 'rock bottom', according to a former chief inspector of schools, who speaks out today as unions warn that a 'perfect storm' of government meddling threatens an exodus of talent from the profession ... The pressure on teachers includes tougher targets [and] a new Ofsted grading system that threatens the current rating of most schools ... Many teachers have also complained of dilapidated conditions in the schools they work in ...

Mayall (2002, p. 13) has commented in relation to policy and decision makers and parents as follows:

> I was alerted as a mother to thinking about childhood ... that children got a raw deal at the hands of policymakers. In the 1970s and 1980s, when other European countries were providing universalist high quality state-run nurseries, British pre-school children were (and still are) the victims of a ramshackle patchwork of poor services. Indeed ... they could not be called services, but rather an ad hoc system which operated certainly not in the interests of children, nor even of the 'working' mothers, who struggled to finance the household in the face of inaccessible, insecure and unaccountable 'provision'.

The social influences upon children in Western industrialized societies are enormous and growing. Recently, in 2006, the UK newspaper the *Daily Telegraph* published a letter signed by over 100 teachers, psychologists and 'other experts' who were beseeching the government to, 'prevent the death of childhood'. They wrote as follows:

> Since children's brains are still developing, they cannot adjust – as full-grown adults can – to the effects of ever more rapid technological and cultural change. They still need what developing human beings have always needed, including real food (as opposed to processed 'junk'), real play (as opposed to sedentary, screen-based entertainment), first-hand experience of the world they live in and regular interaction with the real-life significant adults in their lives. (Fenton, 2006, p. 1)

Some years previously, however, Mayall (2002, p. 163) in drawing upon the work of Buckingham (2000) had commented as follows:

> As David Buckingham describes, the prophets of doom vie with the optimists … The doom-merchants foresee the death of childhood as children are exposed to 'adult entertainment' and are stressed beyond their years; the optimists see children as liberated from adult-controlled childhoods through their access to knowledge, entertainment and networks of children. Buckingham argues that the evidence for a full-blown acceptance of either thesis is poor, and that the claimants exaggerate their theses …

More recently, in July 2012, Martin Beckford the Home Affairs editor for the *Daily Telegraph* reported that, 'Children as young as seven and eight are using ecstasy and cannabis, according to an official report … The youngest reported user of cocaine was nine'.

It is useful at this point to draw once more upon the theoretical work of Bronfenbrenner who has placed much greater emphasis upon the changing and dynamic cultures within which children grow up (Bronfenbrenner, 1979; Bronfenbrenner and Ceci, 2005). As children grow older the nature of their interactions with others changes. Bronfenbrenner has suggested, therefore, that to properly understand development we need to view it within the social, political and economic contexts within which individuals live. He attempted to illustrate this visually by suggesting a number of layers that encompass the growing child and he proposed that these layers directly and indirectly affect the biological maturation of all individuals.

Bronfenbrenner gave names to each layer surrounding individuals. The closest layer to the individual, he called the 'Microsystem'. It is within this layer that children encounter their most direct contact with such influences as their family, the nursery school or playgroup they attend, the communities of which they are a part, their neighbours, and so on. Bronfenbrenner suggested a two-way process within the Microsystem, which influences the child, referring to these influences as 'Bi-directional Influences'. As the child is influenced by the behaviours, actions and beliefs of their parents so, in turn, the child also influences their parents. Bronfenbrenner suggested, therefore, that the relation is bi-directional and saw the influences on the child as being very strong. This is a very important point and one that requires careful analysis.

All children influence their parents, though some to lesser degrees than others. The nature of the way in which parents interact with their young children, including infants, is not always parent-led. Indeed, more commonly, perhaps, very young children will directly influence the behaviours, and indirectly the learning, of their parents through, for examples their cries or their attractive cooing noises and smiles. A very young infant, for example, who is lying in their cot and makes a soft cooing noise or a babbling noise may alert their mother who when hearing the noise comes and picks the infant up and gives it a big hug and then spends time with it. In this example, the infant has initiated (though not intentionally) a behaviour (the cooing or babbling) and the mother's behaviour is altered and then reinforced (see Chapter 2) by the infant with, perhaps, a smile. In a sense they are both reinforcing each other's behaviours – a two-way process – in which learning is taking place for the infant and its mother, although the whole process is at a subconscious level.

Outside of this first layer is the 'Mesosystem', which Bronfenbrenner relates to the forming of connections between, for example, the child's parents and their first teacher, or between their surrounding community and their school. In this way children can relate their experiences gained whilst at school to their experiences gained in the family, and in doing so they can make comparisons between the adults and other children with whom they come into contact; be they brothers and sisters, teachers, teaching assistants, and so on.

The next outer layer is the 'Exosystem', which Bronfenbrenner views as the child's wider social system. It is within this layer that such factors as the commitments that parents have to make to their employers and their working environments influence their children. It is within the Exosystem that the wider social experiences of children impact indirectly upon them. An example can be witnessed with the current economic climate in the UK in which it is being proposed that benefits for many single parents will be reduced. Another example is where the current Coalition Government in the UK has introduced significant changes in the education system by allowing for the introduction of Free schools, giving significantly greater choice to parents.

Outside of the Exosystem lies the 'Macrosystem', which is made up of children's culture, their societal values, the nation's legal structures, and so on. All of these impact upon the children's inner layers. Children, for example, who grow up in traditional societies where adults reject marital separation and divorce may receive less practical support than children growing up in communities that are more accepting of marital separation and divorce. It is within the Macrosystem that the ideological views that are historically dominant in the child's culture are seen as being of central importance. Bronfenbrenner identified a further layer, which he called the Chronosystem. Central to this layer is 'time' and how this interfaces with the environments in which children develop. As children develop they interact with others in different ways and with the environments in which they live. Bronfenbrenner's theory has, however, been criticized in that it fails to pay sufficient attention to the individual psychological needs of the child. In one part of the UK, Northern Ireland, an analysis of underachievement undertaken only three years ago (DENI, 2009, p. 12) offered the following quite worrying statistics:

> Statistics show a pattern of underachievement among children living in or at risk of poverty. Using entitlement to free school meals (FSM) as an indicator of social and economic deprivation, it was reported that in 2006/07, only 27% of pupils who were entitled to FSM gained at least 5 or more GCSEs at grades A*–C ... including English and mathematics by the time they left school, compared with 60% of those who were not entitled to FSM ... 'poor educational attainment can reinforce the cycle of deprivation that many ... marginalised groups experience throughout their lives'.

In addressing concerns regarding the underachievement of children in England, the Chief Inspector of Ofsted, is currently calling for further changes in the way some children might be taught. He is openly critical of the quality of teaching that many children in more affluent rural coastal areas are receiving. His suggestions have been widely reported in the media. Richard Garner, Education Editor for the UK national newspaper *The Independent* commented as follows:

> The country's most talented teachers and heads should be put on central contracts so they can be parachuted into schools that are failing disadvantaged pupils, Chief Schools Inspector Sir Michael Wilshaw will urge today. They would be deployed to improve the teaching of disadvantaged children in the leafy suburbs, rural market towns and seaside resorts – where the gap between the performance of poor and rich pupils is greatest, and where many deprived young people endure 'indifferent teaching'. Sir Michael ... will publish evidence which shows that the schools with the worst records in teaching disadvantaged pupils are no longer those in the inner cities – but deprived coastal towns and rural areas in the east and south-east of England ... These poor, unseen children can be found in mediocre schools the length and breadth of the country. They are labelled, buried in lower sets, consigned as often as not to indifferent teaching ...

> The most important factor in reversing these trends is to attract and incentivise the best people to the leadership of under-performing schools in these areas ...

> This may require government to work with teaching schools (specially designated to aid in the training of teachers) to identify and incentivise experienced and effective teachers to work in less fashionable, more remote or challenging places. (2012, p. 4)

It is clear from the above report, offered in a highly respected national newspaper, that issues regarding the way in which children within the UK are being taught, continue to be of national interest. Garner's report, which must of course be read with a critical mind, highlights the continuing debate that surrounds not only the manner in which children from disadvantaged backgrounds are taught but also how the teaching profession might be organized differently in the future and as a result of government intervention.

LEARNING AND SCHOOLING WITHIN A GLOBAL CONTEXT

It is not possible to fully understand learning and how children are educated in the 21st century without consideration of the global context within which we all now exist. Consider, for example, the current effects on schools in the UK that are being posed by the following: conflict in the Middle East; the extent and ease with which families are relocating to other countries such as New Zealand, Australia and Canada; the reduction in Local Authority governance and the centralization of power in national government; the increase in austerity measures brought about by the downturn in the global economy; and the ease with which most individuals across the world can access information on the World Wide Web.

Much of our thinking in the field of education has been, and continues to be, influenced by research and practice being undertaken in other countries; one only has to look at the rise in international contributions to academic journals researching education and learning and the ease with which these are made available to student teachers and practising teachers undertaking continuing professional development. In addition, most children in the UK now enjoy many of the cultural aspects from other countries, such as the wonderful range of foods, television programmes and literature, and social experiences gained from meeting individuals from other cultures whilst out shopping or travelling, or dining out. All of these experiences add to the learning and social development of children and offer experiences that would have been unheard of 50 years ago. These experiences can be extremely rewarding for children and can open their minds to what exists outside of their own immediate communities and society.

Exercise

Consider the view that schools need to do more to address the changing needs of children in the 21st century.

To understand learning and the education of children more fully within a global context, it is also important to make comparisons between the life experiences of children and young people. It is generally understood, for example, that children in the UK can be employed on a part-time basis if they are 14 years of age and on a full-time basis if they have reached 16 years of age. However, this is not the case elsewhere. A recent report by the International Labour Force (2005) indicated that 246 million children across the world were involved in child labour, that 179 million children from the age of five to 17 were being exposed to types of labour that caused irreversible physical or psychological damage with possible threats to life, and that some eight and a half million children were trapped in patterns of labour which included bonded labour, prostitution and pornography, and even armed conflict (Gray and MacBlain, 2012). It is clear from these startling and very worrying figures that many children across the globe are failing to access anything close to adequate education and schooling. Yet, popular opinion in the Western industrialized world persists in viewing childhood as a period characterized by innocence and playfulness, economic security and regular access to formal education. Woodhead (2005, p. 88), quoted in Smith (2011, p.18) draws attention to the problems associated with adopting this universal view of children's learning as follows:

While universal accounts of normal development offer a powerful basis for realizing rights in early childhood, they also have limitations. Firstly, they tend to overlook the diversities in children's experiences, including differences in the ways children learn, play and communicate … Secondly, any particular account of young children's development is always partial, and can never encompass the varieties of childhood. Thirdly, specific cultural patterns of early development and care risk being normalized and universalized.

Summary

Schooling in the 21st century in the UK is increasing in complexity as the current Coalition Government introduces new types of schools with a shifting emphasis of ideologies. For this reason, it is important that practitioners critically engage with their own practice and draw upon the work of those thinkers and researchers who seek to offer new and purposeful insights into the nature of education at present and, perhaps more importantly, as it will develop in future years in response to economic, political and social change at home and throughout the world.

This chapter sought to highlight the importance of considering learning and schooling within a social, cultural, historical and global context. The function of schools was examined with particular reference to its historical context to alert readers to the need

(Continued)

(Continued)

to see the dynamic character of schooling and the fact that what is being experienced by children in terms of their formal education has not only changed significantly in past decades and centuries but is continuing to change and will change radically in the future. The nature of the curricula on offer to children and the influence of successive governments as well as global economic factors affecting curricula and curricula delivery were also explored. The complex nature of transitions between schools and between stages of education was examined, with consideration being given to the importance of understanding the impact that transitions can have on children. The following chapter now turns to the concept of intelligence and its relationship with learning.

RECOMMENDED READING

Chitty, C. (2002) *Understanding Schools and Schooling*. London: Routledge Falmer.
Cox, S. (2011) *New Perspectives in Primary Education*. Maidenhead: Open University Press.

REFERENCES

Academies Commission (2013) *Unleashing Greatness: Getting the Best from an Academised System. The Report of the Academies Commission*. Pearson/RSA.

Beckford, M. (2012) Children 'are taking Class A drugs aged 7', *Daily Telegraph*, 27 July, p. 2.

Boffrey, D. (2012) Schools 'face talent drain' as teachers' morale dives, *The Observer*, 13 March, p. 1.

Bronfenbrenner, U. (1979) *The Ecology of Human Development*. Cambridge, MA: Harvard University Press.

Bronfenbrenner, U. and Ceci, S.J. (1994) Nature–nurture reconceptualized in developmental perspective: a bioecological model, *Psychological Review*, 101 (4): 568-86.

Bronfenbrenner, U. (2005) *Making Human Beings Human: Bioecological Perspectives on Human Development*. London: Sage.

Buckingham, D. (2000) *After the Death of Childhood: Growing Up in the Age of Electronic Media*. Cambridge: Polity.

Chedzoy, S.M. and Burden, R.L. (2005) Making the move: assessing student attitudes to primary secondary transfer. *Research in Education*, 74 (1): 22–35.

Chitty, C. (2002) *Understanding Schools and Schooling*. London: Routledge Falmer.

Choi, K. (2012) Supporting transition from primary to secondary school using the Protective Behaviours programme, *Educational & Child Psychology*, 29 (3): 27–37.

Cox, S. (2011) *New Perspectives in Primary Education*. Maidenhead: Open University Press.

Crafter, S. and Maunder, R. (2012). Understanding transitions using a sociocultural framework, *Educational and Child Psychology*, 29 (1): 10–17.

Department for Education and Employment (1996) *Education Act*. London: DfEE Publications.

Department for Education (2013) *Education Act 2011*. London: DfE Publications. Available at: http://www.legislation.gov.uk/ukpga/2011/21/notes/division/2 (accessed 10 April 2013).

Department of Education Northern Ireland (DENI) (2009) *The Way Forward for Special Educational Needs and Inclusion*. Bangor: DENI. Available at: http://www.deni.gov.uk/ (accessed 5 February 2013).

Duverger, M. (1972) *The Study of Politics*. Sunbury-on-Thames: Nelson.

Fisher, A. and Rush, L. (2008) Conceptions of learning and pedagogy: developing trainee teachers' epistemological understandings. *The Curriculum Journal*. 19 (3): 227–38.

Fisher, A. , Russell, K., MacBlain, S.F., Purdy, N., Curry, A., and MacBlain, A.D. (2010) Re-examining the culture of learning in ITE: engaging with the new demands of the 21st century, *Critical and Reflective Practice in Education*, 1(2).

Fenton, B. (2006) Junk culture 'is poisoning our children', *Daily Telegraph*, 12 September, p. 1.

Garner, R. (2013) Schools chief: use the best teachers to help failing schools, *The Independent*, 20 June, p. 4.

Geens, W., James, S. and MacBlain, S.F. (2009) Journeyman to master: the changing shape of a PGCE Primary course. *The International Journal of Learning*, 16 (8): 629–40.

Gray, C. and MacBlain, S.F. (2012) *Learning Theories in Childhood*. London: Sage.

International Labour Force (2005) *A Global Alliance Against Forced Labour: Global Report under the Follow-up to the ILO Declaration on Fundamental Principles and Rights at Work 2005*. Geneva: International Labour Force Office.

Jadue-Roa, D.S. and Whitebread, D. (2012) Young children's experiences through transition between Kindergarten and First Grade in Chile and its relation with their Developing Learning Agency, *Educational & Child Psychology*, 29 (1): 32–46.

Kennedy, E., Cameron, R.J. and Greene, J. (2012) Transitions in the early years: educational and child psychologists working to reduce the impact of school culture shock, *Educational & Child Psychology*, 29 (1): 19–30.

Lee, L. (1962) *Cider with Rosie*. Harmondsworth: Penguin.

Long, L., MacBlain, S.F. and MacBlain, M.S. (2007) Supporting the pupil with dyslexia at secondary level: mechanistic or emotional models of literacy, *Journal of Adolescent and Adult Literacy*, 51(2): 124–34.

Lyons, R. and Woods, K. (2012) Effective transition to secondary school for shy, less confident children: a case study using 'Pyramid' group work, *Educational & Child Psychology*, 29(3): 8–26.

Mayall, B. (2002). *Towards a Sociology for Childhood: Thinking from Children's Lives*. Maidenhead: Open University Press.

McCourt, F. (1997) *Angela's Ashes*. London: Flamingo.

Merz, A.H. and Swim, T.J. (2011) 'You can't mandate what matters': bumping visions against practices, *Teacher Development*, 15(3): 305–18.

Office for Standards in Education (Ofsted) (2010) *The Special Educational Needs and Disability Review*. London: Ofsted.

Office for Standards in Education (Ofsted) (2013) *The Most Able Students: Are They Doing as Well as They Should is Our Non-selective Secondary Schools?* London: Ofsted.

Peace, M. and Mufti, E. (2012) *Teaching and Learning and the Curriculum: A Critical Introduction.* London: Continuum.

Schostak, J. (1991) *Youth in Trouble.* London: Kogan Page.

Smith, A.B. (2011) Respecting Children's Rights and Agency: Theoretical Insights into Ethical Research Procedures. In D. Harcourt, B. Perry and T. Walker (eds) *Researching Young Children's Perspectives: Debating the Ethics and Dilemmas of Educational Research with Children.* Abingdon: Routledge.

Smith, M.K. (2001) 'Ragged schools and the development of youth work and informal education', *The Encyclopaedia of Informal Education.* Available at: http://www.infed.org/youthwork/ragged_schools.htm

Smidt, S. (2011) *Introducing Bruner: A Guide for Practitioners and Students in Early Years Education.* London: Routledge.

6 INTELLIGENCE AND LEARNING

This chapter aims to:

- emphasize the controversial nature of intelligence and how such a concept can assist our understanding of learning
- examine the legacy associated with measuring intelligence and controversies surrounding the concept of an Intelligence Quotient (IQ)
- explore issues linked to the measurement of intelligence and intellectual functioning, and the learning needs of children
- highlight alternative ways of thinking about intelligence and learning through reference to the works of Reuven Feuerstein and Howard Gardner
- explore issues relevant to children described as Gifted and Talented
- give consideration to the construct *low ability* and whether such a construct has any place in the 21st century.

INTRODUCTION

Since philosophers and theorists first attempted to explain intelligence, debate as to its nature has raged across most academic disciplines, most notably, psychology and education. Despite decades, and even generations of reflection, evaluation and research, the term can still provoke much heated debate. It is a concept that readers will hear being used frequently and across whole ranges of conversations. '*Try to act in a more intelligent way*' may be a phrase often heard being used by parents and teachers. '*He's not very intelligent*' is possibly another one, as is '*He is highly intelligent*' or '*He's not that bright*'. But, what does the term *intelligence* mean and, more specifically, what can it tell us about learning?

This chapter begins by exploring the nature of intelligence and highlighting two key controversies, that of *eugenics*, and attempts that have been made over the last century to define intelligence. The chapter then explores some of the thinking behind the measurement of intelligence, in particular the use and misuse of Intelligence Quotients, or, as they are more commonly referred to, IQs. Links between intelligence and learning are explored, with consideration being given to the theoretical views of two important contributors to the debate on the nature of intelligence and learning – Howard Gardner and Reuven Feuerstein. Particular reference is made to the learning of those children considered to be *Gifted and Talented* and the chapter closes by questioning the relevance of categorizing children as being of *low ability* in the 21st century.

THE NATURE OF INTELLIGENCE

It is without question that one of the most controversial areas in the psychology of human development is that of 'intelligence'. For centuries, theorists and philosophers have argued about the nature of intelligence – what exactly it is and, perhaps most controversially of all, whether or not it is inherited and if it can be measured. Two decades ago Hayes (1994, p. 178) in her introductory text to the study of psychology cautioned her readers that:

> Intelligence is probably the single most controversial topic in psychology. People hold widely different opinions on what it is, how it develops and how relevant it is for living; and these differences have sometimes developed into highly acrimonious debates. One of the main reasons for this is political: intelligence is not just an academic issue … The political implications of intelligence theory centre on three issues: social stratification, education and eugenics.

Hayes suggested that as the Western world moved towards a meritocratic system where status was accorded to those who were considered to be more intellectually able, the concept of intelligence 'first emerged'. She also drew attention to how theories that attempted to explain the nature of intelligence were largely influential in directing the course of much practice that has occurred within schools over the last two centuries. Arguably, this continues even today and alerts us to the historical and ongoing debate surrounding eugenics, which Hayes has located within the original works of Francis Galton who, Hayes claims, '… argued from studies of the families of eminent Victorians that since intelligence clearly ran in families, it was therefore inherited' (1994, p. 180). She outlines the case proposed by Galton as follows:

> He [Galton] went on to observe with alarm that the 'lower classes' in society were breeding prolifically, and argued that this would result in a lowering of the overall intelligence of the nation, or of the race, contaminating society with an excessively large number of wasters, drunks and degenerates. Consequently, the eugenic argument – which called itself scientific – was that those who were genetically inferior should be prevented from breeding in order to keep society racially 'pure' and to prevent it from becoming 'mongrelised'. (1994, p. 180)

History has shown us that such ideas have been embraced by a number of extreme sections of societies throughout the world, most notably perhaps the Nazis, who, under the leadership of Adolf Hitler, set about the extermination of what they considered to be undesirable individuals. However, not only was this the case in Nazi Germany in the 1930s and 1940s, but examples can also be found elsewhere, even today in some quarters of Western industrialized societies. Hayes again cites an example of laws passed in some parts of the USA, which, 'enforced compulsory sterilization of those with low IQs' (see later for a discussion of the term 'IQ'), a practice she commented upon as continuing as late as 1972 in the state of Virginia.

To gain a better understanding of the nature of intelligence we now turn our attention to the complexities surrounding its definition. Gross (1992, p. 840) has offered a sample of definitions from some influential figures who have sought to define the term:

Binet (1905)	'It seems to us that in intelligence there is a fundamental faculty, the impairment of which is of the utmost importance for practical life. This faculty is called judgement, otherwise called good sense, practical sense, initiative, the faculty of adapting one's self to circumstances. To judge well, to comprehend well, to reason well ...'
Terman (1921)	'An individual is intelligent in proportion as he is able to carry on abstract thinking'.
Burt (1955)	'Innate, general, cognitive ability'.
Wechsler (1944)	'The aggregate of the global capacity to act purposefully, think rationally, to deal effectively with the environment'.

Exercise

Reflect upon the types of behaviours that can be observed in young children when they are playing and consider how these might suggest that intelligence is or is not inherited.

Having emphasized the complexities associated with defining intelligence and the controversial nature of the concept, we now turn to the controversies surrounding its measurement, and particularly the concept of IQ.

THE HISTORICAL DEVELOPMENT OF IQ TESTING: ITS USE AND MISUSE

Perhaps a less than obvious starting point in explaining the concept of IQ can be found in the work of the American psychologist Henry Herbert Goddard (1866–1957). Goddard was a controversial figure in that many of his ideas surrounding the testing of children would now be viewed as wholly unacceptable. He was a Eugenicist who believed that intelligence and mental capacities were inherited and he advocated the institutionalization and sterilization of children and young adults who were considered to be, in the parlance of the time, 'feeble minded'. It was in 1910 whilst at a meeting of the American Association for the Study of the Feeble Minded that he offered a number of classifications for individuals considered to be 'feeble minded'. For those with an IQ of between 51 and 70 he proposed the term 'Moron', for those with an IQ score between 26 and 50 he proposed the term 'Imbecile' and for those with an IQ score of between 0 and 25 he proposed the term 'Idiot'. Sadly, these terms remain in common parlance and readers may still hear them being used by adults to describe others.

Goddard began his career as a teacher and worked with children considered at the time to fall into the category of 'feeble minded'. A significant turning point in Goddard's life came, in 1908 when he travelled to France where he was introduced to the Binet-Simon Intelligence Scales, which he obtained and then brought back to the USA. After translating these from French into English he set about using them with the children with whom he worked and then introduced them subsequently across the USA. So popular were the Scales that over 20,000 were distributed throughout the USA in the 20 years following his return from France. In addition to using the Scales with children he taught, Goddard saw a further use for them when in 1910 he took it upon himself to visit Ellis Island where all the immigrants hoping to enter the USA were initially held in order that they could be screened. Following this initial visit to Ellis Island Goddard returned there two years later and set up a revised screening procedure for newly arrived immigrants as a means of supporting the 1882 law passed by the United States Congress, which prevented individuals considered to be 'mentally defective' progressing beyond Ellis Island into the USA. Goddard used his adapted Binet-Simon Scales as part of this screening process. But what exactly were these scales, where did they come from and why did they become so popular?

Back in France, the government in 1881 had introduced legislation that made formal education in schools compulsory for every child. Prior to this, children considered to have too many intellectual difficulties to attend school remained at home. Because the new legislation called for all children to be educated, the government was faced with the need to set up specialist schools to cater for these children. The challenge then was to determine some process whereby decisions could be made as to what type of school children should attend. This opened the way for attempts at measuring intellectual functioning. In 1905 the French psychologist Alfred Binet and a colleague Théodore Simon were invited to develop a process of assessment through which decisions could be made in regard to placing children in these specialist schools.

At the outset, Binet considered it appropriate to devise a number of tasks that would assess such aspects of an individual's functioning as reasoning and social comprehension. He also considered it important to distinguish between verbal and practical tasks. Binet set about devising these tasks in such a way that they would, he considered, differentiate between performance by age and by ability. In other words, older children would perform better than younger children and children considered more able by their teachers would do better than children considered less able by their teachers. Binet, however, was not alone in attempting to create tasks that could be used to measure intelligence. In 1962, the renowned psychologist George Miller (1962, p. 310) emphasized the naïvety and ignorance that characterized much of the work being undertaken at the turn of the century. Here, he makes reference to the psychologist Raymond Cattell whose work Binet and others (Henri and Simon, for example) took up:

> Cattell … was one of the brightest lights in American psychology at the turn of the century. Yet look at the list of tests he proposed to measure intelligence:
>
> *Dynamometer Pressure.* How tightly can the hand squeeze?
>
> *Pressure Causing Pain.* How much pressure on the forehead is necessary to cause pain?
>
> *Time for Naming Colours.* How long does it take to name a strip of coloured papers?

Following upon the work of Cattell and others, Binet set about attempting to standardize children's performance on these tasks in such a way that standardized scores could be recorded. The result of this was the concept of 'Mental Age' (MA), 'a child's mental age being the chronological age at which most children obtained scores similar to his or her own' (Fontana, 1995, p. 97).

Binet's original work was then developed further in the USA by Lewis Terman whilst working at the University of Stanford, and from this work the concept of *Intelligence Quotient* (IQ) was born. A child's IQ could be calculated by, 'taking the ratio of mental age to chronological age and multiplying it by 100. Thus a child with, say, a mental age of ten and a chronological age of eight would have an IQ of: $10/8 \times 100/1 = 125$' (Fontana, 1995, p. 98).

Fontana (1995, p. 98), however, has identified a number of key issues with the concept of IQ, for example:

> Experience showed that mental age does not appear to improve after age 15 (i.e., in terms at least of intelligence test scores, we seem to peak at around 15) … In consequence we now use what is called a *deviation* IQ, which expresses an individual's score simply in terms of its deviation from the norm of their age, with the norm still being scaled to equal the convenient score of 100.

Despite the original difficulties with the concepts of Mental Age and Intelligence Quotient a systematic appraisal of the original work by Binet took place and through the work undertaken by specialists at Stanford University, which resulted in the Stanford-Binet Scale, a number of significant developments took place. The original Stanford-Binet Scales appeared in 1905 and these were then followed by a revised set in 1908 with a third set following in 1911, the same year that Binet died. The Scales needed to be administered individually and consisted of a series of problems, some of which required the child to provide an oral response and some of which were timed.

The Stanford-Binet Scales, and subsequent similar assessment devices, perhaps most notably the now commonly used *Wechsler Scales*, have been constructed on the principle that intelligence is distributed normally across the population. Such an assumption, however, begs the question as to whether or not intelligence is, in fact, normally distributed. Particular problems have arisen, for example, where these Scales have been used to make decisions about children's levels of intellectual functioning in comparison to their peers and where teachers have placed children in academic sets according to their IQ scores. Take the case of Ben:

Example

Ben is 10 years of age and has just begun attending a local independent school. He has joined this school because he was unhappy at his previous school, which was a local primary school. His new school is considered to be very traditional and places a great deal of emphasis upon achieving good results which will permit its pupils to go on to notable independent senior schools. Reputation, therefore, and the number of its pupils being successful in gaining places at good public schools, is a very important dimension of Ben's new school. As part of their traditional approach to teaching and learning the school sets its pupils according to their abilities and achievements in subjects such as English and Mathematics. In his first week at his new school Ben sits a number of tests prepared by the school, which when marked offer a 'verbal' and 'non-verbal' score. The average score on these tests is 100. Ben's score on these tests will determine which set he is put in. If, for example, he achieves a score of 130 then he will be placed in the 'top set'. If, on the other hand, he achieves a score of 80 then he will be placed in the bottom set of 12 sets. Most teachers at Ben's school believe that if pupils are 'bright' then they will do well and if not then they will do less well. They have been using this system for years and are always keen to obtain test scores from educational psychologists that provide IQ scores, which will help them when they are ranking pupils into sets. A child with a high IQ, they feel, will be capable of achieving more academically than a child with a low IQ. Ben was assessed by an independent educational psychologist prior to coming to the school when he was only five years of age. The psychologist at the time indicated that Ben had an IQ of 95 (average range: 85 to 115). Ben is then assigned to a low set by his teachers as he is considered to be less able than other children who have gained IQ scores above the average range.

It can be seen from Ben's case that his IQ score has been a key determining factor in placing him in a low set. However, what his teachers have not realized is that when Ben's IQ score was calculated he gained extremely low scores on some of the sub-tests because he had specific learning difficulties relating to Working Memory and Speed of Processing. On most other sub-tests he had achieved scores that were above average. When all of the scores were computed his lower scores pulled down his overall IQ score masking the fact that he is, in fact, a very able child of above average ability, and intellectually more able than many of his peers but with learning difficulties of a specific nature. Educational Psychologists now treat IQ scores with great caution, with many, if not most Educational Psychologists never using them.

Now consider the following:

Exercise

What, if any, benefits might Ben's teachers have gained from using his IQ scores and how might they choose to 'set' him differently?

Despite the concept of IQ being open to criticism and continuing to be challenged as a workable construct, it is still popularly used today. Take, for example, the comments written by the journalist Fiona Macrae that appeared in the UK daily paper *The Daily Mail* in August 2012:

> Teenagers who become hooked on cannabis risk long-term damage to their IQ, researchers have warned ... The eminent international research team, including some from the Institute of Psychiatry at King's College London, put more than 1,000 boys and girls through a battery of IQ tests when they were aged 13 and 14. They did the same tests more than 20 years later, at the age of 38, and any differences were noted.

The important point here is that our understanding of *intelligence* is not complete. There are still many aspects of this construct that we simply do not understand. We are, in effect, continuing upon a journey in which we will, over the next decades improve our comprehension as to the nature of intelligence.

Frederickson and Cline (2002, pp. 232–3) offer the following very useful description of the way in which attempts to standardize assessment for IQ tests have taken place:

> A general intelligence scale comprises a wide range of intellectually challenging tasks that are presented to the person being tested in a standard way. During the development of an intelligence scale for children a large, representative sample of children will have been

given these tasks, and data will be available on the average scores of children at each level and on the spread of scores around the average. When individuals are given the scale subsequently, their performance can be compared to the norms for the original 'standardization' sample. Thus the IQ measure is norm-based.

They also draw attention to the benefits that some advocates of IQ and normative testing have put forward, such as the emphasis upon time saving (it is generally fairly quick to administer an IQ battery of test), which are that they:

> provide a reasonably reliable estimate of general mental ability or potential which is stable over time ... draw upon extensive normative information that cannot be accessed without the use of tests ... screen for areas of weakness in thinking and information processing ... provide a baseline index against which to measure future development or learning. (2002, p. 234)

INTELLIGENCE AND LEARNING: THE LINKS

The link between intelligence and learning appears at first glance to be obvious. However, suggesting links between these two constructs is fraught with difficulties, and practitioners working with children need to take great care when making assumptions about how each links with the other. Take, for example, the case of Adam, who was assessed by an educational psychologist following concerns about his lack of progress in school.

Example

Adam is 11 years old and about to enter his final year of primary school. His progress in reading and writing has been extremely slow and he has become anxious about transferring to secondary school. His parents have been very concerned for some time and two years previously had him assessed by an educational psychologist. At that time when Adam was nine years of age the psychologist reported the results of an assessment of Adam's reading and spelling, which are shown in Table 6.1.

Table 6.1   Case study – Adam (initial literacy scores)

Test	Standard score	Centile	Age equivalent
Word Recognition	78	07	6 years 3 months
Reading Comprehension	80	09	6 years 6 months
Spelling	79	08	6 years 6 months

Two-thirds of children are considered to function within the average range of ability, which is represented between the 16th and 84th centiles, with the 16th centile lying at the lowest end of the average range and the 84th centile at the highest. The 85th centile upwards represents increasingly higher ability, with the 95th centile representing the top 1 per cent of ability. At the other end of the range, the 1st centile represents the lowest 1 per cent of ability.

Two years later in his review of Adam the same educational psychologist assessed Adam and reported his findings of Adam's reading and spelling as shown in Table 6.2.

Table 6.2 Case study – Adam (subsequent literacy scores)

Test	Standard score	Centile	Age equivalent
Word Recognition	72	03	6 years 9 months
Reading Comprehension	71	03	6 years 9 months
Spelling	78	07	7 years 3 months

The educational psychologist commented in his later report as follows:
My assessment of Adam using a range of psychometric tests indicated that Adam is a child of at least average ability but with marked specific learning difficulties that affect his progress in all aspects of literacy. In particular, he experiences difficulties in the area of Working Memory and with Processing Speed. In regard to the scores achieved by Adam on the reading and spelling tests it should be recognized that these test scores are not exact measurements and that there may be some variation between different reading and spelling tests as well as variation over time. It is clear that Adam continues to experience marked difficulties in all aspects of literacy and I would suggest that Adam is confused by much of the reading and spelling process. He will benefit particularly from highly structured, cumulative, sequential and multisensory learning that works to address his specific learning difficulties. When asked to say the vowels I observed Adam to become very confused and he responded by saying, 'd', 'u', 'a' and 'e'. Adam was not able to say the alphabet in sequence though he attempted this three times. When asked what sound the letter 'a' made Adam responded by offering the sound made by the letter 'm'.

It can be seen that despite being of '*at least average ability*' Adam is struggling with literacy and with accessing much of the curriculum. So, why might this be the case? Surely, some might argue, if he is that able then why can't he read and spell? It is worth reflecting upon Adam's experience of learning whilst at school and the social and emotional aspects of this and of his overall development. Whilst Adam is intellectually able it is clear that much of his learning at school is not geared to his level of intelligence. In order to make purposeful progress Adam will benefit from having a much better understanding of the language of instruction in the area of literacy development, together with the structural analysis of words. For example, he will benefit from knowing that many words are made up of prefixes, suffixes, roots, and so on, and he should familiarize himself with these so that when he is attempting to read or spell words he is using a more efficient strategy whereby he attempts to analyse the structure as opposed to simply guessing, which is a strategy employed by so many children and young people who are weak readers.

Adam should also follow a highly structured, sequential and cumulative programme in reading and spelling, which incorporates multisensory techniques, which will compensate for his specific learning difficulties in the areas of working memory and processing speed. Daily reinforcement of learning will be important and he could be invited to use a visual timetable for his week, which is broken into time segments, such as before and after break in the morning and before and after break in the afternoon. Reinforcement of new learning should be on a daily basis and should be introduced in as creative a way as possible. The importance of reinforcement was dealt with in Chapter 2.

Adam would benefit from using a cursive script when writing as this will work alongside the development of his kinaesthetic memory and he should be encouraged to sound out letters as he writes them and then say the word as well. Adam could be involved in making his own books (see MacBlain and MacBlain, 2011 for an extensive self-help programme for children with literacy difficulties). Using Information and Communications Technology (ICT) to support his learning with word recognition, reading comprehension and spelling would also be very beneficial and would provide Adam with regular opportunities to record, self-check and proofread his written work. Regular access to high-interest and simple reading material, which links to Adam's natural curiosity, would also be very beneficial as would Paired Reading with adults where Adam could be encouraged to seek connections by talking about his own ideas and those he comes across in the texts he is reading with an adult or another child. He would also benefit from having regular opportunities to develop his self-confidence.

Let us now turn to the case of Gillian, a young woman in her late teens who has succeeded in gaining a place at university to undertake a degree programme in the creative arts:

Example

Gillian is a young woman who is 19 years of age. In order that her learning difficulties would be properly recognized by staff when she begins her university course she referred herself for assessment. The educational psychologist who undertook the assessment commented as follows in his report: *Gillian presented as an intelligent and articulate young woman and she greatly impressed me with her willingness to attempt challenging and difficult tasks. Gillian described her reading as, 'Poor, it's really slow' and her spelling as, 'It's really awful'. She also emphasized that when in class, 'I miss out on a lot of what the teacher is saying and I have to ask my friends to take notes for me otherwise I will miss out a whole lot of what is going on … I read things but afterwards I haven't a clue about what I have just read'.*

Table 6.3   Case study – Gillian (intellectual functioning)

Index	Percentile
Working Memory	21
Processing Speed	2
Verbal Comprehension	91
Perceptual Organization	98

Table 6.4   Case study – Gillian (literacy scores)

Test	Standard score	Centile
Reading accuracy	82	12
Reading comprehension	70	2
Spelling	67	1

It is clear that Gillian is intellectually very able and has the potential to do very well and to develop her creative talents and abilities. However, it is also clear that her learning whilst at school has been affected by underlying specific difficulties of a dyslexic nature. Her results signify a significant discrepancy between her cognitive abilities and her attainments in all aspects of literacy and we must ask how her experiences of learning were throughout her time in primary and, perhaps more worryingly, her post-primary education, where she would have been tasked with reading a wide variety of text and responding to this in oral and written expression in order to access the curriculum. Consideration also needs to be given to Gillian's emotional and social development and how this affected, and in turn was affected by, her difficulties with learning.

Of particular note was Gillian's much weaker performance on those sub-tests that make up the Processing Speed Index. For example, she achieved a below average score on the Coding sub-test, which provides a measure of speed and accuracy of hand–eye coordination, short-term memory and attentional skills. Of note also was Gillian's weaker performance on the sub-tests which are used to gain a measure of Working Memory. For example she achieved a low score on the Digit Span sub-test, which offers useful information relating to short-term auditory sequential memory, attentional strategies and the ability to concentrate. It also provides additional information relating to those processes that underpin reading accuracy and spelling and consists of two parts. Gillian's performance on these sub-tests was in marked contrast to her performance in other areas of functioning. Gillian achieved, for example, a well above average score on the Block Design sub-test – a very useful assessment which attempts to measure the reproductive aspect of visual-motor coordination, perceptual organization ability and spatial visualization ability or abstract conceptualizing ability and generalizing ability.

It is also of note that Gillian achieved well above the average range on the Similarities and Vocabulary sub-tests. The Similarities sub-test assesses the ability to undertake the skills of super and sub-ordinate classification, for example, cows and horses are both types of mammal, coats and shoes are types of clothing. The Vocabulary sub-test consists of a number of words arranged in ascending order of difficulty and individuals are asked to explain orally the meaning of each word. Gillian's score suggests that she has acquired a good fund of knowledge as well as vocabulary, and this will be greatly improved should she increase her level of reading.

Gillian clearly experiences difficulties when expressing her level of understanding of a subject in writing. Problems with spelling and with sentence structure, which affect her ability to produce accurate samples of written work, become quickly apparent, particularly when she is placed under pressure. This would also seem to be the case when Gillian is attempting to carry out a number of operations simultaneously which require the processing of written symbolic information and oral instructions at the same time. Gillian's speed of writing falls below the average expected of students with her ability.

Gillian would benefit from a technical assessment in order that appropriate ICT can be identified, which would make her academic programme readily accessible. In particular, Gillian could be encouraged and supported in using a dictaphone where possible to record lectures and to use this as a means of recording and organizing her own revision, as well as developing her existing skills and knowledge with ICT and exploring how it can help her with her studies in higher education. She would also benefit from having additional time in any formal examinations in order that she can correctly interpret questions and instructions in a limited time and process written symbolic information efficiently and in a manner that demonstrates her ability and potential. This will also allow her to check her accuracy of written work and the meaning of the text she is reading and responding to, and compose and execute written evidence to demonstrate her relevant subject knowledge and understanding in those subject areas in which she is being examined.

THE THEORETICAL WORK OF REUVEN FEUERSTEIN AND HOWARD GARDNER

We now turn to the work of two notable figures who, like other notable theorists and philosophers, have challenged the ways in which we understand and assess intellectual functioning in children and young people. The first of these is Reuven Feuerstein. Feuerstein was born in Botosani, Romania in 1921, and after World War II spent time working with children who were survivors of the Holocaust. This experience was to greatly influence and shape his thinking in terms of the way in which children thought and learned. When these children arrived initially with Feuerstein to be taught they were assessed using standardized IQ tests but Feuerstein observed that typically they did not perform well, though when he intervened to work with them he observed that they did much better and their performance improved. This led him to explore how these children learned and whether or not their abilities were fixed and if these could, in fact, be developed and intellectual skills and abilities taught. This led him to begin exploring the differences between abilities and potential and to develop his approach now known as *Dynamic Assessment*.

Feuerstein has suggested that the belief systems we hold about learning and about intellectual development should view human potential as having almost no limits whilst also recognizing that artificial barriers will be in place which may prevent change in children's development, as well as in the realization of their potential. Feuerstein has also proposed that all children, no matter what the degree of difficulties they may experience, can, with the appropriate support, become effective learners. By adopting such belief systems Feuerstein has argued that practitioners working with children are 'freed' from that type of constrained thinking that can limit their vision in regard to what is possible for all children.

When such a process is adhered to certain consequences occur, the most notable of which is what Feuerstein has termed, *Structural Cognitive Modifiability*, which refers to the recognition that the cognitive structure of an individual's brain may be altered through an enabling process, which allows learners to learn how to learn. In essence, learning becomes cumulative and then positively affects the individual's performance throughout their life (Burden, 1987). This approach, Feuerstein maintains, becomes directed at altering the structural nature of individuals' cognitive development. It should be recognized that Feuerstein sees 'structural change' as an individual's manner of 'acting upon' sources of information and responding to these sources. Feuerstein maintains that the central feature that is involved in learning how to learn is the notion of the *Mediated Learning Experience* and it is this notion that lies at the heart of Feuerstein's *Social Interactionist Theory* of learning. Feuerstein et al. (1980, p. 16) have referred to this as:

> … the way in which stimuli emitted by the environment are transferred by a 'mediating' agent, usually a parent, sibling or other caregiver. This mediated agent, guided by his intentions, culture, and emotional investment, selects and organises the world of stimuli for the child … Through this process of mediation, the cognitive structure of the child is affected.

The central features of mediating learning are: that the mediator should be aware of, make known and ensure that the learner has comprehended what is intended (intentionality and reciprocity); the mediator should explain why they are going to work at a task (investment of meaning); and that the act should be seen as having value over and above the here and now (transcendence) (Burden, 1987).

In the last two decades Howard Gardner (1983) has also offered an alternative view to our understanding of intelligence, and like Feuerstein has challenged academics and practitioners alike to reconsider what is meant by intelligence. Gardner studied under, and briefly worked with, the philosopher Jerome Bruner, who had an enormous impact upon him, in particular his ideas on education and cognitive development. A further influence upon Gardner's thinking was the renowned psychoanalyst Erik Erikson, under whom he also studied as a student whilst at Harvard University.

In particular, he has proposed the view that intelligence is not a unitary concept but, instead, is made up of multiple intelligences, with each of these being, 'a system in its own right' but which, 'interact, otherwise nothing could be achieved' (Gardner, 1983, p. 851). Gardner summarized his Multiple Intelligences as, Linguistic, Logical-mathematical, Spatial, Musical, Bodily-Kinaesthetic, Interpersonal and Intrapersonal, and more recently has explored the notion that there might be others, such as *Naturalist Intelligence,* that could be added to his original list of seven. Though his notion of Multiple Intelligences has not always been readily embraced by academic psychologists, it has, nevertheless, been very popular with many practitioners, in particular, educators (Smith, 2002, 2008).

Gardner's theory of Multiple Intelligences has been criticized on the grounds that it is not possible to test aspects of his theory, which results from, 'an ambiguity of the theory, in that it is not clear to what extent the intelligences are supposed to operate separately or interconnectedly' (Brooks et al., 2004, p. 55).

GIFTED AND TALENTED LEARNERS

Example

Brian is five years old and is in Year 1 at primary school, having completed a successful year in the Reception Class. His parents have referred him to an educational psychologist because they are concerned that his needs are not being recognized. They are particularly concerned that he is not being properly recognized by his school as being very able. In her initial discussions with the educational psychologist Brian's mother describes him as '*very bright*' and '*always on the go*'. When the educational psychologist meets with Brian at his home she observes him completing a range of tasks, talks with him and his mother and invites him to complete a number of tasks from the Wechsler Preschool and Primary Scale of Intelligence (WPPSI) in order to gain some additional baseline assessment data. On this occasion Brian achieves the scores shown in Table 6.5.

Table 6.5   Case study – Brian (intellectual functioning)

	Standard score	Percentile
Verbal IQ	147	99.9
Performance IQ	142	99.7

As indicated earlier, two-thirds of children are considered to function within the average range of ability, which is represented between the 16th and 84th centiles. The 85th centile upwards represents increasingly higher ability with the 95th centile representing the top 1 per cent of ability. At the other end of the range, the 1st centile represents the lowest 1 per cent of ability. Following completion of these sub-tests the educational psychologist asks Brian to read his school reading book and finds that he can read this extremely well and is also able to read such words as, '*distribution*' and '*antibiotic*', which Brian sees printed on a separate piece of paper on the kitchen table.

Brian is quite exceptional and is clearly a very able child who is functioning well above the average range. However, it is also clear that his exceptionally high ability is not being fully recognized by his teachers. Though there will be relatively few children functioning at such a high level as Brian there are also those who are, nevertheless, also extremely able in most areas, as well as those who demonstrate particular strengths in selected areas such as art, music, sport, and so on.

Recently, *The Good Schools Guide* website (2013a) offered the following comments under the heading, 'Educating the Gifted Child':

Gifted is one of a number of issues in education that cause the blood to stir. For some 'Gifted' is an elitist concept that beggars definition ... In England, the Department for Education ... distinguishes between gifted learners and talented children ... **Gifted learners** are those who have particular abilities in one or more curriculum subjects ... **Talented learners** are those who have particular abilities in the creative arts (such as music, art and design, drama, dance) and PE. Some schools (and parents) prefer the term 'more able' or 'high ability' ... but the term 'gifted' is very much part of the official language.

The Good Schools Guide (2013b) also commented under their heading, 'The Gifted Child' how:

Exceptionally bright children often show good hand-eye co-ordination, though sometimes their handwriting lags behind their reading and other skills. Some children may refuse to produce any work on paper because of the frustration caused when they are unable to live up to their own impossibly high standards in handwriting and drawing.

With regard to assessment of children considered to be exceptionally bright the Guide commented as follows:

Others are particularly skilful in playing with ideas, in using their imagination and in being creative. Such characteristics do not always show up on traditional intelligence tests but parents who suspect their child may be gifted should not be afraid to talk things over with the teachers at school.

The Guide highlights a number of challenges facing exceptionally bright children, such as the frequent lack of a positive perception of being very able, and an unwillingness on the part of these children to demonstrate their high levels of ability in front of their peers for fear of embarrassment and being bullied. Other challenges include lack of proper assessment and intervention, special educational needs such as dyslexia and dyspraxia that mask the child's true abilities, a mismatch between academic progress and emotional development, mixing with peers, and boredom and frustration resulting at times in disaffection.

Following a study that began in the 1970s Freeman (2013, p. 8) reported that:

For the 210 individuals in my 35-year sample, their life-stories have shown that the only real difference between the gifted and everyone else is their potential. But the unique challenges the gifted are presented with and how other people reacted to those differences, could affect the way the children grew into adulthood. Their development was clearly influenced by the context of family life, itself a microcosm of the wider society.

In addition, Steiner and Carr (2003), cited in Morris (2013, p. 19) have suggested the following cognitive features that they propose can offer gifted children an advantage with learning, namely: '... speed of processing, a preference for complex, challenging environments and more sophisticated meta-cognitive processes such as strategy forma-tion and problem representation'. However, in regard to more specialized input for young children considered to be gifted, Freeman posed the following questions:

> Two questions to be asked of all special education for the gifted is how much of the initial boost to achievement is due to the Hawthorne effect, that is, to attention and change, and whether the benefits last over years. In fact, in spite of an initially higher measured achieve-ment and participants' feelings of satisfaction during the programmes, the advantage of gifted education tends to disappear over a few years ... (2013, p. 9)

In June 2013 Ofsted published a report, *The Most Able Students: Are They Doing as Well as They Should in Our Non-selective Secondary Schools?* which has raised a num-ber of key issues in regard to the education of the more able children in schools in England. Amongst the key findings offered by the report were the following:

- The most able students in non-selective secondary schools are not achieving as well as they should ...

- Leaders in our secondary schools have not done enough to create a culture of scholastic excel-lence, where the highest achievement in academic work is recognised as vitally important ...

- Transition arrangements from primary to secondary school are not effective enough to ensure that students maintain their academic momentum into Year 7 ...

- Teaching is insufficiently focused on the most able at Key Stage 3 ...

- Many students become used to performing at a lower level than they are capable of ...

- The curriculum and the quality of homework required improvement ...

- Too few of the schools worked with families to support them in overcoming the cultural and financial obstacles that stood in the way of the most able students attending university ...

- Most of the 11 to 16 age-range schools visited were insufficiently focused on university entrance ...

- Schools' expertise in and knowledge about how to apply to the most prestigious universi-ties were not always current and relevant ... (pp. 8–10)

The implications for future practice in schools, and especially secondary non-selective state schools, are significant as it will now be the case that Ofsted will pay particular attention to how the learning of more able children is being managed. However, a num-ber of issues appear to arise here. For example, how will schools determine who is more able and who is not? Will some schools, for example, place greater emphasis upon the attainment of their pupils and less emphasis upon the underlying cognitive and intel-lectual abilities that may be masked by such conditions as dyslexia and dyspraxia (see Chapter 8)? Will secondary schools assume that children transferring from primary schools with high levels of attainment in mathematics, English and science and a strong skills and knowledge base in literacy are the more able and begin to work more extensively with these children, or will they assess the cognitive abilities and potential of each child following transfer? Take the example of Mark and Andrew below.

> **Example**
>
> Mark comes from a family where both parents are well educated and have professional careers. Since commencing school at the age of five his parents have recognized that Mark is not as able as his older brother and less able than most other children in his class. In order to address this situation they have arranged for Mark to be privately tutored in all areas of the curriculum, most particularly, reading and writing and mathematics.
>
> Andrew, on the other hand is an exceptionally able child, but since entering school at the age of five he has presented as a child with behaviour problems. When he was four years of age his father left home, which upset him deeply and he has been reared by his mother since then. His mother has been diagnosed with depression and most weeks since Andrew was a young child his mother has spent time alone in her room not communicating with anyone. Now in his final year of primary school, Andrew is perceived by all of his teachers to be a 'real problem', with a very poor concentration span and an unwillingness to engage with learning. As a young child entering school he found the work boring and lacking in stimulation because he was extremely able but he is now viewed as lacking in ability and as having acquired very poor literacy and numeracy skills.

The examples of Mark and Andrew illustrate the possible difficulties that might arise in the future as secondary schools seek to identify 'more able' pupils and attempt to address their particular needs.

LEARNERS WITH LOW ABILITY: DO THEY EXIST?

What does it mean when we are told that a child is of low ability? More particularly, what will it mean to that child or to their parents? The notion of ability is one that has pervaded a multitude of conversations between teachers and professionals working with children for decades and yet what currency does the word have? Arguably, the notion of ability when applied to learning and development is a false one. Ability is too often judged along a spectrum where children are compared with others. What is all too frequently lacking in these comparisons is a focus on the child's potential. Drawing upon the work of Vygotsky, Bruner and Feuerstein referred to earlier, we need to understand the learning of children not just in terms of what they can or cannot do but also in terms of what they are capable of achieving if given the correct environment.

It is questionable whether the term 'ability' when used to understand or explain children's learning has any place in the 21st century, and especially when freely used by practitioners who have little understanding of the theoretical principles that underpin intelligence and learning and who remain guided by vague observations and their own life experiences. Practitioners of the future should, it might be argued, question whether they serve the needs of children by constructing the learning, and more particularly the cognitive development, of children in overly simplistic terms of what they think the children can or cannot do.

Exercises

- Consider the view that too many practitioners working with children fail to fully understand the links between intelligence and learning. Is such a view justified?
- Does the concept of IQ have any relevance for children's learning in the 21st century?
- What, if any, are the benefits for schools in choosing to measure the intellectual functioning of children using standardized tests?
- Why might it be better to consider children's potential as opposed to their ability? In doing so, would this alter the practice of teachers and Early Years practitioners?

Summary

This chapter sought to explore historical, philosophical and political controversies surrounding the nature of intelligence and in particular the legacy that has come to be associated with the measurement of intelligence. This theme was taken further with an exploration of issues relating to the measurement of intellectual functioning and the individual learning needs of children. Alternative ways of understanding intelligence and learning through reference to the works of Reuven Feuerstein and Howard Gardner were considered, with a focus being given to the particular needs of those children described as Gifted and Talented. The chapter concluded by challenging the continued use of the term Low Ability in the 21st century. The following chapter now looks more closely at emotional aspects of learning and some of the difficulties confronting children in this area.

RECOMMENDED READING

Burden, R.L. (1987) Feuerstein's instrumental enrichment programme: important issues in research and evaluation, *European Journal of Psychology of Education*, 2(1): 3–16.

Feuerstein, R., Rand, Y., Hoffman, M. and Miller, R. (1980) *Instrumental Enrichment*. Baltimore: University Park Press.

Gardner, H. (1983) *Frames of Mind: The Theory of Multiple Intelligence*. New York: Basic Books.
Gray, C. and MacBlain, S.F. (2012) *Learning Theories in Childhood*. London: Sage.
MacBlain, S.F. and MacBlain, A.D. (2011) *Letters Form Words*. Plymouth: SMB Associates SW.

REFERENCES

Brooks, V., Abbott, I. and Bills, L. (2004) *Preparing to Teach in Secondary Schools*. Maidenhead: Open University Press.

Burden, R.L. (1987) Feuerstein's instrumental enrichment programme: important issues in research and evaluation, *European Journal of Psychology of Education*, 2(1): 3–16.

Feuerstein, R., Rand, Y., Hoffman, M. and Miller, R. (1980) *Instrumental Enrichment*. Baltimore: University Park Press.

Fontana, D. (1995) *Psychology for Teachers* (3rd edn.) Basingstoke: MacMillan Press.

Frederickson, N. and Cline, T. (2002) *Special Educational Needs, Inclusion and Diversity*. Maidenhead: Open University Press.

Freeman, J. (2013) The long-term effects of families and educational provision on gifted children, *Educational & Child Psychology*, 30(2): 7–15.

Gardner, H. (1983) *Frames of Mind: The Theory of Multiple Intelligence*. New York: Basic Books.

Gray, C. and MacBlain, S.F. (2012) *Learning Theories in Childhood*. London: Sage.

Gross, R.D. (1992) *Psychology: The Science of Mind and Behaviour* (2nd edn). London: Hodder & Stoughton.

Hayes, N. (1994) *Foundations of Psychology: An Introductory Text*. London: Routledge.

MacBlain, S.F. and MacBlain, A.D. (2011) *Letters Form Words*. Plymouth: SMB Associates SW (email: enquiries@seanmacblain.com).

Macrae, F. (2012) How teenagers addicted to cannabis risk damaging their IQ and show signs normally seen in early Alzheimer's, *Daily Mail*, 28 August.

Miller, G.A. (1962) *Psychology: The Science of Mental Life*. Harmondsworth: Penguin.

Morris, N. (2013) Facing challenge: a phenomenological investigation into the educational experiences of academically gifted pupils, *Educational & Child Psychology*, 30(2): 18–27.

Office for Standards in Education (Ofsted) (2013) *The Most Able Students: Are They Doing as Well as They Should in Our Non-selective Secondary Schools?* London: Ofsted.

Smith, M.K. (2002, 2008) Howard Gardner and multiple intelligences. In *the Encyclopedia of Informal Education*. Available at http://www.infed.org/thinkers/gardner.htm.

The Good Schools Guide (2013a) Available at: http://www.goodschoolsguide.co.uk/help-and-advice/your-child/gifted-talented-able-children/439/educating-the-gifted-child (accessed 5 March 2013).

The Good Schools Guide (2013b) Available at: http://www.goodschoolsguide.co.uk/help-and-advice/your-child/gifted-talented-able-children/214/the-gifted-child (accessed 5 March 2013).

THE EMOTIONALLY INTELLIGENT LEARNER

This chapter aims to:

- explore the nature of emotional intelligence
- examine characteristics of emotional learners
- explore aspects central to the development of emotional intelligence
- introduce the reader to a number of intervention programmes
- highlight the importance of children feeling that it is okay to be different
- emphasize the importance of learning to give appropriate emotional responses.

INTRODUCTION

This chapter addresses the growing realization amongst practitioners that it is important to think about children and their learning not only in terms of knowledge acquisition but also in terms of the feelings and emotions they experience and bring to learning situations. In recent decades a number of key authors (Salovey and Mayer, 1990) and more recently Goleman (1996) have given this aspect of children's learning and development a much greater profile, with the result that practitioners now seek to explore and understand the ways in which children manage their emotions and the effect this has upon their learning. Whilst this aspect of children's learning and development has received much recent attention, it must also be acknowledged that in the case of too many children it is largely ignored.

This chapter explores what it is to be an emotional learner. Before doing so, however, it is important to understand what is meant by the construct *emotional intelligence*. The chapter also builds upon many of the ideas expressed in previous chapters, for example Chapter 4, which addressed early attachment, Chapter 5, which explored transitions between stages, Chapter 6, which examined links between intelligence and learning, and of course the first chapter, which set out the ideas of a number of key thinkers who, over the generations, have taught us to think in terms of the 'whole child'. This last point is especially relevant as we observe the rapidly changing nature of society around us today, and the immense pressures placed upon children and young people learning to grow up in cultures increasingly defined by materialism, image, instant access, and the increased blurring of what many of us previously considered to be clear boundaries for children.

THE NATURE OF EMOTIONAL INTELLIGENCE

In order for children to function positively and effectively within society and meet the vast range of demands made upon them they need to be able to manage feelings and emotions. Not only do they need to understand the emotions of others but they also need to understand their own emotions and feel capable of managing these. To fail to do so brings its problems. Many researchers and practitioners now employ two terms to account for this process, *emotional intelligence* and *emotional literacy*, which though different are frequently used interchangeably. Salovey and Mayer (1990, p. 189) have defined emotional intelligence as:

> ... the subset of social intelligence that involves the *ability to monitor one's own and others' feelings and emotions, to discriminate among them and to use this information to guide one's thinking and actions.* [original emphasis]

Salovey and Mayer have suggested four key elements or stages in developing emotional intelligence, which are: perceiving emotions, reasoning with emotions, understanding emotions, and managing emotions. With the first of these, children start from an early age to develop their ability to correctly perceive emotions, which might include picking up on another's body language, facial expressions, and so on. They learn to observe the emotions of those around them through understanding their behaviours and language. The degree to which children develop their sensitivities in this area depends on many factors, perhaps most notably the observations and explanations provided by adults and older siblings and friends who are close to them. Children then use their own emotions to engage in reasoning with their emotions. For example, they may extend their thinking about and understanding of situations they encounter and by doing so they extend their cognitive capacity. They will, for example, begin to make judgements as to whether or not it is appropriate to respond to the emotions of others and if so, how. With the third of these the individual gives meaning to emotions through a process of making accurate interpretations. For example, a teacher may experience a child being very aggressive towards them and may interpret the child's aggression purely in terms of it being an angry outburst when in fact the child's aggression may be due to the fact that he feels very embarrassed and guilty because of something he believes he has caused.

The final element or step involves the ability to manage, and more specifically regulate, emotions. This requires, for example, the individual making appropriate responses to the emotions they are observing and experiencing from others. Salovey and Mayer have posed the following question:

> People who have developed skills related to emotional intelligence understand and express their own emotions, recognize emotions in others, regulate affect, and use moods and emotions to motivate adaptive behaviors. Is this just another definition of a healthy, self-actualized individual? (1990, p. 200)

Drawing upon the work of Mayer (co-author with Salovey referred to above) Goleman (1996, p. 48) has commented as follows:

> Mayer finds that people tend to fall into distinctive styles for attending to and dealing with emotions.
>
> - *Self-aware.* Aware of their moods as they are having them ... When they get into a bad mood, they don't ruminate and obsess about it, and are able to get out of it sooner ...
>
> - *Engulfed.* These are people who often feel swamped by their emotions and helpless to escape them ... They are mercurial and not very aware of their feeling, so that they get lost in them ... As a result, they do little to try to escape bad moods... They often feel overwhelmed and emotionally out of control ...
>
> - *Accepting.* While these people are often clear about what they are feeling, they also tend to be accepting of their moods, and so don't try to change them ...

Early Years practitioners as well as teachers in both primary and secondary schools will be aware of children with the second of these distinctive styles and who present as being engulfed by their emotions. Readers may also be aware of adults they have met who also display this distinctive style and who appear to struggle to manage difficult feelings and confront their emotions. Teachers working with young people during the period of adolescence may, for example, interpret behaviours in boys as being outward facing and aggressive and, in girls, inward facing and as being masked by an apparent unwillingness to communicate with adults, and even withdrawal. This is, of course, overly simplistic, but in some instances may actually be the case.

Exercise

Consider examples of behaviours you have observed in children when they have been upset. How did you interpret those behaviours and what led you to interpret them in the way you did?

In the recent report, *An Intelligent Look at Emotional Intelligence* (ATL, 2005, p. 6) commissioned by the Association of Teachers and Lecturers, Professor Guy Claxton commented as follows:

> In school, young people's emotions are much more present in classrooms – and playgrounds – than they used to be. For example:
>
> - With what sociologists call the 'decline of deference' (and what teachers simply label as 'bad behaviour'), pupils and students bring more of their complicated emotional selves into the classroom with them.
>
> - Living with the consequences of 'inclusion', teachers are sometimes faced with challenging behaviour and displays of strong emotion that they struggle to know how to deal with.

Claxton (ATL, 2005, 9) goes on to suggest that emotional intelligence differs from more traditional understandings and representations of intelligence in two important ways. Firstly, emotional intelligence:

> ... values different ways of being bright. It asserts that understanding someone else's point of view, or knowing how to deal with stress, are forms of intelligence, just as useful – indeed, quite possibly more so – than being able to solve logical brainteasers fast under pressure.

The second difference proposed by Claxton is that, unlike popular notions of intelligence as being fixed in some way, such as in the case of IQs, emotional intelligence:

> ... focuses on the extent to which emotional competence can be developed. Whereas a child of 'low (intellectual) ability' tends to be seen as a prisoner of their genes, Emotional Intelligence is of interest to so many teachers because they believe they can do something to help.

This last point is important and suggests why the whole concept of emotional intelligence or emotional literacy has become so popular with teachers across the entire span of education, not just in the UK, but throughout the world. By promoting the notion of emotional intelligence and moving away from the more traditional view of intelligence as being something that one is born with (see Chapter 6), teachers and Early Years practitioners are recognizing that what they do and how they do it, in terms of children's learning can really have a significant impact upon how children think and how they can interact meaningfully and purposefully with their environments and with those around them. More importantly, perhaps, it also emphasizes the challenge facing teachers, especially those working with young children in regard to creating learning environments in which children are supported in realizing their potential, as opposed to simply acquiring and developing abilities that allow them to 'get by' in learning and in life.

Claxton draws particular attention to the importance of gaining some kind of measure when we talk of emotional intelligence in order for the concept to be accorded greater credibility, in the same way that the concept of Intelligence Quotient has (see Chapter 6). He suggests two means by which this can be achieved, namely self-reporting by individuals themselves using, for example, questionnaires and interviews, and what he terms 'performance measures' or asking individuals to engage with particular types of tasks and then observing how successful they are. Claxton makes reference to one particular attempt, by the Israeli psychologist Reuven Bar-On – the 'Emotional Quotient Inventory' (EQ-1) – in developing self-report measures, which Claxton proposes, are typically more cost effective:

> The EQ-I divides Emotional Intelligence into five components, each assessed by a different sub-scale. Drawing on Howard Gardner's terminology, Bar-On calls these *intrapersonal intelligence* (which contains self-awareness, self-esteem and assertiveness); *interpersonal intelligence* (empathy, social responsibility and social awareness); *adaptability* (problem-solving, reality testing and flexibility); *stress management* (stress tolerance and impulse control); and *general mood* (happiness and optimism). Respondents indicate the extent to which they agree or disagree with a range of statements designed to tap these qualities, and the replies are statistically aggregated into scores and sub-scores in the normal psychometric ways. (ATL, 2005, p, 11)

Clearly, some of these components identified by Bar-On can be difficult to define and even more difficult, perhaps, to observe and record. For example, how do we define happiness and optimism or flexibility?

Exercise

Consider experiences you have had where you might have described a child as *happy* or *unhappy* or as having *low self-esteem*. In what ways do you think that you might have measured these constructs and would others have been in agreement? What potential problems might Early Years practitioners and teachers have when recording such descriptions of children and sharing these with other professionals?

THE EMOTIONALLY INTELLIGENT LEARNER

Recently, the popular author and psychologist Oliver James (2012) has drawn attention to the importance of children having love in their lives with his introduction of the notion of 'Love Bombing' (see also Chapter 4). Making particular reference to temper tantrums and defiance in young children, James comments on the importance of love and consistency in children's lives and the need for parents to take time to explain to children how their actions affect others:

> It takes time for children to learn to tolerate frustration of their wishes without becoming furious. It is completely natural for small children to use physical force to impose their will and for them to become incensed when thwarted ... The capacity for self-regulation – the ability to press a 'pause' button before taking physical action – has to evolve slowly ... But until he has language and a relatively sophisticated mind, he is still prone to being swamped by emotion – the 'red mist' coming down ... If the consequences of his actions are constantly explained to the child ... and if he is consistently shown love and support and sympathy for his predicament, he will come to be able to know his own feelings and feel safe enough that his needs will be met without having to impose himself. (2012, pp. 27–8)

Children with strong emotional intelligence will typically feel secure in the love their parents have for them. Readers may wish to reflect once more upon the ideas offered by Erich Fromm (Chapter 4) who talked of love in terms of care, responsibility, respect and knowledge. Children with strong emotional intelligence typically learn from an early age that their needs will be met within a caring framework, which by necessity has its boundaries. Routines will have been established and will be consistent and have purpose. These children will have been encouraged to explore and take measured risks, to engage with others in a collaborative way, to feel satisfaction when they have achieved, learn to associate effort with outcome and internalize their perception of adults as being there to help and support them and to care for them. They will typically have stronger resilience and will have been accustomed to praise from their parents and significant others when young. When with others they demonstrate a capacity to communicate their feelings with purpose, and, very importantly, they can be observed to appraise challenging situations and events through applying thinking that is characterized by higher levels of problem solving.

It almost goes without saying that in schools children will view their teachers differently. The perceptions they form of their teachers, however, will be heavily influenced by past experiences with adults, as well as by interactions with their peers. In turn, teachers will also view their pupils differently and they themselves will be influenced by past experiences, perhaps from their own childhood and the nature of the parenting they will have experienced when young. The challenges facing teachers working with children with poor emotional intelligence have been well expressed by Colverd and Hodgkin (2011, p. 20) who have characterized this as follows:

> Each child sees its teacher through a separate pair of eyes ... Each child sees its teacher as a powerful figure. This can have an immense effect upon the child's emotional and academic life ... The teacher must balance a feeling of dislike or non-connection with a child with the need to connect the child with the learning and with itself. Children with challenging behaviours can be difficult to like. They may be working hard to make you not like them, so as to confirm their feelings of worthlessness.

Clearly, the importance of teachers viewing children in a balanced and non-judgemental way cannot be over emphasized. After all, it is a fundamental part of the teacher's role to promote emotional intelligence in their pupils and in doing so prepare them for their future transitions between stages of formal education and those natural transitions between early childhood, adolescence and adulthood. This said it is worth readers reminding themselves of the challenges facing many teachers in primary schools and Early Years practitioners today. The reality for many teachers and Early Years practitioners is that significant numbers of children are entering schools with few of the skills that children in previous generations might have had. This offers its challenges and brings with it problems, not only in terms of behaviour management, but also the challenges of teaching important social skills and even developing expressive language and perhaps more importantly receptive language. Early Years practitioners, in particular, will recognize the need for children to learn to listen and to be attentive to the adults around them. Often, the environments within which some children begin their formal education can seem to them to be very alien, and may even appear hostile to them if they have had limited experience of mixing in different social situations outside of the home. Some children may even, for the first time in their lives, be where they are experiencing consistency, stability, sensitivity and care.

Exercise

What factors contribute to the development of emotional intelligence? Should teachers and Early Years practitioners be doing more to cultivate this aspect of children's development and, if so, what measures could they take?

DEVELOPING EMOTIONAL INTELLIGENCE

Developing emotional intelligence is a process that begins from birth. Take the following comment from Colverd and Hodgkin (2011, pp. 14–15):

> The mother who always wakes her 1-year-old toddler in the morning with soft words and a cuddle ... is creating a pattern of experience that will structure the child's brain to expect this behaviour ... to believe they are cared for and that the experience of touch and being looked after is pleasurable. If a child has a negative or painful experience of caregiving, if caregiving is frightening or neglectful, the child's expectations of caregiving and of adults in the future will be equally frightening and painful.

In respect to the importance of those first experiences between infants and their primary caregivers Goleman (1996, p. 22) has emphasized how:

> ... many potent emotional memories date from the first few years of life, in the relationship between an infant and its caretakers. This is especially true for traumatic events, like beatings or outright neglect ... the interactions of life's earliest years lay down a set of emotional lessons ...

Goleman goes on to emphasize that:

> The risks are greatest for those children whose parents are grossly inept – immature, abusing drugs, depressed or chronically angry, or simply aimless and living chaotic lives ... A survey of maltreated children found the neglected youngsters doing the worst of all: they were the most anxious, inattentive, and apathetic, alternately aggressive and withdrawn. The rate for having to repeat first grade among them was 65 percent. (p. 195)

Now let us look at the case of Billy:

Example

Billy is three years of age and already concerns have been expressed by neighbours about his lack of care and the possibility of physical abuse. His mother is a heroin addict and she lives with Billy in a rundown part of town. She has never worked and gave birth to Billy when she was 16 years old. Billy's father left her when he found out that she was pregnant and although he lives a few miles away has only visited Billy on a few occasions. When he has visited he has been very aggressive towards Billy's mother. Billy has observed their arguing and their shouting loudly at each other. Billy is rarely picked up by his mother and she frequently leaves him in the evenings with a teenage girl who lives a few doors away when she goes out socially, generally not returning until well after midnight. Billy appears thin and undernourished and generally lethargic. He presents as an unhappy little boy who rarely smiles. At home he is rarely praised by his mother for taking the initiative to do things such as brush his teeth, wash himself and put his clothes on – if he gets any of these wrong she shouts at him and even, on occasions, belittles him. When starting nursery school staff observed him at times to be excessively clingy and tearful when his mother was making moves to leave, and when picked up by his mother he gave her little attention, preferring instead to absorb himself in what was happening around him. Nursery staff describe Billy as having frequent temper tantrums and angry outbursts when he is prevented from doing things. He is often observed to be aggressive towards the other children and finds making friends a challenge. He rarely appears to play collaboratively with other children, preferring instead to snatch toys away from others or to play alone. Staff in the nursery also express their concerns that Billy appears to be very mistrusting of adults.

It is clear that Billy lacks the type of care that most children have in their first months and years of life. His mother struggles to cope with life and resorts to substance abuse as a means of managing her own sense of loneliness and rejection as a child, her worries and fears about finance, and her relationship problems with boyfriends and with her own parents and siblings. If we apply the principles of Behaviourist theory (see Chapter 2) in trying to understand the nature of Billy's learning and his emotional intelligence then we can observe how his mother and the adults around him model behaviours to him, which will be constantly reinforced and which he will imitate. Equally, we can also observe how important behaviours such as talking, touching, cuddling, actively listening to others, initiating purposeful actions, and asking questions may not be reinforced by his mother and the adults around him. Because they are not devoting time to him the quality of the time they spend with Billy is very poor. Here, the expectations that Billy is learning to have of the adults around him are essentially negative. When he attempts new behaviours such as climbing or jumping he is typically chastised and told to stop. Billy is learning within his home background that adults are not caring. When he makes a transition to the local nursery school he will take these expectations with him and his expectations of the adults he will come into contact with at the nursery, whilst similar, will need to change. Because the adults at the nursery will manage his behaviours differently he will start a new process of learning.

Clearly, in the case of Billy it will be important for the adults working with him in his nursery to understand his behaviours and, especially, to understand that these have been learned at home, and through continual reinforcement have become internalized as structures within his brain. If we apply Vygotsky's theoretical approach to Billy's situation then we begin to examine, more critically, the nature of the environments within which Billy is learning and the particular need for the nursery staff to create an enriching environment in which Billy can develop his social language and become part of an informing culture that is qualitatively different to his home. If we employ Piagetian theory to Billy's situation then we look to Billy's cognitive development and the importance of the nursery school in maturing Billy's thinking, and supporting him in interacting positively and meaningfully with his environment.

Salovey and Mayer (1990, p.201) have suggested that individuals with good levels of emotional intelligence are:

> ... aware of their own feelings and those of others. They are open to positive and negative aspects of internal experience, are able to label them, and when appropriate, communicate them. Such awareness will often lead to the effective regulation of affect within themselves and others, and so contribute to well being. Thus, the emotionally intelligent person is often a pleasure to be around and leaves others feeling better.

They also suggest, however, that:

> Many problems in adjustment may arise from deficits in emotional intelligence. People who don't learn to regulate their own emotions may become slaves to them. (p. 201)

It is clear that the development of emotional intelligence can be approached in many ways. Developing resilience is another very effective approach. Two important contributions to our understanding of resilience can be found in the work of Garmezy (1985) and Grotberg (1995) who have both identified a number of 'protective elements', which, they argue, are apparent in resilience. The elements, identified by Garmezy were:

1. Personality features such as self-esteem
2. Family cohesion and the absence of discord
3. The availability of external support.

Grotberg, however, identifies different factors: 'personality factors', 'family and external support structures', and the 'child's own social and interpersonal skills', with the following illustrations (Barnard et al. 1999, p. 57): '*I am*', or the personality features, for example self-esteem, which include the child feeling that s/he is a person who is loved and who is happy to please others and be respectful of themselves and those they meet and is able to take responsibility for their actions; '*I have*', or the family and external support structures, which might include, for example, the child feeling they have individuals around them who they can trust, who love them and who actively support them in their learning, who set boundaries and rules and who encourage independence and autonomy; '*I can*', or the child's own social and interpersonal skills, for example, where the child feels they can communicate such feelings as fear and anxiety to others, explore ways of finding solutions to problems, exercising control over their emotions and behaviours, and approach others when they feel they need support.

Grotberg argued that with the first of these, the '*I am*' factors, it was possible to strengthen these but not create them. With the '*I have*' factors she argued that it was possible to provide these and strengthen them but with the '*I can*' factors, she argued that these must be learned and could not be taught. Grotberg viewed the child as an active participant and argued that any child having experienced loss following bereavement would need more than one of the above factors to be present in order to exercise resilience in the face of trauma. When none of these 'protective elements' are present, she suggested, and when the child is not functioning as an active participant, then mental health issues can arise.

Now, let us look again at the case of Billy in the earlier example. Imagine now that Billy has been asked by his mother to sit down at the table to eat his lunch time snack, which she has ensured contains some important elements such as fruit and protein. Billy, however, refuses to eat any of it and begins to throw a tantrum, which consists of throwing some of his food on the floor and kicking and screaming. In this situation his mother should really try to understand why he is behaving as he is, in particular why he does not want to eat. She should speak to him calmly and talk to him about why he is not eating. She may lift him up and hold him as she is doing this, and when he is calm talk to him about the importance of eating well when he is still very young. In this way she will be modelling appropriate behaviour to Billy. By being with her and observing her Billy will come to learn the nature of positive responses, which will become part of his own repertoire as he grows older. As she talks with Billy she should encourage him to articulate his feelings. Through holding and talking to Billy she will also encourage him to learn that boundaries and rules are important and are there to benefit him. In this way she is helping him learn for the future so that when he is older he will understand why his teachers set boundaries and make demands upon pupils. She could also talk with Billy about the importance of eating and the choices he has in regard to eating or refusing to eat as well as the consequences of his actions.

It is by engaging Billy in this way that his mother can also have her own needs met, but it would appear that Billy's mother may do none of these things, preferring instead to take his food away and shout at him or even smack him and ignore him until his tantrum ends. It is also likely that she will put him away in his bedroom and refuse to talk to him for several hours. Billy, on the other hand, has, through his tantrum, displayed a need to impose his will on his mother but is failing to learn that there must be consequences to his behaviours and that there must be limits to how he acts. He is also failing to learn about his own emotions and feelings. Instead, he is internalizing emotions through which he perceives that he is being punished and rejected, and not being loved by his mother. Perhaps, most importantly, he is failing to learn how to effectively communicate his own emotions and feelings, and to understand that there are other ways of behaving as opposed to being aggressive and screaming.

Taking Billy as an example and applying Grotberg's three *I have, I am, I can* illustrations, discussed earlier, we can surmise that, amongst other things, Billy is lacking in the first of these – trust in the relationship he has with his mother, continuity and structure with clear boundaries, and positive and purposeful role modelling. With the second of these, he is lacking feelings of being loved and being proud of himself and being trusted by his mother to behave independently and responsibly. With the final one of these illustrations, Billy is failing to learn how to communicate effectively and appraise situations in a problem-solving manner, as opposed to emotionally reactive responses where he fails to learn that it is necessary to manage his feelings and behaviours differently when he becomes upset.

Having focused on the development of emotional intelligence within the family, we now consider the important role that schools and Early Years settings need to play in the lives of significant numbers of children. Goleman (1996, p. 279) has commented:

> As family life no longer offers growing numbers of children a sure footing in life, schools are left as the one place communities can turn to for correctives to children's deficiencies in emotional and social competence ... Emotional literacy implies an expanded mandate for schools.

It almost goes without saying that schools need to offer an ethos that promotes emotional intelligence in all of their children. It is in primary schools, for example, during the first years of formal education that many of the foundations for children's future social and emotional development are laid down. Central to any school's ethos, however, is the importance of all teachers and adults who work in the school recognizing and fully understanding that the negative behaviours they observe in children arise, in the main, from past experiences of living within their own unique families, their communities, and particularly the interactions they have had with their parents and immediate caregivers. To fail to properly understand this means that in many cases teachers may attribute unacceptable behaviours presented by children within the classroom and school environment as arising from choices made by these children. Furthermore, it needs to be recognized that an important aspect of a teacher's role is to guide and support children in their social and emotional learning and not just their academic learning. It is very debatable as to whether this can be achieved by offering children regular blocks of time such as weekly sessions when they work through particular commercial programmes geared to addressing personal issues underpinning social and emotional development. Rather, this is an ongoing dynamic process in which relationships between adults and children, and children and their peers, are fostered in such a way that the children come to develop resilience, learn coping strategies, recognize their feelings and emotions for what they are, and acquire and internalize appropriate and effective strategies for managing their feelings and emotions.

Exercise

Consider examples of how children first begin to develop emotional intelligence and the roles that parents and siblings can play in this process. What contributions can language and play make in the development of emotional intelligence in children before they start formal education? In the case of Billy, in the above example, how might Early Years practitioners and Key Stage 1 teachers have developed his resilience and taught him effective coping mechanisms?

For adults to effectively and purposefully promote emotional intelligence in children it is important that they, also, are emotionally intelligent. This may not be the case in the homes of some children, and in such cases it will be even more important for practitioners to have acquired strong levels of emotional intelligence, typically characterized by self-awareness, assertiveness, high self-esteem, self-confidence, sound knowledge of child development and learning, and the ability to identify and manage their own emotions. Goleman (1996, p. 279) suggests that '…teachers need to be comfortable talking about feelings'. Take the following example of Miss B., a relatively new member of the teaching profession:

Example

Miss B. is in her mid twenties and was appointed to her school three years ago after she graduated with a degree in Primary Education. It is September and she has just started with her new Key Stage 2 class. She has been told by their previous teacher who had them for two years that they are a 'lively class with a few troublemakers, one in particular called Bob, who you will have to watch very carefully … his father died a few years ago and since then his behaviour has deteriorated, I think he runs circles round his mother'. Miss B. had an uneventful start to her first two weeks with her new class but in week 3 she found herself having to discipline Bob several times each day because he frequently shouted out, left his seat when he was supposed to be working and interrupted her when she was talking to the

(Continued)

(Continued)

class, even though she had asked him not to on a number of occasions. In week 4 she asked the classroom assistant to remove Bob from the classroom because he was being very disruptive and calling out and laughing at the other children. The classroom assistant took him to the library and sat with him until he promised to go back into the classroom and work quietly. When Bob returned to the class room he sat for a few minutes and then shouted out. The other children laughed and Bob was again removed by the classroom assistant. In the weeks that followed Bob's behaviour deteriorated and the decision was made by his class teacher and by the head teacher to invite the Educational Psychologist to become involved and to meet with Bob's mother at the school.

It would appear from the above example that Bob is presenting Miss B. with significant challenges. One might also go as far as suggesting that she wishes he was not in her class. Now let us look at the example of Miss B. when she meets with the educational psychologist (EP) for the first time:

Example – *Continued*

EP: *Tell me about Bob.*

Miss B.:   *I have tried everything with Bob since the beginning of term. He is constantly disruptive and a distraction to all of the other children. He refuses to do what he is told and most days he is argumentative. As I said, I have tried everything with him but nothing seems to work. I find myself most days trying to persuade him to settle down and get on with his work but he just seems to ignore me whenever he wants to. I get really stressed some days and at the end of the week I feel exhausted with him. You're the expert, I was hoping that you would tell me what to do, as I said I have tried everything but nothing seems to work with him. I don't have any problems with the other children, they're all fine.*

This is an interesting exchange between the Educational Psychologist and Miss B. It becomes quickly apparent, however, that Miss B. views all of the problems she has with Bob as emanating from him. She is not giving enough critical consideration to the fact that Bob's behaviours have been learned, that they have been and continue to be reinforced (see Chapter 2) most likely by his home background and, most importantly, that he is, in fact, not actively choosing to behave as he does. In addition, Miss B. is displaying quite non-assertive behaviour, which in itself fails to meet her own needs as a teacher and as an adult, as well as those of Bob. In effect, Bob is learning from Miss B.

that it is possible to manipulate her, and in doing so maintain a sense of control over her and over the classroom environment, and the other children, by distracting them and making them laugh. This whole situation is failing to support Bob in recognizing and understanding his own behaviours and emotions, which are inappropriate for a classroom. Miss B. needs to implement clear and consistent boundaries and to spend time with Bob in helping him to recognize that he needs to adapt his behaviours and understand the feelings of others, including his teachers.

A further aspect of the dialogue between Miss B. and the educational psychologist is that her comments tell the psychologist very little about Bob. They are, in effect, vague fuzzy statements, which lack specificity. They also lack objectivity and are more an indication of Miss B's subjective feelings. They are really an account of the emotions that Bob causes within her. To this end, they are not very helpful and suggest that the manner in which she is responding to Bob's behaviours is essentially at an emotionally reactive and non-assertive level. Because of this, there is little hope for Bob developing his emotional intelligence within this type of relationship.

One very useful approach to developing emotional intelligence can be found in the use of creative activities such as play and drama. Colverd and Hodgkin (2011, p. 73), for example, make particular reference to the important role that drama can play in developing emotional intelligence. They make particular reference, for example, to *Positional Drama*, which they conceptualize as follows:

> When we work with children on positional drama our aim is to place them in another pair of shoes – the metaphor for another life, another person, another set of social circumstances, possibly another historical time.

Colverd and Hodgkin see Positional Drama as giving children opportunities to experience the lives of others and, more particularly, to learn through this experience. Children can create characters and events and work through social and emotional aspects of the lives of others as well as observing played-out behaviours and reflecting upon these through discussion with their teachers. Colverd and Hodgkin refer to this as, 'The entire model drives through an engagement in the learning through ownership, emotional connection and imagination' (2011, p. 73). Positional Drama would be a most useful approach to helping Bob understand how he should behave in classroom situations.

Exercise

How might teachers and Early Years practitioners work to develop resilience in children and young people and assist them in developing effective coping strategies for managing problems in their lives?

DEVELOPING THE RIGHT EMOTIONAL RESPONSE: IT'S OKAY TO BE DIFFERENT

To feel different can be one of the greatest challenges for children and young people. How often do parents, teachers and Early Years practitioners find themselves comforting and consoling one of their children who has been made to feel different and has been subsequently teased by those around them? Such situations are not confined to very young children but can be observed occurring throughout the primary and post-primary phases of children's formal education. These situations are also not confined to formal educational environments but, again can be observed elsewhere at a wider community level. For a young child or adolescent the feelings that come with being teased and in more extreme cases marginalized and isolated because of perceived difference can not only be difficult to manage but also difficult to understand. And yet, in some respects it can be these very hurtful feelings that can help children to grow as individuals. Sadly, however, this may not always be the case, for confronting complex emotions can be for many children extremely painful and for a few, a bridge too far. In commenting upon the complexity of emotional intelligence Salovey and Mayer (1990, p. 201) have made the following important point:

> The emotionally intelligent person … attends to emotion in the path toward growth. Emotional intelligence involves self-regulation appreciative of the fact that temporarily hurt feelings or emotional restraint is often necessary in the service of a greater objective.

For the emotionally intelligent person, then, painful and hurtful feelings can be perceived as having an important role because it is through experiencing feelings of sadness and pain that we may come to understand happiness and contentment and grow as individuals. For children who experience such negative feelings they may be painful in the short term, but by being helped to understand them they can benefit in the longer term. Negative experiences, therefore, can be viewed as having a purpose. In a sense, the individual learns to view experiences within a much wider framework and as part of their overall life experiences and journey. Again, Salovey and Mayer, have commented:

> Thus, emotionally intelligent individuals accurately perceive their emotions and use integrated, sophisticated approaches to regulate them as they proceed toward important goals. (1990, p. 201)

In extreme cases, failing to cope with painful emotions can lead some young people to fall into ways of expressing themselves through, for example, substance abuse, promiscuity, eating disorders and depression. It is vital, therefore, that parents and teachers understand the difficulties faced by children and young people, and in the case of the latter have the knowledge and skills to identify problems and offer appropriate support.

In recent decades schools have addressed the nature of diversity and difference and the potential effects upon their pupils. This has been done with varying degrees of success. Various initiatives such as *Social & Emotional Aspects of Learning* (SEAL) have been developed, which aim to build underlying knowledge, qualities and skills in children and, thereby, support positive behaviour and effective learning through, for example, focusing on self-awareness, motivation and the management of feelings. A particular difficulty with such initiatives, however, lies in the fact that some teachers may see such programmes as part of the curriculum and allocate particular times in the week for 'doing SEAL' as opposed to incorporating the principles that underpin these initiatives into their teaching and in all aspects of their work with children.

Teachers and Early Years practitioners working with children who present with behavioural difficulties need to understand that these children may not be choosing to disobey, but as Colverd and Hodgkin (2011, p. 25) put it:

> They are simply conditioned to read the social and emotional signals that are coming their way. Children who have suffered severe parental neglect will often present with inappropriate behaviours ... This can be misinterpreted as confrontational behaviour, but the child will not read the signals telling them to give space and pull back. This inappropriate behaviour comes from a background in which the child has not been taught the absolute basics of social behaviour – the reading of emotional and social signals; they find it extremely difficult to interpret their own or others' emotions.

Teachers and schools can offer such children a strong sense of security with clear boundaries, consistency and stability, routines, and the modelling of appropriate relationships and social behaviours. In doing so, they can offer children the means of developing many important aspects of their personality that will come to serve them well as adults and also when they themselves become parents. In making reference to the importance of these factors in the early education and learning of children, Miller and Pound (2011, p. 92) have drawn upon the Steiner philosophy (see Chapter 1) and commented as follows:

> Steiner practitioners observe that young children are nurtured by the security of rhythm and repetition – within which their inherent skills and abilities can flourish ... Having well thought through and repeated routines builds habits that are useful (properly washed hands), respectful (creating a peaceful mood at the table) and comforting ('this is how we always do it here').

Some decades ago the psychologist Albert Bandura, who is perhaps best known for his theory of Social Learning (Bandura, 1977a), proposed that children not only observe physical behaviours but also observe verbal behaviours in those around them, including, for example, the expectations that others have of them (Linden, 2005). He further proposed that children observe adults around them as they communicate verbal narratives and descriptions of events to others and as they employ spoken language and gestures to convey their ideas, thoughts, and so on. Bandura also proposed a form of symbolic modelling in which children can be observed engaging in imitation and identification of fictional characters such as those found in fairy tales, cartoons, children's television, the cinema and, increasingly, computer games.

Another important and relevant factor offered by Bandura (1977b) is that of self-efficacy, which he viewed as children's belief in their abilities to do well and, through their capacity to exercise control over their own actions, achieve success. Bandura saw self-efficacy as being directly related to how children think and behave as well as to their emotional state. Children with poor self-efficacy, for example, typically demonstrate a tendency towards avoiding tasks they find challenging, preferring instead to focus their thoughts on negative factors, thus framing their thinking around constructs whereby they come to convince themselves that they are not able to achieve success. Typically, children with poor self-efficacy present themselves in social situations as having poor self-confidence.

Directly linked to the capacity that children have to achieve success are those feelings that children have about themselves and others, and the way in which they interpret and understand the world around them. Tasked with having to identify personal learning goals and targets, children with poor self-efficacy will generally do less well than children with strong self-efficacy. They may, for example, show a lack of interest in attempting tasks and then completing them, and may also appear less committed to collaborating with their peers. In some cases, they may even demonstrate anxiety when asked to engage in problem-based learning tasks. Colverd and Hodgkin (2011, p. 36) have stressed how children in learning situations may:

> ... place limits on what they think is possible, believing a task is beyond their capability. Lack of self-belief affects their motivation and their commitment to learning. 'I can't do this, it's boring' signals 'I don't believe I can be successful with this and therefore I don't want to take the risk – it may or may not be boring'.

Bandura suggested that a central factor in developing self-efficacy was the development of 'mastery' through experiences, for example by observing others succeeding, receiving affirming comments from peers and understanding one's feelings and emotions. Developing self-efficacy, therefore, is an important and integral part of the early learning experiences of children. The implications of this for practitioners working with children in primary schools and Early Years settings are obvious.

Exercise

Identify occasions when you have observed children demonstrating a strong sense of self-efficacy. Consider how this developed within the children and what factors might have contributed to this process. Give some consideration to how the modelling of positive behaviours by adults might have had an influence.

Summary

This chapter explored the nature of emotional intelligence and the characteristics that facilitate emotional learning in children and young people. Aspects central to the development of emotional intelligence were discussed and a number of intervention programmes were highlighted. The importance of children learning to feel confident in their own differences and giving the 'right' emotional responses was also highlighted.

It is clear that the needs of children in the 21st century are in many ways different to those of children 10 and even 20 years ago. Schools are having to play an increasingly important role in supporting the social and emotional development of children and this is likely to increase as children find that they must remain at school throughout their adolescence and into the early stages of adulthood when the nature of their needs will change and the foundations that have been laid down for them in terms of their social and emotional development will take on much greater importance.

It is an encouraging fact that many new initiatives in education in the UK have placed the principles of emotional intelligence at their core. The extent to which this will continue in the future is, however, open to question as it appears that an increasing emphasis is being placed upon results. The following chapter picks up on this theme and addresses the complex nature of learning for children with a range of additional needs.

RECOMMENDED READING

Barnard, P., Morland, I. and Nagy, J. (1999) *Children, Bereavement and Trauma: Nurturing Resilience.* London: Jessica Kingsley.

Colverd, S. and Hodgkin, B. (2011) *Developing Emotional Intelligence in the Primary School.* London: Routledge.

Linden, J. (2005) *Understanding Child Development: Linking Theory to Practice.* London: Hodder Education.

Miller, L. and Pound, L. (2011) *Theories and Approaches to Learning in the Early Years.* London: Sage.

REFERENCES

Association of Teachers and Lecturers (ATL) (2005) *An Intelligent Look at Emotional Intelligence*. London: Association of Teachers and Lecturers.

Bandura, A. (1977a) *Social Learning Theory*. Englewood Cliffs, NJ: Prentice Hall.

Bandura, A. (1977b) *Self-efficacy: The Exercise of Control*. New York: Freeman.

Barnard, P., Morland, I. and Nagy, J. (1999) *Children, Bereavement and Trauma: Nurturing Resilience*. London: Jessica Kingsley.

Colverd, S. and Hodgkin, B. (2011) *Developing Emotional Intelligence in the Primary School*. London: Routledge.

Garmezy, N. (1985) Stress resilient children: the search for protective factors. In J. Stevenson (ed.) *Recent Research in Developmental Psychopathogy*. Oxford: Pergammon Press.

Goleman, D. (1996) *Emotional Intelligence: Why It Can Matter More than IQ*. London: Bloomsbury.

Grotberg, E. (1995) *A Guide to Promoting Resilience in Children*. The Hague: Bernard van Leer Foundation, Netherlands.

James, O. (2012) *Love Bombing*. London: Karnac Books.

Linden, J. (2005) *Understanding Child Development: Linking Theory to Practice*. London: Hodder Education.

Miller, L. and Pound, L. (2011) *Theories and Approaches to Learning in the Early Years*. London: Sage.

Palmer, S. (2006) *Toxic Childhood*. London: Orion Books.

Salovey, P. and Mayer, J.D. (1990) Emotional Intelligence. Available at: http://www.unh.edu/emotional_intelligence/EIAssets/EmotionalIntelligenceProper/EI1990%20Emotional%20Intelligence.pdf (accessed 20 March 2013).

8 ADDITIONAL SUPPORT NEEDS AND LEARNING

This chapter aims to:

- give consideration to the fact that too many children in the UK are being assessed as having special educational needs
- explore the context within which children with additional needs are now educated
- consider the difficulties and challenges experienced by children with the specific difficulties of dyslexia, dyspraxia, dyscalculia, ADHD and Asperger's Syndrome, and identify factors that contribute to positive and measurable progress
- discuss the implications that problems in the areas of Working Memory and Speed of Processing can have on children's learning
- explore the concept of Conduct Disorders and how these impact upon learning.

INTRODUCTION

Writing in the UK national newspaper the *Daily Mail* on 13 July 2012, educational correspondent Laura Clark commented as follows:

> Children as young as one are being labelled as having special educational needs by their nurseries ... By the age of five, more than one in six children – 173,525 – has been diagnosed as having special needs ... Most are diagnosed during their first year at school ... Figures released yesterday by the Department for Education showed that 19.8 per cent of children across the school system – more than 1.6 million – have been given the label.

The reporting of such statistics in a popular newspaper is worrying and presents a stark picture. Perhaps more worrying, however, is the following, again offered by Clark:

> Ofsted revealed two years ago that schools may have wrongly labelled as many as 450,000 children as having special needs ... the Government's former adviser on speech and language, warned that this was often 'used as an explanation for failure'.

Some months earlier the journalist Peter Stanford, writing in another UK national paper, the *Daily Telegraph* commented as follows:

Many experts fear that funds earmarked to help children with learning difficulties are being redirected to cope with a new tide of social deprivation that is washing up in the classroom. Children from troubled homes, who turn up at schools with behavioural problems, are being routinely put on the SEN register alongside those with more specific learning difficulties, such as dyslexia and dyspraxia.

PERCEPTIONS OF LEARNERS AND LEARNING

How we perceive learners and the act of learning is crucial. To fully engage in this process, however, requires that we stand back and examine not only the child but also the child's environment. Such a view finds support not just in countless pieces of research but also in the work of major theorists, perhaps most notably Vygotsky and Bruner, whose work was discussed in Chapter 2. Learning does not happen in a vacuum. It is not a discrete process but rather a dynamic process that draws into its dynamic such key factors as: parenting; teachers' skills and knowledge bases; policy and decision makers' views of education and schooling; diet; the media, and so on. Practitioners working with children, and especially those with additional needs, who take time to stand back and reflect upon the environments within which children learn and the manner in which they, themselves, manage these environments will have far greater insights into the learning of children than those practitioners who don't.

ACQUIRING LITERACY

The United Nations considers an entitlement to literacy to be one of our most basic human rights (MacBlain et al., 2005, p. 54). Children who experience difficulties with reading and writing become seriously disadvantaged and all too frequently fail to realize their potential and life chances. The extent of this problem offers major challenges to Early Years Practitioners and primary school teachers in terms of their responsibility for the early identification and assessment of difficulties with the acquisition of literacy, since it is only through proper identification and assessment that children with literacy difficulties will receive appropriate interventions and provision.

EXAMPLE

Years ago when I (the author) was training teachers to gain a postgraduate diploma that qualified them to teach children with dyslexia, I was struck by one particular case that has never left me. As part of the course, which was validated by the Royal Society of Arts and the British Dyslexia Association teachers taking the course had to work with a primary-aged child, a secondary-aged child and an adult, all of whom had significant problems with literacy. One of the teachers began working with an elderly lady in her late sixties who was, for all intents and purposes illiterate – she had never learned to read or write. She was intelligent and had a lovely sense of humour. When the teacher began working with her it became clear that this lady had one aim in her mind – to open a bank account, acquire a cheque book and go to the local toy store and buy a large red tractor for her little grandson of five years of age *using her cheque book.*

The teacher began working with her, teaching her initially how to write her name in capital letters and then her signature. As the weeks progressed she learned how to write her address, how to write the letters up to 100, the name of the toy store, and so on. The teacher then took her to the bank where she opened a bank account. A week later she received her cheque book and after many, many trials writing out the amount of '*Twenty eight pounds and 50 pence only*' on spare paper and practising her signature she set out with the teacher to the toy shop where they collected the large red tractor from the shelf and approached the checkout. With the teacher standing right behind her the grandmother then produced her cheque book, asked the till attendant how much the tractor was and then wrote a cheque for the correct sum.

The above example illustrates clearly how a lack of literacy can affect people's lives. This was an incredible lesson for the teacher and her student group with whom she subsequently shared it, and illustrated the importance of individuals acquiring the ability to read and write from an early age.

At the heart of all that children do in schools lies the acquisition of literacy. For those children who struggle with this the repercussions and impact can be devastating. Much has been happening recently within the UK in regard to the teaching of phonics in primary and also secondary schools. This is largely in response to the fact that significant numbers of young people are leaving school after as many as 12 years of formal education with little if any literacy skills. Successive governments have been very worried by this. Too many children, for example, who struggle with literacy in the post-primary years, become disaffected, with many ending up withdrawing from school and society and becoming involved with crime.

It is sometimes difficult to comprehend how children can attend school for so many years and then leave with very low levels of literacy, with some being almost unable to read basic text. It would appear that much still needs to be done in schools to address this most important aspect of children's learning. By examining models of intervention and focusing on the learning of children with a range of specific learning difficulties, as well as the importance of Working Memory and Processing, it is intended that readers will gain a deeper and more critical understanding of many of the key factors that contribute to the poor acquisition of literacy and failure.

MODELS OF ASSESSMENT AND INTERVENTION

As implied in the quotations at the start of this chapter the assessment and identification of young children experiencing difficulties in learning needs to be radically challenged. In particular, identification, assessment and subsequent intervention needs to be viewed within the wider context of how children are first engaged with learning; how they are subsequently taught; the nature of their learning experiences; and the knowledge and skills base of those who are responsible for undertaking the assessments, designing subsequent interventions and managing the overall learning of the children.

In 2009 the Office for Standards in Education (Ofsted) commenced a substantial and detailed review of special educational needs and disability in England (Ofsted, 2010). During the review they visited a large number of providers including those from the Early Years private, voluntary, independent and maintained sectors, primary and secondary schools, including independent and non-maintained special schools, as well as residential schools, further education colleges and independent specialist colleges. Following their review Ofsted highlighted the fact that the term 'special educational needs' was too widely used. Approximately 50 per cent of the schools and Early Years providers that they visited employed the concepts of 'low attainment' and 'relatively slow progress' as the main indicators for deciding on whether or not a child had a special educational need. In fact, the inspectors reported on schools which, they observed, identified children as having special educational needs when their needs were, in actual fact, not significantly different to the majority of the other children. The report concluded that whilst these children were underachieving, this was, in part, due to the fact that the provision offered by schools was 'not good enough' and that expectations of these children were 'too low'. The results of this, the report suggested, were that in some instances children were being incorrectly identified as children with special educational needs and that some of the provision that was additional and that required further funding was being used, 'to make up for day-to-day teaching and pastoral support'. The report also highlighted the fact that:

> In the case of children and young people who need complex and specialist support from health and other services to enable them to thrive and develop, the term 'educational needs' does not always accurately reflect their situation. Both these considerations suggest that we should not only move away from the current system of categorisation of needs but also start to think critically about the way terms are used. (Ofsted, 2010, p. 9)

In addition to identifying barriers to the learning of children and young people with special educational needs and disabilities the report also identified key elements that underpinned successful learning, for children and young people, as follows:

- they looked to the teacher for their main learning and to the support staff for support

- assessment was secure, continuous and acted upon

- teachers planned opportunities for pupils to collaborate, work things out for themselves and apply what they had learnt to different situations

- teachers' subject knowledge was good, as was their understanding of pupils' needs and how to help them

- lesson structures were clear and familiar but allowed for adaptation and flexibility

- all aspects of a lesson were well thought out and any adaptations needed were made without fuss to ensure that everyone in class had access

- teachers presented information in different ways to ensure all children and young people understood

- teachers adjusted the pace of the lesson to reflect how children and young people were learning

- the staff understood clearly the difference between ensuring that children and young people were learning and keeping them occupied

- respect for individuals was reflected in high expectations for their achievement

- the effectiveness of specific types of support was understood and the right support was put in place at the right time. (Ofsted, 2010, p. 47)

THE SPECIFIC LEARNING DIFFICULTIES OF:

Dyslexia

Example

Arthur is 11 years and six months old and spells badly. His reading is also very poor and he has never been able to master his times tables. Mathematics is for Arthur a bit of a mystery. He has only recently learned to tell the time and gets easily flustered if asked to engage in even basic numerical operations. His handwriting is difficult to read and he has developed strategies for avoiding reading. Over the years his teachers have praised Arthur for his creativity and abilities in art. Arthur is due to transfer to his local secondary school and he is excited but fearful. His biggest fear is being asked to read aloud. Arthur's parents have spoken with his teachers over the years and expressed their concerns but have been told that whilst he is struggling in some areas he is, nevertheless, making progress. After speaking with the parents of another child,

(Continued)

(Continued)

Arthur's parents requested an independent assessment by an educational psychologist. Following this assessment the educational psychologist discussed her findings with Arthur's parents and sent her report, extracts of which are given below:

Current level of intellectual functioning

In order to gain additional information in regard to Arthur's cognitive functioning I administered the Wechsler Intelligence Scale for Children [Table 8.1]. On this occasion, Arthur achieved the following scores:

Table 8.1   Case study – Arthur (intellectual functioning)

Index	Centile
Working Memory	0.1
Processing Speed	5
Verbal Comprehension	47
Perceptual Reasoning	39

Two-thirds of children are considered to function within the average range of ability and this range is represented between the 16th and 84th centiles, with the 16th centile lying at the lowest end of the average range and the 84th centile at the highest. The 85th centile upwards represents increasingly higher ability where the 95th centile represents the top one per cent of ability. At the other end of the range, the 1st centile represents the lowest one per cent of ability.

Discussion of statistical results

The above results suggest to me that Arthur has specific learning difficulties that are severe and that are typically found amongst children with dyslexia. Of particular note, are Arthur's centile scores on Working Memory and Processing Speed Indexes [Table 8.1], which are well below the average range ...

Literacy

Arthur was assessed on his Reading Accuracy (Word Recognition), Reading Comprehension and Spelling. He achieved the following reading and spelling results.

Table 8.2   Case study – (Arthur literacy scores)

Test	Centile
Basic Reading	25
Reading Comprehension	50
Spelling	04

It is clear from Table 8.2 that Arthur experiences marked difficulties with literacy. In particular, Arthur experiences significant difficulties with individual word recognition and decoding as well as with spelling … I formed the opinion that Arthur is quite confused by the whole process of 'spelling'. This confusion, combined with the use of inefficient strategies underpinned by very weak working memory, suggests to me that Arthur finds the whole idea of 'spelling' to be extremely challenging and somewhat of a mystery. For these reasons I would suggest that Arthur will need to acquire new and more efficient strategies for tackling spelling, as well as word recognition and decoding …

Summary and recommendations

In summary … Arthur's difficulties in the areas of Working Memory and Processing Speed [Table 8.1] are significant and may mask underlying abilities. It is important that Arthur's true abilities and potential are fully recognised by those responsible for managing his education. This will be especially important when he commences secondary school … Central to improving Arthur's learning in the areas of word recognition, spelling and numerical operations will be the need for him to develop new and efficient strategies for approaching tasks … Given Arthur's weaknesses with Working Memory I would recommend that significantly greater emphasis is placed upon developing and using kinaesthetic memory and giving Arthur opportunities each day to engage in this … In particular, I would recommend the following:

- *Arthur will benefit from precision teaching and learning, which offers carefully considered and graded steps that are small, that avoid any sense of failure and that are combined with lots of focused and appropriate reinforcement.*
- *Teaching and learning should be as creative as possible and there should be much over-learning of new material.*
- *Arthur needs to develop appropriate strategies for improving his Working Memory and Speed of Information Processing.*
- *Arthur needs support in managing his time and developing his organisational skills.*
- *Arthur needs to gain a much better understanding in regard to how he approaches new learning situations and how he organises work schedules in relation to the type of demands he faces.*
- *Spelling and word recognition programmes should be highly structured, cumulative and sequential and should incorporate a great deal of multi-sensory learning.*
- *Arthur should gain a better understanding of the language that is used by teachers, working to remediate literacy such as learning what prefixes and suffixes are and how words are made up.*
- *He needs to gain a better understanding of basic spelling principles.*
- *Increasing Arthur's knowledge of sound/symbol correspondence will be extremely important as will be the development of his knowledge and understanding of syllabification.*
- *Arthur still uses print when writing and he should be encouraged to develop cursive writing, and especially where this can be linked to multi-sensory approaches, which develop kinaesthetic memory.*
- *Information and Communications Technology (ICT) should be central to supporting Arthur in many aspects of literacy and he could be supported in developing his keyboard skills, which will be important for him when he attends secondary school.*
- *Arthur will also benefit from having opportunities to demonstrate his abilities in front of his peers. This will help him internalise a more positive view of himself, and his abilities and potential.*

The profile of difficulties offered in this example is typical of many, though not all, children with dyslexia and illustrates the complexities that underpin the learning of many children with this condition, and more particularly the underlying problems that can frequently be hidden from even the most well-meaning of teachers.

Dyslexia is perhaps one of the most contentious and most argued about conditions within the field of education and one that is surrounded by much confusion and a great deal of controversy. Everatt and Reid (2009) have, for example, commented as follows:

> ... there is still no clear explanation that is universally accepted of what exactly constitutes dyslexia. Identification is still riddled with controversies despite the emergence of a number of new tests to identify dyslexia ... Indeed, there is still an ongoing debate on the value of dyslexia as an identifiable syndrome ...

For decades, the professional practice of those working in the field of dyslexia has been confounded by problems of definition, lack of clarity as to what exactly the condition is, whether or not it exists, how it is identified, and how schools and other professionals should respond to it. A very pertinent quotation offered by Cruickshank (1968), cited in Pumfrey and Reason (1991, p. 15) demonstrates the confusion of the time and, arguably, still holds some relevance today:

> If a child diagnosed as dyslexic in Philadelphia moved to Bucks County, ten miles north, he would be called a child with a language disorder. In Montgomery County, a few miles south, he would be called a child with special or specific language problems. In Michigan, he would be called a child with perceptual disturbance. In California he would be called either a child with educational handicaps or a neurologically handicapped child. In Florida and New York State, he would be called a brain injured child. In Colorado, the child would be classified as having minimal brain dysfunction ...

The crucial question is one of how dyslexia affects learning. Crombie and Reid (2009, p. 71) have suggested that:

> The responsibility for early identification should not rest solely on the teacher or school, but it should be a planned and integrated activity involving parents and professionals working together in the context of both home and school ... Yet, if early identification is to be effective then it is important that it focuses on pre-school children as well as children in the early years of primary school.

This is a crucial point and raises the importance of working together and of having clear, comprehensive and agreed identification and intervention strategies for supporting children who in the early stages of education are experiencing problems with the acquisition of literacy. To fail to have these may well result in children's specific difficulties going unnoticed and appropriate support not being provided. Crombie and Reid (2009, p. 71–2) again, rather worryingly, emphasize how:

> It is often the case, in a local authority context, that a child has to *fail* to learn to read and write before difficulties are recognized, and certainly before the term 'dyslexia' can be used. This means there is a delay in providing effective provision ...

Such an assertion is concerning and highlights not only the wasting of potential where many young children fail to have the support they need, but also the anxiety and worry that is experienced by the parents of those children who are struggling to master reading, spelling and writing. It can be seen in the case of Arthur above that whilst his parents persisted in their concerns about Arthur's reading they were unable to access an assessment by the Local Authority's educational psychologist and had to pay for a private independent assessment, by which time Arthur had been failing for many years. The secondary problems that frequently arise with failing to read and spell can, all too often, be seen in children's lowered self-esteem, self-confidence and self-efficacy (MacBlain et al., 2005; Long et al., 2007).

With regard to the issue of 'planning' to meet the needs of children with dyslexia, Reid and Came (2009, pp. 198–9), have emphasized the importance of gaining a detailed knowledge of the strengths as well as the weaknesses that children with dyslexia display. They also emphasize the importance of viewing difficulties and challenges presented by these children as being the responsibility of the school as a whole and not just the individual teacher who is working with a particular child. They also call for '… accurate and full assessment' of each child's attainments as a necessary part of any planning and any programme designed to support the child. In particular, they call for accurate assessment of listening comprehension in addition to a child's accuracy in reading and their reading fluency, 'Indeed it is often the discrepancy between listening or reading comprehension and reading accuracy that can be a key factor in identifying dyslexia' (Reid, 2009, p. 199). They also highlight the importance of cultural factors, for example, in the case of bilingual children. Given the large number of children now in schools whose first language is not English, this needs to be seen as a key factor in the planning of schools (MacBlain et al., 2006).

Perhaps Drysdale (2009, p. 237) has struck one of the key elements in understanding and managing the learning of children with dyslexia; that of multisensory teaching when she alludes to the fact that:

> To become a skilled reader, the young learner must create entirely new neurological circuitry connecting visual, auditory and motor systems at lightning speed. Development of the skills within any one of these systems and the learner's ability to make neural connections at speed will affect success in learning to read.

Dyspraxia

> ### Example
>
> Annie is eight years of age and attends a local school where she is described by her teacher as a *'lovely little girl'* who *'struggles to keep up with the other children, is hopelessly disorganized and never finishes written work on time'*. Her teacher has expressed concerns regarding Annie's handwriting and her *'very poor organization'*. In PE Annie comes across as having difficulty following the rules of games and activities. Since starting school Annie has been considered by her teachers to be clumsy, overly sensitive and very quick to cry. She gets very frustrated when working on construction activities, and her parents report that she has only just managed to ride a two-wheel bicycle without stabilizers. Tying her shoelaces remains an activity that presents significant problems. Spelling and reading, and especially the former, are presenting significant challenges to Annie.

Annie has the condition known as dyspraxia, which is not well understood by many practitioners working with children. She is typical of a number of children who present with difficulties in the area of movement and her case offers insights into the type of challenges that face many teachers working with children with this condition. A particular problem for Annie appears to lie in the manner in which her behaviours are perceived by her teachers, who largely describe her behaviours as problematic and give little apparent attention to environmental factors. Some teachers working with children whose dyspraxia has not yet been identified may perceive them as simply children with very poor concentration, who lack motivation, are easily distracted and inattentive, take little care over their handwriting and pay scant attention to neatness. They may also be heard to express their frustration with these children, who typically fail to complete written work within set periods of time, have a strong tendency towards being disorganized and have poor short-term memory. But what is dyspraxia and how common is it?

In addressing our understanding of what dyspraxia is Boon (2010, p. 7) has commented as follows:

> If you ask different professionals what dyspraxia is, you get different answers, depending on their field of expertise … The Dyspraxia Foundation … defines dyspraxia as 'an impairment or immaturity of the organization of movement. Associated with this there may be problems of language, perception and thought.' It is fundamentally an immaturity in the way that the brain processes information, which results in messages not being properly or fully transmitted to the body.

The Dyspraxia Foundation suggests that dyspraxia affects up to 10 per cent of the general population, with two per cent being affected severely. The Foundation also suggests that, in general, males are more affected than females and that statistically it is likely that in a class of 30 children there is likely to be one child with dyspraxia. To gain some understanding of this complex condition (as well as the related condition of *Developmental Coordination Disorder*) and its impact upon children, we need to look more closely at 'movement' and more especially the relationship between movement and the brain. It almost goes without saying that movement is fundamental to the learning of all children, and especially young children, and can be observed in nearly every activity in which children engage.

The brain consists of literally millions of nerve cells, which facilitate learning, and which, as Macintyre and McVitty (2004, pp. 5–6) have proposed:

> … work together to receive, analyse and act on information from both external, i.e. environmental sources, and internal feelings, i.e. pain, hunger and the different emotions. As different experiences occur, these neurons join into networks that work together as systems to facilitate specific functions such as vision or hearing, movement or paying attention …

> Each neurone has an axon, a long spindle that leads to branching dendrites. These connect to other dendrites over a synapse, i.e. a gap, to approximately one hundred thousand other neurons. Chemicals such as dopamine act as neurotransmitters, passing messages from one cell to the next. The vast number of cells and connections mean that an infinite number of connections can be made and unmade …

> Myelin is a thin fatty coating that acts as an insulator around the axons, allowing signals to proceed smoothly and quickly to their designated ports. There is a gradual maturing of the brain that continues over thirty years but the 'majority of the maturation has occurred by the age of three to four years'. (Winkley, 2003)

As children grow and develop so their brains develop also and with it the basis of learning. Every part of our body is connected with the brain, with some parts having many more neurons than others. Hence, some parts of our body are much more sensitive than others and more receptive to stimuli such as touch, pain and so on. In children with dyspraxia this process is different in that it is characterized by immaturity.

Young children with dyspraxia typically face challenges with everyday activities such as getting dressed, eating, climbing stairs, balancing and playing games. Indeed, movement is involved in almost all activities that children engage in, for example, running and jumping, writing and drawing and speaking, and for children with dyspraxia these activities can also present significant problems. When muscles in the child's mouth or throat are affected their speech and general language processing may be compromised and they may, for example, experience problems with articulating words, phrases and ideas, rendering speech, in some instances, incomprehensible (Macintyre, 2002).

Movement is also very important in the development of self-esteem, and many teachers will be familiar with those children who present with significant difficulties in this area. Children's poor self-esteem may have resulted from problems such as an unwillingness of their peers to choose them for games, difficulties with riding two-wheeled bicycles, poor handwriting and presentation of written work at school, problems with organization, learning to read the time, and so on.

One particular way that children with dyspraxia are affected is with planning their thoughts and actions. For example, children with dyspraxia can have problems with planning their ideas for a written story, and it is of interest that many children come to be referred for assessment at around the age of nine when their teachers are expecting them to write longer stories as opposed to sentences to match pictures. These children may also be very easily distracted during their planning by, for example, others around them, their own thoughts, and by noises or visual stimuli around them, meaning that they fail to finish their written work within time limits. They can also experience difficulties sitting for even relatively short periods of time and will often be observed to move about or 'squirm' in their seats. Physical education (PE) and games lessons can be particularly challenging for many children with dyspraxia, and their immaturities in the area of motor coordination often mean that they can struggle to keep up with other children when running and jumping, and may display much poorer skills with, for example, ball control when playing soccer, basketball or rounders. Throwing and catching can also be especially problematic for the young child with dyspraxia.

Teachers working with children with dyspraxia should take account of a number of key factors in meeting the needs of these children. For example, they should at the very least gain a sound understanding of the condition, and especially the effects upon the child's social and emotional development. Finally, it is worth proposing that class teachers working with young children who are presenting with difficulties with movement, in particular persisting and marked problems with coordination, short-term memory and especially language, should involve the SENCo prior to considering involving parents and working towards possible multi-sensory assessment.

ADHD

Example

Jack is 11 years of age. On a personal level he presents as a caring, thoughtful and sensitive child but his teachers all describe him as '*unable to sit still; always out of his seat; constantly interrupting and at times very rude; he doesn't seem to know where the boundaries lie*' and as '*a huge distraction to the other children*'. They claim that '*he never appears to be where he should be*' and when he arrives in the morning for school, '*he invariably arrives late and has the wrong books or homework assignments with him'*. During unstructured time, for example at break times, he is described by his teachers as, '*at times he is dangerous, he takes risks that other children wouldn't take and he doesn't seem to be able to play with the others in a constructive way'*.

Jack has been recently assessed as having ADHD and the descriptions of his behaviours offered by his teachers will be familiar to those teachers and Early Years practitioners who have worked with children with ADHD. The condition of ADHD is complex. Macintyre and McVitty (2004, p. 130), for example, have proposed that there are two distinct types, 'The first has key factors of impulsivity and hyperactivity, the second (often known as ADD) predominantly houses inattention'. It is generally the first type that causes teachers and Early Years practitioners most concern.

ADHD is a neurological condition typically characterized by observable behaviours such as hyperactivity, impulsivity, marked problems with focusing and sustaining attention, and difficulties with managing behaviours and feelings. The condition is not confined to children and there are many adults who have this condition. Children with ADHD are frequently delayed in their development; it is thought to affect around five per cent of the population, with more boys being affected than girls. It is now accepted that ADHD is co-morbid with other conditions, that is children with ADHD may also, though not always, have characteristics found, for example, in dyslexia. Children with ADHD typically demonstrate poor understanding of the link between behaviours and consequences and tend to respond poorly to being offered bribes to change their behaviours. As these children progress through schooling, they may, if they are not appropriately supported, develop secondary conditions such as anxiety and in severe cases depression.

It is important that practitioners working with children with ADHD are open to looking at the 'whole child' and take time to make informed and purposeful assessments and interventions, rather than making rash judgements based solely on presenting behaviours. It is all too possible for practitioners to focus almost entirely on the negative behaviours of the child, as appears to have been the case with Jack. Practitioners should, where possible, aim to focus on the positive aspects of the child's functioning and should endeavor to identify the needs of the child as opposed to trying to make a diagnosis of the condition and spend their time concentrating entirely upon presenting behaviours.

Certain stimulant medications have been prescribed for children since the 1960s, one example of which is Ritalin. It has been estimated (Kring et al., 2013, p. 405) that in 2006 there were around 2.5 million children in the USA who were taking stimulant medication. Kring et al. (2013, p. 406) also suggest that amongst the treatments for ADHD, other approaches that do not require medication have been found to offer positive results, such as providing training for parents and altering the manner in which teachers manage their classroom environments, in particular making use of Operant Conditioning (see Chapter 2), the tutoring of children with ADHD by their peers, and closer liaison between teachers and parents in shaping behaviours through the use of positive reinforcement and reward.

Kring et al. (2013, p. 406) also emphasize how research in this area has supported the view that when teachers vary their style of presentation during lessons as well as the materials they use, and engage the child with ADHD in short tasks where feedback is given immediately afterwards, positive results are gained. They also draw attention to the positive effects that teachers can have when they adopt an enthusiastic and task-focused style and provide the child with regular periods of physical activity. Here we see, in the work of Kring et al., much greater emphasis being placed upon environmental factors such as the learning context, and the behaviours of the teacher and the parents, as opposed to 'within-child' factors and medication.

We now turn to a further complex condition, which has only recently begun to be properly understood.

Asperger's Syndrome

> **Example**
>
> Paul is 10 years old and attends a local school. He has just been referred to the educational psychologist because his teachers are concerned by a number of his behaviours. In their referral to the educational psychologist they stress that, *'Paul has difficulty making friends and is a bit of a loner ... he is extremely good with maths, easily the best in his class and probably better than many children at secondary school ... but gets very anxious when he is asked to engage in creative writing'*. His teacher is especially concerned about his behaviours when he is outside during break times. She reports that he does not *'... really play with the others, always on the periphery of a game or an activity but never really involved'*.

Paul's behaviours are typical of a number of children with Asperger's Syndrome (AS). It was considered at one time that AS was due to parenting. This is not the case. Research has led us to a place where we now accept that 'Asperger's Syndrome is due to a dysfunction of specific structures and systems in the brain. In short, the brain is "wired" differently, not necessarily defective ...' (Attwood, 2007, p. 327). Mayes and Calhoun (2003, p. 15) have commented as follows:

> Many experts now agree that autism is a spectrum disorder and that Asperger syndrome (AS) is high-functioning or mild autism... However, controversy persists, and 'Asperger syndrome' remains a popular term used by clinicians and parents alike.

Having a better understanding of AS has led to changing perceptions of the way in which children with AS can be best supported as they move through their schooling and manage, for example, transitions from preschool to primary school, from primary to post-primary school and then into adulthood. Much of our understanding of AS has arisen because of research studies that have sought to understand how the brain functions. Attwood (2007, p. 327) has put the case as follows:

> Research studies ... have confirmed that Asperger's Syndrome is associated with a dysfunction of the 'social brain', which comprises components of the frontal and temporal regions of the cortex ... There is also evidence of dysfunction of the amygdala, the basal ganglia and cerebellum ... The latest research suggests that there is weak connectivity between these components ... There is also evidence to suggest right hemisphere cortical dysfunction ... and an abnormality of the dopamine system... Thus, we now know which structures in the brain are functioning or 'wired' differently.

Attwood has suggested that for most individuals with AS the reason that the brain has developed differently is due to genetic factors (2007, p. 328).

In making reference to the work of Attwood (1993), Herbert (2005, pp. 187–8) has offered a number of interventions for teachers with children with AS:

- provision, as far as possible, of a predictable environment and consistent routines ...;
- allowing opportunities for social interaction and facilitation of social relationships in fairly structured and supervised activities;
- preparation for alterations in routines or timetabling;
- issuing of brief, precise, and specific instructions ...;
- reducing tasks into manageable segments ...;
- not expecting the student to have the ability unaided, to generalize instructions ...

Creating classroom environments where the child with AS can feel supported and where there are clear boundaries and rules for all of the children is essential. The child with AS may, at times, appear overly keen to talk about a particular subject and in doing so may talk over the adults or interrupt. This is not intentional and the child will need to have their awareness of boundaries raised. The child with AS will need to acquire strategies that can be used within the classroom to support new learning. One simple and very effective strategy is the use of visual timetables for the child so that they can see at a glance what they need to do. Visual timetables that also show where change is due to occur are especially valuable and can, more often than not, prevent the child with AS becoming anxious and fearful.

Some wonderful insights into AS have been offered by those who have been diagnosed with the condition. Wendy Lawson (2003, p. 190), for example, has offered the following:

> For me there are some good things about being autistic. I can enjoy the quiet and peaceful feeling of my own space. I can focus upon a desired object … for hours. This means that being committed to the study of my choice isn't difficult for me. Whilst some students easily become tired, bored, or distracted, I am in my element!

Talking about her experiences during her early years she commented:

> If people only see the negative and constantly tell you what you are doing wrong, then your self-esteem plunges … I was fortunate to encounter a couple of people who decided to give me some of their time … I tended to be left to my own devices often. This isn't ideal for children with autism. We benefit more from early intervention and activities that keep us 'connected' to life. (2003, pp. 188–9)

Having a diagnosis can help young people, as well as adults with AS, to understand themselves and to know that they are not, for example, unintelligent and that whilst they have limitations these are not just confined to them. One further important insight offered by Wendy Lawson is in regard to her social and verbal interactions with others:

> Someone might just be speaking to me. However, I experience it as someone projecting into my thinking or conversation, and I feel almost violated! 'How dare they interrupt my space and distract me from my course. Didn't they understand that now I would have to start over again, recapping my thoughts or plans, and schedule it all again … understanding everyday life requires an understanding of "concepts" – concepts such as right, wrong, time, space … Most of the time I got into trouble at school because I didn't have a concept for what was being said, done, or expected'. (2003, p. 192)

Our understanding of this condition has grown in the last 30 years. Before that, little was known about it. For children with AS to have appropriate learning opportunities it is essential that teachers and Early Years practitioners become much more informed as to what AS is and especially how it affects the social and emotional lives of children as well as their families.

Dyscalculia

Example

George is 10 years of age. His teacher describes his reading as '*reasonably good, much bet-ter than his spelling, which is very poor*' and his maths as '*This is a real problem area for George*'. Despite continual attempts at learning his multiplication times tables they appear to be beyond him. Fractions, decimals, area and volume present George with enormous challenges. He still has not mastered the skills and knowledge to subtract higher numbers from lower numbers where hundreds, tens and units are involved. From an early age he found counting in 'twos' and 'threes' very difficult. Handling and calculating money has also been problematic as well as telling the time. Directionality has also presented its prob-lems for George and he frequently gets his right and left mixed up. This also appears to cause him problems for example with map reading in geography. When asked about his abilities in maths George is quick to respond with such answers as, '*I'm no good at maths*' and, more recently, with '*I hate maths*'.

George is typical of many children who struggle in the area of mathematics, though it is important at the outset, as with any child, to determine what the causes of his difficul-ties are and if they are 'within-child' factors or in fact more to do with the way in which he has been introduced to mathematics. Two decades ago Westwood (1993, pp. 149–50) commented that, 'Not infrequently the instruction given in mathematics is poor, in that it does not match the current aptitude or learning rate of the slower children'. He went on to suggest a number of factors at the heart of poor instruction in mathematics, including the pacing of work, which outstripped the child's capacity to assimilate new concepts and new skills, and poor structuring of discovery learning, which resulted in the children failing to '… abstract or remember anything from it'. Westwood also drew attention to the type of language used by teachers, which for many children failing with mathematics failed to match their level of understanding. He also drew attention to the introduction by teachers of abstract symbols at too early a stage and '… in the absence of concrete materials or real-life examples'. Children failing in mathematics were, he suggested, all too often introduced to calculations involving place-values before they had grasped simple computations involving single numbers. He also emphasized the linear nature of some teaching where a small number of teaching sessions were given to a particular topic before that was left behind for a new one. Given that there may be elements of teaching that militate against all children making progress in mathematics and result in confusion, it is now important to address the notion that there may be a group of children who have specific difficulties within this area.

The National Numeracy Strategy: *Guidance to Support Learners with Dyslexia and Dyscalculia,* cited by Chinn (2009, p. 127), offers the following in relation to the concept of Dyscalculia:

> Dyscalculia learners may have difficulty understanding simple number concepts, lack intuitive grasp of numbers and have problems learning facts and procedures ... Purely dyscalculic learners who have difficulties only with numbers will have cognitive and language abilities in the normal range and may excel in non-mathematical subjects. It is more likely that difficulties with numeracy accompany the language difficulties of dyslexia.

Chinn (2009) has further commented:

> ... dyscalculia is a complex concept, not least because there is unlikely to be a single reason behind the problem of the many, many people who fail to master maths, not all of whom will be diagnosed as dyscalculic. (p. 127)

In 2012 the British Dyslexia Association offered the following definition of dyscalculia on its website:

> A condition that affects the ability to acquire arithmetical skills. Dyscalculic learners may have difficulty understanding simple number concepts, lack an intuitive grasp of numbers, and have problems learning number facts and procedures. Even if they produce a correct answer or use a correct method, they may do so mechanically and without confidence.

The Association suggests that dyscalculia, of which very little is known is a 'congenital condition', which is caused by '... the abnormal functioning of a specific area of the brain'. Estimates of dyscalculia offered by the Association suggest an occurrence of between three and six per cent of the population, that is, children who are 'purely' dyscalculic – that is they only have difficulties with maths but have good or even excellent performance in other areas of learning. It is also of note that the Association suggests that between 40 and 50 per cent of dyslexics do not present with signs of dyscalculia and may perform at least as well as other children in maths, with some 10 per cent performing even higher. However, the Association also estimates that between 50 and 60 per cent of dyslexics do present with difficulties in maths and makes the point that, '... difficulty in decoding written words can transfer across into a difficulty in decoding mathematical notation and symbols'.

Symptoms of dyscalculia indicated by the Association on its website, which are typically found in children are:

- **Counting**: Dyscalculic children can usually learn the sequence of counting words, but may have difficulty navigating back and forth, especially in twos and threes.

- **Calculations**: Dyscalculic children find learning and recalling number facts difficult. They often lack confidence even when they produce the correct answer. They also fail to use rules and procedures to build on known facts. For example, they may know that 5+3=8, but not realise that, therefore, 3+5=8 or that 5+4=9.

- **Numbers with zeros**: Dyscalculic children may find it difficult to grasp that the words ten, hundred and thousand have the same relationship to each other as the numerals 10, 100 and 1000.

- **Measures**: Dyscalculic children often have difficulty with operations such as handling money or telling the time. They may also have problems with concepts such as speed (miles per hour) or temperature.

- **Direction/orientation**: Dyscalculic children may have difficulty understanding spatial orientation (including left and right) causing difficulties in following directions or with map reading.

The Association also indicates that currently there is no formal diagnostic test for dyscalculia, though there is a screening device available to teachers. The Association has also acknowledged that, compared with dyslexia, there has been very little research into dyscalculia.

WORKING MEMORY AND SPEED OF PROCESSING

Lack of progress in literacy and numeracy are, for many children, due in large part to problems in the area of short-term memory, or as it is more commonly referred to, Working Memory. Whitebread (2012, pp. 98–9) has proposed that Working Memory has three distinctive features, which he describes as: rehearsal and the articulatory loop, multi-sensory representations, and limited capacity. Because the capacity to store information in Working Memory is very limited and information that is held quickly decays (after about 30 seconds), individuals need another means of holding information for longer. This is done through the use of rehearsal. By rehearsing information when it is in Working Memory it is possible to store it longer. Rehearsal of information also facilitates the transfer of information into the long-term memory where it can be stored for considerably longer. Not only do we begin to develop our ability to engage in rehearsal from a very early age and throughout primary and post-primary education, but we also improve the quality of this process. As we grow older, then, our use of Working Memory typically, though not in all cases, improves. The second feature of Working Memory proposed by Whitebread is its multi-sensory nature or more particularly the 'visuo-spatial scratch pad', which facilitates the storing and manipulation of visual images. Having the capacity to represent sensory information in Working Memory in different ways increases the strength of the memory trace. Though this seems a relatively simple assertion, it is nonetheless, of crucial importance to the learning of children with, for example, dyslexia who typically struggle to retain information such as words or calculations in working memory long enough and in a way that the information can be transferred to the long-term memory where it can be recalled at a later date. Using different senses together and in unison, therefore, can be a very useful means of improving the memory capacity of children with dyslexia and, ultimately, their learning.

Whitebread's third feature of Working Memory is its limited capacity. It has been accepted for some time that adults, for example, can typically hold around seven bits of information in their short-term memory. However, as new bits of information come in to short-term memory other bits already in the short-term memory store become pushed out. Children have smaller storage than adults and, therefore, can hold fewer bits or items of information in short-term storage.

CONDUCT DISORDERS

A recent guide published by The Children and Young People's Mental Health Coalition (CYPMHC, 2012) aimed at helping head teachers prevent emotional and behavioural difficulties in children in their schools suggested that pupils with conduct disorder and severe ADHD are much more likely to experience marked difficulties with the acquisition of literacy and numeracy skills. In their guide, CYPMHC draw a distinction between conduct disorder, which they define as '… a repetitive and persistent behaviour problem, where major age-appropriate societal norms or the basic rights of others are violated' and emotional disorder, which they suggest refers to '… conditions such as depression and anxiety' (p. 4). The guide also offers the following rather startling facts:

> 1 in 10 or at least 3 young people in every class has a behavioural or emotional difficulty … Almost half of young people with fewer than five GCSEs graded A* to C said they 'always' or 'often' feel down or depressed compared with 30% of young people who are more qualified … and 7 will have been bullied (Faulkner, 2011) … 1 in 4 young people of secondary school age will have been severely neglected, physically attacked or even sexually abused at some point in their lives.

It is clear to most practitioners working with children that behavioural and emotional difficulties can significantly impact upon the academic achievement of children. This is an important point as pupils with persisting conduct or emotional disorders are more likely to have special educational needs and, perhaps more worryingly, to be excluded from their schools. A significant number of these pupils will leave school with few if any qualifications.

More recently, Kring et al. (2013, p. 407) refer to the *Diagnostic and Statistical Manual of Mental Disorders* (DSM-5) in their discussion of conduct disorder, which they indicate focuses upon those types of acts that are illegal and that can be construed as violating the rights of other individuals and breaking the consensus of agreed social norms. They emphasize that in meeting the criteria for being a conduct disorder these acts have to be characterized by such factors as, aggression and cruelty, lack of remorse and a degree of callousness and high rates of frequency. Kring et al. (2013, p. 407) also suggest that:

> A related but less well understood externalizing disorder in the DSM-IV-TR is **oppositional defiant disorder** (ODD). There is some debate as to whether ODD is distinct from conduct disorder, a precursor to it, or an earlier and milder manifestation of it … Commonly comorbid with ODD are ADHD, learning disorders, communication disorders, but ODD is different from ADHD in that the defiant behavior is not thought to arise from attentional deficits or sheer impulsiveness.

It is often the case that children and young people with conduct disorder engage in substance abuse and experience higher levels of anxiety and depression than is typical of their peers. It is generally accepted amongst professionals that interventions that involve the parents and immediate family members are more likely to yield positive outcomes, especially if such interventions can take place as early as possible in the child's life. Kring et al. (2013, p. 412) make reference to the work of Gerald Patterson and his colleagues who developed and evaluated a behavioural programme called '*Parent Management Training*' (PMT), where the parents of very young children are introduced to ways of modifying their own responses to their children. Parents were encouraged to reward 'prosocial' as opposed to 'antisocial' behaviours in a consistent manner or, as Kring et al. suggest, 'Parents are taught to use techniques such as positive reinforcement when the child exhibits positive behaviours and time-out and loss of privileges for aggressive or antisocial behaviours' (p. 412). Kring et al. go on to assert that though this type of programme has been modified over the years by others, in fact, it is the 'most efficacious intervention' for those children who present with symptoms of conduct disorder and ODD. Children who attend nurture groups are much more likely to gain from their experience and to go on to be better learners. In essence, their emotional intelligence is likely to develop more.

It is worth, at this point, drawing attention to the concept of Nurture Groups that has developed within the UK over recent years, with there now being well over a thousand of these. Having their basis within the area of 'attachment', the rationale that underpins Nurture Groups is that of understanding the gaps in young children's emotional and social development and problems they may have with establishing secure attachments to others. Nurture Groups work to meet the particular and individual needs of preschool children, many of whom have been born into dysfunctional families and have lacked access to positive parenting models and secure and positive relationship formation. It is generally recognized that these Nurture Groups have been very successful. Cowie (2012), for example, cites a number of evaluations of Nurture Groups (Cooper and Whitbread, 2007; Ofsted, 2011) who have reported very positive outcomes of the work in Nurture Groups, particularly in terms of the children making better transitions to primary schooling, engaging more positively with their peers and adults and presenting with behaviours that suggest more secure attachment.

The implications for the learning of these children are immense. Children who learn to manage their emotions and behaviours will be more productive learners and should gain more from their time at school. In addition, it is probable that their behaviours in the classroom will be less disruptive of others, thus allowing their peers to gain more from their lessons. One particular initiative that is increasingly being used in schools is the Social and Emotional Aspects of Learning programme, more commonly referred to as SEAL, which aims to promote those social and emotional skills considered to contribute to purposeful and effective learning, positive behaviour and the emotional health and well-being of pupils.

ENGLISH AS AN ADDITIONAL LANGUAGE: THE CHALLENGES

Just under five years ago it was estimated (DCSF, 2009) that in England alone there were around 856,670 children in schools learning English as an Additional Language (EAL), suggesting 200 different native languages. Pupils with EAL were considered to represent just over 15 per cent of the primary population and 11 per cent of the secondary school population in England. Within inner London, it was estimated that just over 50 per cent of pupils were learning English as an additional language. In other parts of the UK it was recognized that there was also a growing number of children in schools who were learning English as an Additional Language. For example, in Northern Ireland inward migration over the past two decades has had a significant impact on schools. Figures released by the Department of Education Northern Ireland (DENI, 2010) suggested that there had been a six-fold increase in what was termed 'newcomer children' between 2001–2 and 2009–10 in 2001/2, 1,366 children and 2009/10, 7,899 children in all schools in Northern Ireland, with the majority of these newcomer children being educated in primary schools. Whilst in previous decades immigrants had come to Northern Ireland for short periods of employment, government statistics have indicated that families were now intending to settle and rear their families in this part of the UK. A recent interview with a specialist EAL teacher working across a wide range of schools offered the following:

> **Example**
>
> What factors do you think contribute to effective learning for children with EAL in schools?
> *I would say for someone to take the lead for that specific group of children and their families...it often falls into the role of the SENCo ... I would say that is bad practice ... I think it works best if the EAL coordinator or the person with responsibility for EAL is someone else ... there's also that stereotyping, oh yeah EAL children they're below average, stick them in the bottom groups ... if you think of good role models for speech and language then lumping them in with your bottom group, your SEN group, well it's not the best role models ... and good examples of English tend to be found in your middle or above average groups ...*
> Have you identified examples that you consider to be good practice?
> *Where a school sees EAL as a whole school issue rather than the responsibility of one person ... so that the coordinator's role is to facilitate but not to take control of the assessment, the resourcing, contacting parents ... the class teacher should be responsible for this ...*
> Why do you think it works better in some schools than others?
> *I would say it is because they have embraced EAL, multiculturalism as a positive rather than, ah – oh no! There's these children who can't speak English ... it's schools who have brought EAL children and their families into their community ... they support the families with, for example, buying school uniforms, filling in forms, they see EAL as a bonus not an add on ... it's an attitude, obviously it comes from the head teacher down ... you can see in some schools they foster that multicultural ethos and they are proud of it ... they have events, they have parents in to share their own cultures ...*
> What factors prevent effective learning for EAL children in schools?
> *I think if it's the role of one person ... in the past there was a lot more support ... the economy is having a significant effect as Local Authorities are being cut back ... and that pastoral and emotional support has completely gone in some areas ... it is now the responsibility of the school ... there's no accountability now for the spending of the money that used to go to Local Authorities that now goes directly to schools ...*

The above interview emphasizes a number of key points in regard to EAL. Firstly, meeting the needs of children with EAL should be a whole school responsibility, led from the senior management, and not the responsibility of one member of staff. Secondly, the school should seek to embrace the child's culture as well as their family as part of the school community. Thirdly, this group of children is not a separate homogenous group but should be recognized as having differing individual needs. Fourthly, these children should not be 'lumped' together with children with special educational needs and/or disabilities. In offering advice to teachers in secondary schools, Brooks et al. (2004, p. 275) comment that:

You are likely to come across two main categories of pupils learning EAL:

- Those who were born in Britain and who have progressed through the education system. Some of these pupils may have entered school with little or no English;

- Those who have recently arrived in this country either because their families are seeking asylum or because one or both of their parents is studying or working in the United Kingdom.

Kenner (2006, p. 75) quotes Saxena (1994) who describes a typical day experienced by a four-year-old child from a Panjabi family living in Southall, London:

> This boy observes his parents and grandparents reading newspapers and novels, and writing letters and shopping lists in Panjabi, Hindi and English. As a result, he can distinguish between three different types of script, although his school literacy experience is restricted to English only.

Teachers may not always be fully aware of the range of language and literacies that many children use and there may be scarce opportunities for children to use or even develop the range of literacies they have acquired within their school settings. Brook et al. (2004) also make the point that the acquisition of EAL depends, amongst other factors, upon the child's own proficiency in their own first language.

RESOURCING LEARNERS AND LEARNING

It is a common complaint made by many teachers and Early Years practitioners that there are never enough resources. Often one hears the case that class sizes are too large, that there is a lack of ICT equipment such as personal computers and that more additional adults are required to work within the classroom. The challenges that face many teachers in meeting the needs of their pupils can be many and, in some cases, can affect the motivation and morale of teachers, especially those in their first years of teaching. Most practitioners would argue the case for more resourcing in terms of equipment, additional staffing, space and ICT. Indeed, different schools and Early Years settings engage with the challenges of resourcing on a yearly if not monthly and even daily basis.

All too often, however, the identification and assessment of children with additional needs is driven by a desire for additional resources, which in some cases can mean that assessment becomes more about the pursuit of, for example, additional adults working in the classroom than accurate assessment with subsequent and appropriate intervention strategies being put in place.

Summary

The past three decades have seen the emergence of new and more sophisticated ways of thinking about children with additional needs. Legislation, combined with research and a willingness to explore and understand the learning of children, has meant that practitioners and schools have embraced the challenges of working with children with a range of special educational needs and/or disabilities, as well as those children with special needs and especially those children in the UK whose first language is not English.

To effectively meet the needs of children presenting with such conditions as dyslexia and dyspraxia requires that schools and Early Years settings are properly resourced and that practitioners are adequately trained and prepared to meet the widening and diverse range of difficulties, learning styles, parenting, and so on, that characterize the learning and early development of many young children today.

Exercises

- Take time to critically reflect upon and evaluate the statement that 'teaching is a caring profession'.
- In the light of our growing understanding of conditions affecting children's learning, critically reflect upon the view that too many teachers and Early Years practitioners need to be much better prepared to work with children with additional needs.

RECOMMENDED READING

Attwood, T. (2007) *The Complete Guide to Asperger's Syndrome.* London: Jessica Kingsley.
Boon, M. (2010) *Understanding Dyspraxia: A Guide for Parents and Teachers* (2nd edn). London: Jessica Kingsley.
Chinn, S. (2012) *The Trouble with Maths: A Practical Guide to Helping Learners with Numeracy Difficulties* (2nd edn). London: Routledge.

REFERENCES

Attwood, T. (1993) *Asperger's Syndrome: A Guide for Parents and Professionals.* London: Jessica Kingsley.
Attwood, T. (2007) *The Complete Guide to Asperger's Syndrome.* London: Jessica Kingsley.
Boon, M. (2010) *Understanding Dyspraxia: A Guide for Parents and Teachers* (2nd edn). London: Jessica Kingsley.

British Dyslexia Association (BDA) (2012) *Dyscalculia, Dyslexia and Maths*. Available at: http://www.bdadyslexia.org.uk/about-dyslexia/schools-colleges-and-universities/dyscalculia.html (accessed: 9 January 2013).

Brooks, V., Abbott, I. and Bills, L. (2004) *Preparing to Teach in Secondary Schools*. Maidenhead: Open University Press.

Chinn, S. (2009) Dyscalculia and learning difficulties in mathematics. In G. Reid (ed.) *The Routledge Companion to Dyslexia*. New York: Routledge.

Clark, L. (2012) Nurseries label one-year-olds 'special needs', *Daily Mail*, 13 July, p. 12.

Cowie, H. (2012) *From Birth to Sixteen: Children's Health, Social, Emotional and Linguistic Development*. London: Routledge.

CYPMHC (2012) *Resilience and Results: How to Improve the Emotional and Mental Wellbeing of Children and Young People in Your School*. The Children and Young People's Mental Health Coalition, 25 September.

Everatt, J. and Reid, G. (2009) Dyslexia: an overview of recent research. In G. Reid (ed.) *The Routledge Companion to Dyslexia*. New York: Routledge.

Crombie, M. and Reid, G. (2009) The role of early identification models from research and practice. In G. Reid (ed.) *The Routledge Companion to Dyslexia*. New York: Routledge.

Department for Children, Schools and Families (DCSF) (2009) *Statistical First Release*, August 2009. London: DCSF.

Department of Education Northern Ireland (DENI) (2010) *Statistics on Education*. Bangor: DENI.

Drysdale, J. (2009) Overcoming the barriers to literacy: an integrated, contextual workshop approach. In G. Reid (ed.) *The Routledge Companion to Dyslexia*. New York: Routledge.

Fenton, B. (2006) Junk culture 'is poisoning our children', *Daily Telegraph*, 12 September, p. 1.

Frederickson, N. and Cline, T. (2002) *Special Educational Needs, Inclusion and Diversity*. Maidenhead: Open University Press.

Gray, C. and MacBlain, S.F. (2012) *Learning Theories in Childhood*. London: Sage.

Herbert, M. (2005) *Developmental Problems of Childhood and Adolescence: Prevention, Treatment and Training*. Oxford: Blackwell.

Kring, A., Johnson, S., Davison, G., Neale, J., Edelstyn, N. and Brown, D. (2013) *Abnormal Psychology* (12th edn). Singapore: John Wiley & Sons.

Kenner, C. (2006) Using home texts to promote L1 and L2 literacy learning in the classroom. In T.M. Hickey (ed.) *Literacy and Language Learning: Reading in a First or Second Language*. Dublin: Reading Association of Ireland.

Lawson, W. (2013) Remembering school. In M. Prior (ed.) *Learning and Behavior Problems in Asperger Syndrome*. New York: The Guilford Press.

Long, L., MacBlain, S.F. and MacBlain, M.S. (2007) Supporting students with dyslexia at secondary level: an emotional model of literacy, *Journal of Adolescent and Adult Literacy*, 15(2): 124–34.

MacBlain, S.F., Hazzard, K. and MacBlain, F. (2005) Dyslexia: the ethics of assessment, *Academic Exchange Quarterly*, 9(1).

MacBlain, S.F., O'Neill, A., Weir, K. and MacBlain, M. (2006) Supporting pupils with dyslexia: emotional or mechanistic approaches to literacy. In T.M. Hickey, (ed.) *Literacy and Language Learning: Reading in a First or Second Language*. Dublin: Reading Association of Ireland.

MacBlain, S.F. and MacBlain, A.D. (2011) *Letters Form Words*. Plymouth: SMB Associates SW (enquiries@seanmacblain.com).

Macintyre, C. (2002) *Play for Children with Special Needs: Including Children Aged 3–8*. London: David Fulton.

Macintyre, C. and McVitty, K. (2004) *Movement and Learning in the Early Years: Supporting Dyspraxia (DCD) and Other Difficulties*. London: Paul Chapman.

Mayes, S.D. and Calhoun, S.L. (2003) Relationship between Asperger Syndrome and high-functioning autism. In M. Prior (ed.) *Learning and Behaviour Problems in Asperger Syndrome*. New York: The Guilford Press.

Office for Standards in Education (Ofsted) (2010) *The Special Educational Needs and Disability Review*. London: Ofsted.

Prior, M. (2003) (ed.) *Learning and Behavior Problems in Asperger Syndrome*. New York: The Guilford Press.

Pumfrey, P. and Reason, R. (1991) *Specific Learning Difficulties (Dyslexia): Challenges and Responses*. London: Routledge.

Reid, G. (ed.) (2009) *The Routledge Companion to Dyslexia*. New York: Routledge.

Reid, G. and Came, F. (2009) Identifying and overcoming the barriers to learning in an inclusive context. In G. Reid (ed.) *The Routledge Companion to Dyslexia*. New York: Routledge.

Stanford, P. (2012) Can 20% of school children really have special needs? *Daily Telegraph*, 12 May, p. 23.

Westwood, P. (1993) *Commonsense Methods for Children with Special Needs*. London: Routledge.

Whitebread, D. (2012) *Developmental Psychology and Early Childhood Education*. London: Sage.

COMMUNITIES OF LEARNING

INTRODUCTION

Children from the moment of birth belong to communities, most typically their immediate family and their extended family. It is within these communities that their learning first begins. Not only do they learn language and facts about the world around them but they also learn to be part of these communities and to understand their place and the role they must play. For example, children learn to be younger brothers or sisters, nephews or nieces and grandchildren. This is an important aspect of their learning and prepares them for the time when they make the transition to external communities such as playgroups, nursery schools, primary schools, church groups, and so on. Rather worryingly though, many children, even from a very young age, are tasked with taking on the role of carer, often for a very ill parent. For them, the demands of the family community within which they grow up can be extremely challenging.

Being a part of various communities enables young children to learn how to adapt to the role of learner, which they will need as they progress throughout their formal education. In particular, children come to learn how to interact with adults, who in teaching/learning relationships have a much greater degree of power and authority. In this way, it can be argued that children are prepared to become effective citizens and responsible members of their wider social communities and society as a whole.

Early Years settings and schools, therefore, play a significant role in preparing children for their future role as adults and, more importantly perhaps, as parents. Adults working in Early Years settings and schools will typically model appropriate behaviours and ways of acting in different situations, effective and purposeful language, the managing of emotions, positive relationships and interactions, and so on.

The degree to which Early Years settings and schools actively and purposefully involve children in understanding their own involvement in this learning process and thinking independently is extremely important. In one sense, they are giving children a voice and in doing so developing their unique identity as individuals and as future members of the communities in which they will live and work. This natural, but complex, process begins in the family, and the extent and degree to which children take up and engage with this process when at school will be influenced by early experiences in their family. It is for this very reason that practitioners in Early Years settings and teachers have sought to develop close links between, and partnerships with, parents.

Drawing upon findings of *The Home School Knowledge Exchange Project* which explored how valuable learning experiences in the home and school could be brought together for young children, Cox (2011, p. 117) has offered some practical means by which this might be attempted, together with some of the challenges that exist around the perceived balance of power between parents and teachers:

> One way that this was achieved in practice was for children to bring into school shoeboxes of artefacts that were important to them; another was giving disposable cameras to the children to record aspects of their own lives of their own choosing. It is interesting that both teachers and parents initially found it difficult to accept the idea of the 'transfer of knowledge' from the home to the school, reflecting the established balance of power.

Not all children in the UK, however, follow the same path throughout their education. Some will be taught in state primary and secondary schools whilst others will attend independent schools, newly formed academies or *Free* schools. Some will even be educated almost totally at home. There are those who will attend Grammar Schools and Comprehensive Schools or *Faith* Schools, whilst others will attend schools belonging to the Steiner tradition, and so on. The way in which children are educated in the UK and the learning communities to which they belong are diverse and appear to be increasing in their diversity. There are those who argue that it is right and just for all children to belong to the same education system, whilst others celebrate the diversity of communities into which young children are introduced and come to be educated.

This chapter now explores a number of issues, debates and dilemmas that underpin our perceptions of communities of learning, beginning with an examination of the contribution that a number of key factors can make to effective learning communities, before identifying economic and social factors that impact upon these communities. The chapter then explores issues surrounding segregation, with particular emphasis being given to the place of Grammar Schools, newly formed Academies and the Independent sector often referred to as 'private' schools. Consideration is also given to the increase in immigration in the UK and the impact this has on communities of learning.

CREATING EFFECTIVE LEARNING ENVIRONMENTS

What is an effective learning environment? A useful starting point in considering this question is to reflect upon why young children might gain success in one environment whilst experiencing failure in another. Equally, consideration might also be given as to why some children appear to experience significant levels of failure in particular learning environments whilst their peers appear to achieve significant levels of success. Are success and failure, therefore, due to children's abilities, motivation and backgrounds or are they in some significant way connected with the environments in which they learn? The creation of effective communities of learning needs to be explored against those challenges that currently face, not only schools, but society as a whole.

When one begins to critically engage in a consideration of the nature of the environments in which children learn, such a task takes on much greater proportions. The range of environments in which children learn is enormous. It is worth readers taking some time to reflect upon the different learning environments they themselves have experienced, as well as those they have heard of in the course of their reading or through talking with others or simply by tuning into different television programmes reporting on children throughout the world. What is also worth considering is the manner in which learning environments within the UK have changed over the last decades and since the beginning of the 20th century. Once tasked with sitting quietly in rows for hours and being fearful of speaking in case of receiving physical punishment from a teacher, children now sit in groups in their classrooms and are encouraged to talk and express themselves. It would be fairly safe to propose the view that schools are now much happier places than they were 30 or 40 years ago. This said, learning communities such as schools and Early Years settings are now also faced with challenges that did not face teachers decades ago and which alter the nature of those communities in quite radical ways.

The past three decades have witnessed an increasing diversity of children's needs in schools and Early Years settings, which can be related to the growing numbers of children with special educational needs (SEN) attending mainstream schools following international strides towards greater inclusion (UNICEF, 1989; UNE-SCO, 1994) in addition to more recent legislation in the UK (SENDA, 2001). In England, for example, it was estimated that in 2008 there were slightly fewer than one and a half million children with SEN, around 20 per cent of the school population. More than half of the children in England with Statements of Special Educational Needs (just under quarter of a million) were, in the same year, attending mainstream school (DCSF, 2008) – these are children who decades ago would more than likely have been placed in special schools. In other parts of the UK, for example Northern Ireland, there were in 2009 around 60,000 pupils with SEN (just under 20 per cent of the school population) (DENI, 2009), with over 60 per cent of pupils with Statements of Special Educational Needs being placed in mainstream schools.

More recently, the Department for Education (DfE) (2012a) reported that in primary schools funded by the state the most frequent types of primary need were: Speech, Language and Communication (29.1 per cent), Moderate Learning Difficulty (21.8 per cent), and Behaviour, Emotional and Social Difficulties (18.6 per cent). The DfE also reported that in secondary schools that were state funded the three most common types of primary need were: Behaviour, Emotional and Social Difficulties (29 per cent) followed by Moderate Learning Difficulties (22.7 per cent) and Specific Learning Difficulties (15.9 per cent). Rather surprisingly given the push to move children with special educational needs and/or disabilities into mainstream schools, the DfE also reported that whilst the most common types of primary need in special schools were Severe Learning Difficulties (24.6 per cent) followed by Autistic Spectrum Disorder (20.4 per cent), the category of Moderate Learning Difficulties made up 18.6 per cent. Children with Moderate Learning Difficulties have been that group of children who have, over the last decades and especially since legislation in the early 1980s, been moved out of special schools and into mainstream education. Added to the growing number of children with SEN in mainstream schools has been the growth in numbers of children learning English as an Additional Language (discussed in Chapter 8).

At this point it is worth making an important distinction between Special Educational Needs and Special Needs. In drawing upon the work of Robson (1989), Frederickson and Cline (2002, p. 37) offer the following:

> In the case of black and ethnic minority groups, Robson (1989) has suggested four areas in which special or additional needs may be identified without any implication that individual pupils have learning difficulties in the same sense as those with SEN:
>
> 1. *language* – a particular need for help with English and, if possible, with the development and maintenance of their first language(s);
>
> 2. *culture* – a particular need for the school curriculum to include reference to and respect for a broad cultural range, including their own cultural heritage.

3. *overt racism* – a particular need for support from the school in opposing racist behaviour and in promoting a positive picture of other cultures.

4. *socioeconomic disadvantage* – a particular need for educational policies and provision that combat the negative effects of socioeconomic disadvantage on school achievement.

All of these special needs are group phenomena … In this sense they are distinct from the individual experience of learning difficulty that is the foundation of SEN.

It almost goes without saying that practitioners working with children with special needs should not rush to make judgements about their abilities and potential but should seek to properly assess each child's needs and then determine the best and most effective means of meeting that child's needs. If we take Robson's first area above, that of *language,* it will be important, for example, that teachers fully recognize and understand the difficulties that some children with special needs might experience and, thereby, maintain high expectations in all areas of the curriculum. This is equally the case with Robson's fourth category, that of *socioeconomic disadvantage,* where teachers might have low expectations of children's abilities when in fact some children who are socioeconomically disadvantaged may fail to progress because they do not have the facilities at home to properly complete homework tasks, because there is little if any emphasis upon reading at home, and they may have little if any access to ICT other than at school.

A further consideration in exploring what factors contribute to the creation of effective learning environments is the extent to which teachers and Early Years practitioners reflect upon and critically engage with their own practice, the learning that occurs within the environments they create, and the nature of the pedagogies and contexts created by their schools and settings. Researching their own practice is, some would strongly argue, a very necessary part of the role of an effective teacher. Research is also central to the knowledge and skills base of teachers. As students, they will themselves have been expected to become familiar with various theoretical viewpoints and to have read the work of researchers investigating learning and teaching. They will also have been expected to critically evaluate and synthesize selected research through discussion in seminars and tutorials, and through written assignments. As practitioners, teachers are expected to keep abreast of new developments in the field of education, usually through attending in-service training and reading.

Despite accessing new learning and updating their skills, many teachers, however, may not perceive the possibilities that researching their own practice and their working environments can offer. Some, in fact, may view themselves as consumers of research and believe that research should really be the domain of academics working in colleges and universities. It can be argued, however, that all teachers have the potential to conduct relevant, useful and significant research. What they may need, however, are the tools to conduct research and, perhaps more importantly, methodologies that are accessible to them and which they can relate to as practitioners. Such a view, of course, has enormous implications for teachers and, perhaps more importantly, student teachers in training who will be entering the teaching profession over the next years. All teachers are in a privileged position to promote change (Kearns, 2003), which will benefit children within the learning communities of which they are a part as well as wider social communities and society as a whole. As researchers they can seek to understand this process in more detail and at a more critical level. In doing so, they can gain greater confidence in their own abilities and create even better and more effective learning environments for the children they teach.

Each day, teachers involve themselves, wittingly or unwittingly, in the life stories of their pupils. They do this at a variety of levels, and in doing so they exert power and influence that can be significant. Teachers, perhaps now more than ever before, are seeking to understand the didactic and dynamic nature of their work with children in what is an increasingly complex society. This has led many teachers to move away from focusing more on delivering a curriculum to understanding those complex social processes of which they themselves are a dialectical part (Kearns, 2003). The interactions between teachers and their pupils, and particularly the emotional and sensory elements they experience on a daily basis, do not, however, come about as isolated fragments of experience. Rather, they exist as connected and interrelated events or episodes in the evolving stories or biographies of the children they work with (Schostak, 1985). Every day, teachers and pupils share with one another verbal accounts of events as experienced by themselves in relation to others. Teachers, therefore, can be viewed as playing a unique and central role in how pupils construct their world views and come to internalize new understandings and self-knowledge. To this extent, it can be proposed that teachers have available to them increased opportunities to redefine themselves as teacher-researchers, and in doing so create more effective learning environments.

Teachers experience interactions with pupils and interpret that experience through the structure of their own life histories, their needs and drives, and through their life interests, motivations, relationships, and so on. When they come to relate events to others, for example other teachers or professionals such as educational psychologists or social workers, they may do so in ways that become accounts with a narrative structure. Accounts, then, can serve as central structuring devices through which experiences become interpreted. Narrative accounts, therefore, and the process of telling a story, can become key methodological devices, which are used to represent, explain and comprehend the social world within which teachers and their pupils exist. Constructing such accounts, therefore, can offer a powerful research method by which teachers, acting as researchers, can pull together the complex worlds of their pupils. Narrative accounts of particular cases can also offer teachers a medium which is easily recognized, interpreted and evaluated by others. The benefits can be far-reaching. As long ago as the 1970s, the celebrated educationalist Lawrence Stenhouse (1975, p. 78) commented as follows:

> The portrayal of cases offers to inform the judgement of … administrators, teachers, pupils or parents … by opening the research accounts to recognition and to comparison and hence to criticism in the light of experience.

When accounts are narrated, they do not stand alone but exist within a tradition, most commonly the tradition of that particular school or community, and become reference points to other accounts. This is also the case where accounts are narrated as texts such as reports, though with text time can be taken to reflect and organize thoughts, to draft and redraft. Accounts, therefore, exist in history and within wider cultures, which have at their heart those uses of language and discourse that occur between individuals, and within specific social contexts. Often, schools and those working within them will have devised their own aspects of language to explain phenomena to one another. Individuals, however, exist only in relation to others, and those relationships through which their life experiences have been constructed and expressed. Indeed, social contexts such as schools or Early Years settings exist only because there are individuals who create them.

Teachers and Early Years practitioners may often use anecdotes to share narrative accounts of sequences of behaviours and actions involving children and their families. Anecdotes, it can be argued, do have structures within themselves and can relate to other anecdotes as well as to the unique conceptual schema of the adults sharing them. They are never just personal to an individual but also refer to, and in the narrating come to form a part of, the social and cultural heritage of the school or community within which the individual exists. Anecdotes, therefore, have meaning as well as a social function, in addition to personal significance. Indeed, individuals, in their social conversations, frequently employ anecdotes as one of their many repertoires. Without anecdotes, individuals might even be construed as being socially illiterate. Anecdotes, therefore, can provide insights for the teacher and Early Years practitioner into how children in their care structure their experiences within the context of their own unique interests. They also offer insights into how children's social and physical environments impact upon their consciousness, and upon their needs, desires and motivations (Schostak, 1985, 1986).

ECONOMIC AND SOCIAL FACTORS AND THEIR IMPACT UPON COMMUNITIES OF LEARNERS

As indicated earlier, all children start their lives in communities, most typically the home. The nature of their communities, however, can vary dramatically with, for example, the number of others living there, the number of rooms available to siblings, garden space for play activities and privacy, whether the home is in a rural or urban setting, and so on. Two key elements, however, that affect the nature of homes and that can impact directly upon the development of children and their learning, are economic and social factors. Whilst some children have access to much comfort, good diets and a strong sense of security and stability from the outset, there are also many who do not and who grow up in homes characterized by economic deprivation. In a recent report, *Deprivation and Risk: The Case for Early Intervention* published by Action for Children (2010), Dr Ruth Lupton wrote as follows:

> The relationship between deprivation and educational attainment is striking. Across the UK, children from the poorest homes start school with more limited vocabularies and greater likelihood of conduct problems and hyperactivity ... During primary school UK children fall further behind, and even the brightest children from the most disadvantaged backgrounds are overtaken by the age of 10 by their better-off peers who start off behind them ... (Action for Children, 2010, p. 12)

Lupton goes on to emphasize the fact that the level of parental financial income is not the only factor that adversely affects the development of children in families. She stresses the importance of the environment that is created within the family and the crucial fact that positive and effective environments can, in fact, greatly militate against disadvantage. She stresses, for example, how regular reading to young children around the age of three, '... matters twice as much for their development by age five as family income'.

Drawing upon a recent study by Cullis and Hansen (2009) Lupton, rather worryingly, comments on the importance of financial income within families, particularly after birth and in the first months and year of life:

> Recent research shows that every £100 of additional income in the first nine months of life makes the difference of about a month's development by age five. The poorest families cannot afford books, computers, equipment and extracurricular activities and their children's education is also more likely to suffer from poorer nutrition, household overcrowding and stress. (Action for Children 2010, p. 13)

Such statements are clearly very concerning and readers will no doubt reflect upon the degree and extent to which parents throughout the UK and the Western industrialized world are experiencing increasing financial hardship as austerity bites and major economies face possible recession. It almost goes without saying that many more low income families now face significant problems in buying books for their children, providing them with computers, and funding out-of-school activities that would develop their children's learning and general knowledge, as well as in the provision of adequate living space in what may well be overcrowded homes, and so on. In addition, there appears to be a growth throughout the UK of centres that have been established to provide basic food stuffs to families who are experiencing poverty. The impact of all of these factors, including the impact upon children's diets and the subsequent knock-on effect this has upon their learning, is an unfolding factor that deserves much greater scrutiny. A growing concern in the UK, as in other countries, is the stress that many parents are increasingly experiencing in regard to facing possible unemployment and the problems that go hand-in-hand with this, most particularly having their homes repossessed. The effects upon children of living in such homes must be significant.

The effects of austerity in the UK can be seen in most places, with schools being no exception. Services that were once readily available have been increasingly cut, with more schools now having to 'buy in' services such as those offered previously by Educational Psychology services employed by Local Authorities. School budgets are now under closer scrutiny than ever before, with many head teachers having to face the challenges that are being brought about by the wider economic and social factors that are contributing to increased poverty in some areas, most worryingly perhaps the growth in the drug culture that appears to permeate many areas of society and defines some more socially and economically deprived communities. In many respects the challenges facing teachers and schools, as well as parents, in the 21st century are considerable and require new ways of understanding childhood and the learning paths that are taken by many children.

One group of children who deserve much greater attention are those who from an early age are tasked with caring for other members of their family, most typically perhaps a parent who suffers from very ill health. In order to more fully understand the nature of their life experiences it is useful to consider what is generally perceived to be the course of 'normal' development. A useful entry point can be found in the work of the celebrated psychologist Erik Erickson, whose work, though mostly associated with the 1980s and 1990s is, nonetheless, still relevant today.

Erikson viewed the course of normal development as progressing through eight stages (the first five are especially relevant to our understanding of learning in children). His theory, known as the Theory of Psychosocial Development proposed that when individuals move successfully through each stage they achieve balance and develop healthy personalities. However, he also proposed that when individuals do not move successfully through these stages the result is that they fail to develop personalities that are healthy. His theory has significant implications for helping us to understand the lives and more specifically the learning opportunities and barriers that confront many children tasked with caring for another family member.

Stage 1. Trust versus Mistrust (birth to 1 year). Erikson suggested that during this stage young children develop a sense of trust in the world around them and especially in relation to those who care for them. At this stage, trust is largely dependent upon the consistency and reliability of the care that is given and received. Erikson argues children who receive this type and quality of care learn to take this into their own future relationships and in doing so develop a strong sense of security. If the care, however, lacks consistency and reliability then the child learns to mistrust, and will, again, carry this into their own future relationships with the result that they may acquire and internalize associated anxieties.

Stage 2. Autonomy versus Shame and Doubt (2 to 3 years). It is during this next stage that Erikson proposed children develop independence and autonomy. They are now learning to walk and run and can put physical distance between themselves and their immediate caregivers. They are learning that they can have choice concerning, for example, what they eat, how they play, and so on. Play is now becoming very important, with the manner of play being engaged in being characterized increasingly by their interactions with others. Parents play an important part at this stage in supporting their children's growth towards independence and in providing them with important opportunities to gain success and thereby develop their self-confidence and self-efficacy. Successful progression through this stage leads to confidence and security. Unsuccessful progression, however, through this stage, where, for example, children are scolded and overly disciplined or 'put down' by their immediate caregivers can lead later on in life to over dependency on others, feelings of self-doubt and low self-esteem.

The implications at this stage for children who live in a household where an older sibling may be tasked with caring for others can be significant. It is usual at this stage for parents to introduce their children to community toddler groups, pre-school playgroups, nurseries, and so on. In the case of a child, for example, who has a mother with mental health issues such as acute phobias or who is confined to bed, these experiences may at best be very limited and at worst non-existent. For some parents, this will be a cause of distress as their child is visibly seen to be missing out on opportunities that are readily available to other children. Some parents who are being cared for by their children may even feel very isolated and at times may, because of stress, be overly critical of their children, even mistaking the child's failings for an unwillingness to be helpful.

Stage 3. Initiative versus Guilt (3 to 5 years). During this next stage children are still developing at a rapid pace. Their language is improving and they are internalizing the ability to empathize with those around them and to be empathetic. Parents who are being cared for may try to restrict the activities of their children either because they are concerned about potential risks or because they simply do not have the capacity to physically support their children with such activities. Because of this the child's social and physical experiences may be very limited as they come to spend more time indoors. In addition, a parent who is being cared for may, because of their own stress and anxiety, exert too much restriction on the child and even punishment. At this stage, over-control will, Erikson suggested, result in feelings of guilt within the growing child, which are frequently manifested as lack of initiative.

It is during this stage that children can be observed to typically engage in asking lots of questions. Should the child's requests for answers and knowledge go unheeded then the child's questions will fail to have been given the appropriate status and again feelings of guilt, accompanied by embarrassment and even shame may follow and reduce the degree to which the child then seeks to interact with those around them. Difficulties at this stage might be linked directly to a lessening of creativity in the child. It is at this stage that children also begin to acquire a sense of purpose. Implications for children who are tasked with caring can be many. They may, for example, become limited in expressing their own emotional needs. Creativity may be adversely impaired and they may find it increasingly difficult to develop a sense of purpose in their lives and in what they do from day to day. For the child's parent, important opportunities to move their child on beyond the 'baby' stage may be very restricted.

Stage 4. Industry versus Inferiority (6 to 12 years). During this stage children are now attending primary school and the nature of their learning is much more formal. Their teacher and their immediate peer group have now become very important role models and come to guide much of the child's own activities. Winning the approval of their peers at this stage of development is hugely important, as it is through this that the child develops their sense of pride in who they are and in what they can do. Successful progression through this stage leads to children acquiring feelings of being confident and industrious, with growing confidence in what they feel they can succeed at. Unsuccessful progression through this stage typically results in feelings of inferiority and self-doubt. It is also during this stage that children come to develop their sense of competence. Many children who are tasked with caring may have limited time to spend with their peers and may, throughout their days at school, find their minds drifting back to the person they are caring for, with strong feelings of anxiety and worry, which will affect their concentration and their learning, and even their enjoyment of school and spending time with their classmates

5. Identity versus Role Confusion (13–18 years). All readers will appreciate the importance of transition from adolescence to adulthood. At this stage children typically gain much more independence and develop new and different types of relationships. They start to look more actively towards their futures. For children who are caring this may not prove to be the case as they are caught up daily with spending their free time outside of school at home looking after a family member. Erikson saw this stage as being central to the formation of identity and suggested that there were two key identities that were formed during this stage, namely, sexual identity and occupational identity. The child's physicality is altering and successful progression through this stage, he argued, leads to fidelity.

Example

Pedro is eight years of age and lives at home with his mother who has a serious debilitating illness. Each day before going to school he helps his mother out of bed and helps to wash her. He then makes some sandwiches for his mother and prepares some vegetables that will be ready for the evening meal, which he cooks when he returns home each day from school. He rarely plays outside with his friends after school and is too embarrassed to tell them what he does at home to help his mother. He dearly loves his mother but spends a lot of his time being frightened as he finds himself thinking that he might return from school one day to find that she has died.

Exercise

Considering this example, should staff at Pedro's school know about his situation and if so how involved should they become?

LEARNING AND SEGREGATION: NEW PATHWAYS TO LEARNING

Segregating children for the purpose of learning can be observed almost everywhere. But what do we mean by the term segregation? Take the system of education in Northern Ireland, for example, where many children attend different schools based on their parents' religious beliefs, where many boys and girls attend single sex schools, where children are separated at about the age of 11 to attend highly academic grammar schools, and where many children with special educational needs and/or disabilities attend special schools. In England there has been a growth in the number of Faith Schools in the past decades with parents choosing to send their children to these schools. With the recent introduction of Free Schools parents and children now have even greater choice. All of this will mean that in practice some children growing up together in the same Early Years setting or primary school may become separated from their friends as a result of the choice made by their parents to send them to a different type of school. But is this segregation?

The whole concept of Free Schools, which are an extension of the Academies Programme, whilst not entirely new is, however, an important development as it is a concept that is being supported by the current Coalition Government in the UK. The Department for Education (DfE) website (2013) offers the following in regard to Free Schools and demonstrates the high level of support it is giving this initiative:

> Free Schools are all-ability state-funded schools set up in response to what local people say they want and need in order to improve education for children in their community. The right school can transform a child's life and help them achieve things they may never have imagined. Through the Free Schools programme it is now much easier for talented and committed teachers, charities, parents and education experts to open schools to address real demand within an area.

Free schools can be established by groups such as parent groups, charities, religious groups, and so on, who submit their application to the Department of Education. Start-up grants are provided and funding is in line with locally controlled schools maintained by the state. Free Schools are expected to offer a broad and balanced curriculum and are subject to inspections by Ofsted.

Writing in the popular UK newspaper the *Telegraph* in April 2013, the paper's Education Editor, Graeme Paton, drew public attention to the fact that there appeared to be a significant increase in demand for places at Free Schools. He wrote as follows:

> Figures released by the Department for Education show that almost nine-in-10 of the schools – new primaries and secondaries established by parents' groups and charities – received more applications than places for September. Overall, an average of three pupils are competing for each place at free schools, it was revealed. The most popular school, West London Free School in Hammersmith, had 1,196 applications for just 120 places – leaving 10 pupils competing for every spare desk. Dixons Trinity Academy in Bradford had 676 applications for 112 places – a ratio of around six-to-one. Ministers insisted that the figures showed 'how popular free schools are with parents'. (Paton, 2013)

There can be little doubt that the whole concept of Free Schools, which has existed for some time in other countries such as Sweden, is controversial. Within the UK, views are very divided, with some suggesting that these new schools will increase segregation and division whilst others see them as a necessary and appropriate response to the desires and wishes of parents. Only time will tell.

A further consideration when discussing learning and segregation is that of special school versus mainstream school. Throughout the past decades policy and decision makers, academics, practitioners, theorists and the general public have been challenged by the notion of 'inclusion' and whether children's needs are best served in mainstream schools or in 'special' schools. As yet, no definitive position has been reached and debate still rages over this topic. Within 'special' schools children with complex needs have been catered for by having significantly smaller class sizes, a much higher teacher – pupil ratio and, most typically, additional specialist resources. However, in the last decades and especially since the publication of the seminal Warnock Report in 1978, there has been a significant 'push' to include children who would have previously attended 'special' schools within mainstream schools.

A particular feature at the centre of this debate has been the view that children who attend 'special' schools are typically part of much smaller communities of learning where their individual needs can be more readily assessed and understood, and where there is more time and more resources to implement necessary and effective interventions. In many instances parents are very pleased that their children attend these smaller communities of learning where there are more opportunities, especially at post-primary level, to get to know the school staff, which may include, for example, Speech and Language Therapists or Physiotherapists, and to become more directly involved in their children's education. Other parents, however, strive to have their children moved from 'special' schools and attend mainstream schools where they feel they will be part of the mainstream population of children. This situation is not easy to resolve and different practitioners continue to have different, and often very strong, views about whether 'special' schools have a purpose that is in line with thinking in the 21st century. What is interesting, however, is the fact that there is an emerging move from some quarters to open Free Schools that will serve as communities of learning for children with a wide range of special educational needs and/or disabilities.

Now let us turn to the case of Edward.

Example

Edward has just reached his fifth birthday and his parents have made their final decision about his schooling. Edward has severe and complex learning difficulties and requires close supervision and a high level of resourcing. His parents have visited a number of schools in

(Continued)

(Continued)

their area and also some specialist schools. They have finally decided upon a specialist school where all of the children have severe and complex difficulties, where class sizes are very small and where there is a high level of resourcing. The school has its own occupational therapist and each class has at least two Learning Support Assistants working with the teacher. The decision to send Edward to a specialist school has not been an easy one and Edward's parents have found themselves on many occasions being overcome by their emotions. They have particularly struggled with the fact that Edward's older brother and sister attend the local primary school, which is within walking distance. On meeting the head teacher and Special Educational Needs Coordinator in the school, however, they came away feeling that the school was of the opinion that they could not accommodate Edward because, as the head teacher explained, '*We simply do not have the resources to meet Edward's needs*'. Because the specialist school that Edward will attend is quite some distance away it will mean that he will have to leave home very early in the morning when he will be picked up by organized transport from the school and then returned home quite late in the afternoon at around 5pm. His parents worry that he will grow up spending much of his time in a different school community, to his brother and sister and to all of the other children who live close to Edward. They worry particularly that when he is in his mid to late teenage years he will have become quite isolated from his own local community.

It is clear that many children with special educational needs and/or disabilities are educated in specialist schools, with some having to travel many miles each day. It is also the case that significant numbers of children with severe learning difficulties are educated very far away from home where they have to board, either on a weekly or termly basis.

Exercise

Consider the argument that by attending a specialist school Edward is being segregated because of his special educational needs and/or disabilities. Is it reasonable or unreasonable to propose that children with needs as severe as those that Edward has should not be educated alongside the children with whom they grow up in their own local communities?

We now turn to the issue of 'class' and explore how, if at all, children are segregated because of their background. As recently as April 2012 Alison Kershaw, writing in the UK i-Newspaper, *The Independent*, felt able to draw public attention to comments made by Dr Mary Bousted, general secretary of the Association of Teachers and Lecturers (ATL) as follows:

Dr Mary Bousted ... said stratified schools are 'toxic' for deprived youngsters .... 'We have, in the UK, schools whose intakes are stratified along class lines. We have schools for the elite; schools for the middle class and schools for the working class. Too few schools have mixed intakes ... The effect of unbalanced school intakes is toxic for the poorest and most dispossessed. And whilst teachers and school leaders strain every sinew in these schools to raise aspiration and achievement, they struggle always against the effects of poverty, ill health and deprivation and children in these schools routinely fail to make the educational progress achieved by their more advantaged peers.' ... She claimed that the Government has cut funding for Sure Start centres, scrapped the education maintenance allowance for poorer teenagers, removed protected funding for school meals, cut council budgets and made tax reforms that are likely to hit low to middle-income families ... 'Schools cannot vanquish these inequalities; they can ameliorate them, but in vastly unequal societies only the brightest will escape the lasting effects on inequality.'

It is of course important to recognize that the above comments were offered by an individual who was representing union members, though perhaps not every single member of that union. Here, it is possible to locate different ideologies that are underpinning perceptions of learning and the communities into which children arrive for their formal education as well as those communities that they come from.

Exercise

Reflect upon the ideas of those more modern of philosophers in Chapter 1 and consider why different politicians, policy and decision makers, and members of the public view the impact of 'class' on education differently.

GRAMMAR SCHOOLS, ACADEMIES AND THE PRIVATE SECTOR

Grammar Schools

The Department for Education (DfE) website offered the following in April 2012:

Grammar schools are defined ... as maintained ... schools which select all, or substantially all, of their pupils by reference to high academic ability. Grammar schools can also operate selection by aptitude, but must apply this after the selection by ability. Between 1973 and 1998, the number of grammar schools fell from 809 to 164. The only legally recognised grammar schools are those designated as such by the Secretary of State and named on a designation order. The term 'grammar' is not protected – hence many schools call themselves grammars even when they are not. Because the definition only includes maintained schools, grammar schools which convert to academy status are no longer classed as grammar schools ... By 1 July 2011, 75 grammar schools had converted ... they will no longer be included in the count of grammar schools. (2012a)

Since the release of *Circular 10/65* by the then Labour government in 1965, which called upon Local Education Authorities to commence a process whereby they would begin to convert secondary schools into the new Comprehensive System, the debate about the role of Grammar Schools has raged. With the introduction of Comprehensive Schools came the closure of many Grammar Schools and a move away from testing children at the age of 11 using the controversial Eleven Plus examination. Recently, in 2013, the National Grammar Schools Association (NGSA), which was founded in 1970, indicated on their website that currently there are 164 Grammar Schools in England and 69 in Northern Ireland. The concept of Grammar Schools, however, remains highly controversial and highly political, as indicated by the comments below, which appeared in one of the UK's most popular newspapers.

In 2010 Graeme Paton, the Education Editor of the UK newspaper the *Telegraph* wrote as follows:

> More than three-quarters of adults believe more academically-selective schools should be opened, particularly in inner-city areas with poor education standards, it was disclosed. Support for grammar schools has actually increased over the last four years, figures suggest. The disclosure, in a survey by ICM, comes amid growing concerns over provision for the brightest pupils in state comprehensives ... Labour introduced legislation when it came to power more than a decade ago banning the opening of any more grammars and Ed Balls, the Schools Secretary, has recently accused them of condemning many young people to 'failure' at the age of 11.

Two years later, (Paton, 2012) with the new Coalition Government in power, Graeme Paton offered the following:

> Stephen Twigg, the Shadow Education Secretary, said the party opposed an overhaul of national admissions rules that gives England's 164 state grammars the freedom to take more pupils. He accused ministers of attempting to expand academic selection 'by the backdoor' without full consultation with parents. In an attempt to trigger a Coalition split over the issue, he also said he would write to Liberal Democrat MPs seeking their support to oppose the move. The comments come just days after it emerged that the rule change could pave the way for a significant expansion in the number of grammar school places ...

There are still those older individuals in the UK who like to assert with pride that they attended a Grammar School when younger. In some respects they may perceive this as an indication of their intellectual abilities and higher levels of intelligence as entry to Grammar Schools was traditionally through open competition involving written examinations, the examination most popularly associated with this transition being the 'Eleven Plus'. Equally, there are also many older individuals who will still recount their feelings of failure associated with not gaining a place at a Grammar School because they 'failed' the Eleven Plus. Many of this latter group may even acknowledge some inner emotional struggles as a result of being separated from friends at a relatively young age who 'won' places in Grammar Schools. They may even feel that their life chances were adversely affected and that had they gone to a Grammar School they might have, for example, sought a place at university. There may also be those individuals who failed to win a place at a Grammar School and who may acknowledge that they spent many years trying to prove to themselves and to others that they were 'as good as' their peers who had been successful in attending this type of school.

Academies

The Department for Education website (February 2013, p. 1) offered the following information in regard to Academies, which are independent and publicly funded:

Academies benefit from greater freedoms to innovate and raise standards. These include:

- freedom from local authority control;
- the ability to set their own pay and conditions for staff;
- freedoms around the delivery of the curriculum; and
- the ability to change the lengths of terms and school days ...

Some academies ... will have a sponsor ... from a wide range of backgrounds including successful schools, businesses, universities, charities and faith bodies. Sponsors are held accountable for ... improving the performance of their schools. They do this by challenging traditional thinking on how schools are run ... They seek to make a complete break with cultures of low aspiration and achievement ...

Academies receive the same level of per-pupil funding as they would receive from the local authority ... plus additions to cover the services that are no longer provided for them by the local authority ...

Schools which already select some or all of their pupils will be able to continue to do so if they become academies, but schools becoming academies cannot decide to become newly selective schools ...

The growth of Academies in the UK has been quite dramatic, with just over 200 in 2010 rising to just under 2,500 towards the end of 2012. More recently, the Report of the Academies Commission (2013, p. 5) emphasized the following in regard to the expansion of Academies:

The Commission believes that a fully academised system is best seen as a community of schools, each independent but working best if connected to the rest of the system. These schools would work with one another to accelerate school improvement... Collaboration across this national community of schools should enable a balance to be struck between independence and interdependence ...

Academies now range from the first early sponsored academies, set up to replace failing schools in poor areas and highly resourced strategic investments in change, to those established from 2010 as a result of the Coalition government's decisions to encourage good and outstanding schools to convert to academy status and to extend the sponsored academy programme into primary schools ... This report argues for a new phase of academy development ... to provide such support for improvement.

The Report also called for a new and determined focus on implementing the Academies programme and suggested three key imperatives in the future development of Academies as follows:

- to ensure that there is a forensic focus on teaching and its impact on pupils' learning so that the gap between the vision for academies and practice in classrooms is reduced and the words 'academisation' and 'improvement' become inextricably and demonstrably linked

- to ensure that an increasingly academised system is fair and equally accessible to children and young people from all backgrounds

- to ensure that academies demonstrate their moral purpose and professionalism by providing greater accountability to pupils, parents and other stakeholders. The role of governors is more important than ever in an academised system, and their scrutiny and challenge should ensure effective accountability. (pp. 4–5)

The private sector

Private or independent schools have been the source of heated debate for years with much of the debate centring upon the notion of 'class' and inequality. Typically, parents pay fees for the education of their children, class sizes are much smaller than in the state system, and it is frequently asserted that discipline is better and standards higher. Independent schools are often characterized by their emphasis on sport and competition and the wide range of additional activities and resources that they offer.

The renowned author Robert Graves who lived until 1985 wrote the following in his much celebrated autobiographical text *Goodbye to All That*, published in 1929, in relation to his own education at a Preparatory (independent) school where children boarded:

... preparatory schoolboys live in a world completely dissociated from home life. They have a different vocabulary, a different moral system, even different voices. On their return to school from the holidays the change-over from home-self to school-self is almost instantaneous, whereas the reverse process takes a fortnight at least. A preparatory schoolboy, when caught off his guard, will call his mother 'Please, matron,'... school life becomes the reality, and home life the illusion. In England, parents of the governing classes virtually lose all intimate touch with their children from about the age of eight, and any attempts on their parts to insinuate home feeling into school life are resented. (p. 24)

Of course, not all independent schools are boarding schools and of course much has changed since Graves published his text in the years prior to World War II. However, some aspects of schooling and education that Graves would have encountered remain today, perhaps most notably the fact that many children continue to live away from home, typically as termly boarders and, in more recent years, as weekly boarders. Fees continue to be a necessary condition of attendance in many independent schools and children attending those independent schools where boarding is an integral part of school life are expected to have high aspirations. The author of this text worked as a teacher at such a school for two years and subsequently as an educational psychologist for many independent schools and was struck by their strong sense of community, and particularly the way in which teachers and parents alike looked out for one another when the need arose.

At the time of writing this text Ofsted has released a new report (June, 2013) *The Most Able Students: Are They Doing as Well as They Should in Our Non-selective Secondary Schools?* which has raised many issues in regard to how the more able children in 'non-selective state' secondary schools are progressing. The report offered the following:

> This survey investigated why so many of our brightest students in non-selective state secondary schools, including academies, fail to achieve their potential compared with students who attend selective and independent schools ... We also examined why relatively few students from non-selective state schools apply to, or gain places at, the most prestigious universities. The survey focused on two key questions.
>
> • Are the most able students in non-selective state secondary schools achieving as well as they should?
>
> • Why is there such disparity in admissions to the most prestigious universities between a small number of independent and selective schools and the great majority of state-maintained non-selective schools and academies? (pp. 6–7)

The report, in particular, emphasized their finding that too many of the most able children and young people in these schools are, in fact, underperforming in state non-selective schools and offered the following rather stark results from their study:

> Too many of our most able children and young people are underperforming in our non-selective state secondary schools. Many of these able students achieve reasonably well when compared with average standards but, nevertheless, fail to reach their full potential. This is most obvious when we consider the pupils who did well in both English and mathematics at primary school and then examine their achievement at GCSE five years later. At the national level:

- Almost two thirds (65%) of high-attaining pupils leaving primary school, securing Level 5 in both English and mathematics, did not reach an A* or A grade in both these GCSE subjects in 2012 in non-selective secondary schools. This represented over 65,000 students.

- Just over a quarter (27%) of these previously high-attaining students attending non-selective secondary schools did not reach a B grade in both English and mathematics at GCSE in 2012. This represented just over 27,000 young people.

- In 20% of the 1,649 non-selective 11 to 18 schools, not one student in 2012 achieved the minimum of two A grades and one B grade in at least two of the facilitating A-level subjects required by many of our most prestigious universities. (Ofsted, 2013, p. 5)

The Ofsted report concluded that such outcomes were 'unacceptable' in a global world, which is becoming increasingly competitive. This report raises the debate between selective schools such as independent schools and state-maintained schools to a new level and it will be most interesting to see how this debate is now played out over the next few years. It is clear at this stage that many teachers and head teachers working in state-maintained non-selective schools will feel 'bruised' by this report.

LEARNING AND IMMIGRATION

Readers will be aware of the growth in numbers of children entering the UK with their families and attending local schools. In some cases members of these newly arrived families may not speak English or have a poor command of the language. In addition, they may bring with them different views of parenting, of disciplining their children, different aspirations, and so on. They may also bring with them new ideas, new cultures, new insights and many other elements.

For some families and their children the move to the UK can be effortless and enjoyable whilst for others it can be extremely difficult and fraught with challenges and problems for which they may not be prepared. In school, the children will need time to adjust and to learn not only aspects of the UK curriculum but also perhaps new ways of interacting with their peers and engaging with teachers and Teaching Assistants. Most schools in urban areas within the UK are prepared for meeting the needs of newly arrived children from other countries. This, however, can be less so in more rural areas where few immigrant families choose to settle with their children. Indeed, some very rural schools in the UK may not have had any experience of working with children of immigrant families. Because of this, much greater emphasis is being given to how teachers are trained to work with children whose first language may not be English or who have recently arrived from another country.

Some aspects of immigration have given rise to concerns. For example, the UK charity Barnardo's (2007), cited in Cowie (2012, p. 1), indicated that 27 per cent of white

British children are currently living in poverty in comparison to 48 per cent of black and black British children and 67 per cent of Pakistani and Bangladeshi children. Rather worryingly, Cowie has also emphasized how families who live in poverty typically have poorer health and reduced life expectancy. The Barnardo's report (2007, p. 16), written by Neera Sharma, goes on to stress the role of government in the UK and presents the case that unless government implements appropriate and targeted policies, ethnicity will remain a key factor in determining children's futures and the life chances and opportunities open to them. The report indicates, for example, that '... the achievement gap between 16-year-old white pupils and their Pakistani and African-Caribbean classmates has almost doubled since the 1980s. 'In some urban authorities, African Caribbean pupils are now entering compulsory schooling as the highest achieving group based on baseline assessments but leaving as the group least likely to gain five high GCSEs' (p. 21). The importance of quality preschool provision is also stressed, though a rather worrying statistic offered in the report was the fact that '... around 75 per cent of Asian children have not accessed any form of formal childcare in the last year, compared to only 54 per cent of white children' (p. 20)

The report made mention of a number of initiatives, such as *Aiming High*, which have had some impact, but also stressed the importance of governments taking action to offer appropriate funding, tackling racism and bullying in schools, addressing disadvantage in the early years, offering suitable childcare provision and being more proactive in their work with Early Years providers, such as offering subsidized, and even free places for children from the poorest families.

Exercise

Consider the argument that newly established Free Schools will not have the necessary resources or capacity to effectively meet the individual learning needs of children who have recently arrived from countries outside of the UK and who have a range of learning difficulties.

 Summary

There can be little doubt that the nature of education and schools is changing significantly within the UK. Although the UK has experienced a great deal of change in education over the last decades, the rate of this change has increased markedly since the election of the

(Continued)

(Continued)

current Coalition Government in 2010. Children and their parents now have much greater choice than ever before and the extent of the choices open to them is accelerating. Parents can now send their children to Free Schools or Academies, which simply did not exist a few years ago. The nature of these schools is changing as they undertake a process of establishing their own identities. As part of this evolving process, some schools are recruiting different types of teachers to fit in with their visions, implementing new aspects of the curriculum, embracing new initiatives, and, perhaps more importantly, creating new communities within which the future parents of children in the UK will have been educated.

This chapter sought to explore the concept of communities of learning and the diverse range of communities in which children within the UK are educated, in particular Grammar Schools, the new Academies and Free Schools, and schools in the independent sector. Issues relating to the effective creation and maintenance of learning communities were explored, with a focus on economic and social factors, segregation and immigration. The following chapter addresses how learning for children in the future might be.

RECOMMENDED READING

Academies Commission (2013) *Unleashing Greatness: Getting the best from an Academised System. The Report of the Academies Commission*. Pearson RSA.

Cowie, H. (2012) *From Birth to Sixteen: Children's Health, Social, Emotional and Linguistic Development*. London: Routledge.

Gray, C. and MacBlain, S.F. (2012) *Learning Theories in Childhood*. London: Sage.

REFERENCES

Academies Commission (2013) *Unleashing Greatness: Getting the best from an Academised System. The Report of the Academies Commission*. Pearson RSA.

Action for Children (2010) *Deprivation and Risk: The Case for Early Intervention*. London: Action for Children.

Barnardo's (2007) *It Doesn't Happen Here: The Reality of Child Poverty in the UK*. Ilford: Barnardo's.

Cowie, H. (2012) *From Birth to Sixteen: Children's Health, Social, Emotional and Linguistic Development*. London: Routledge.

Cox, S. (2011) *New Perspectives in Primary Education: Meaning and Purpose in Learning and Teaching*. Maidenhead: Open University Press.

Cullis, A. and Hansen, K. (2009) *Child Development in the First Three Sweeps of the Millennium Cohort Study*, DCSF Research Report RW-007.

Department for Children, Schools and Families (DCSF) (2008) *Special Educational Needs in England*. London: DCSF.

Department for Children, Schools and Families (DCSF) (2009) *Statistical First Release, August 2009*. London: DCSF.

Department for Education (2012a) *Statistical First Release: Special Educational Needs in England, January 2012*. London: DfE.

Department for Education (2012b) Grammar Schools, Available at http://www.education.gov.uk/schools/leadership/typesofschools/maintained/a00198400/grammar-schools (accessed 21 May 2013).

Department for Education (2013) What is an academy? Available at http://www.education.gov.uk/schools/leadership/typesofschools/academies/b00205692/whatisanacademy (accessed 20 February 2013).

Department of Education Northern Ireland (DENI) (2009) *The Way Forward for Special Educational Needs and Inclusion*. Bangor: DENI. Available at: http://www.deni.gov.uk/) (accessed 5 February 2013).

Department of Education Northern Ireland (DENI) (2010) *Statistics on Education*. Bangor: DENI.

Graves, R. (1929) *Goodbye to All That*. London: Penguin.

Frederickson, N. and Cline, T. (2009) *Special Educational Needs, Inclusion and Diversity: A Textbook* (2nd ed). Buckingham: Open University Press.

Kearns, H. (2003) University accreditation of professional development in schools: can professional development serve two masters?, *Journal of In-Service Education*, 29(1).

Kershaw, A. (2012) School intake 'segregated by class', *i-Newspaper, The Independent*, 4 April, Available at http://www.independent.co.uk/news/education/education-news/school-intake-segregated-by-class-7618824.html (accessed, 18 April 2013).

Office for Standards in Education (Ofsted) (2013) *The Most Able Students: Are They Doing as Well as They Should in Our Non-selective Secondary Schools*? London: Ofsted.

Paton, G. (2010) Grammar schools 'should be expanded', *Daily Telegraph*, 9 February.

Paton, G. (2012) Labour seeks Lib Dem support to oppose grammar schools, *Daily Telegraph*, 16 January.

Paton, G. (2013) Nine-in-10 of the Coalition's free schools 'oversubscribed', *Daily Telegraph*, 10 April.

Schostak, J. (1985) Creating the narrative case record. *Curriculum Perspectives*, 5(1): 7–13.

Schostak, J. (1986) *Schooling the Violent Imagination*. London and New York: Routledge and Kegan Paul.

Special Educational Needs and Disability Act (SENDA) (2001) London: HMSO.

Stenhouse, L. (1975) *An Introduction to Curriculum Research and Development*. London: Heinemann Educational.

United Nations Children's Fund (UNICEF) (1989) *Convention on the Rights of the Child*. UNICEF.

United Nations Educational, Scientific and Cultural Organization (UNESCO) (1994) *The Salamanca Statement and Framework For Action On Special Needs Education*. UNESCO.

10 FUTURE LEARNING

This chapter aims to:

- examine the changing nature of childhood in the 21st century
- explore links between creativity, learning and success
- consider the challenges facing children as they learn to work in societies increasingly driven by economic factors
- explore the nature of entrepreneurship and its links to learning
- examine the unfolding nature of cyber communication and its relevance for children learning in the 21st century.

INTRODUCTION

In looking to the future we must not leave the past behind but learn from it. We must also recognize the importance of asking ourselves not only how children learn but, perhaps more importantly, why so many children continue to fail in fundamental aspects of their learning. Why, for example, are significant numbers of young people in the 21st century leaving schools in the UK after years of learning with poor literacy and numeracy skills and limited knowledge in even the most basic of subject areas, and in too many instances being unable to read and write and accurately process basic numerical operations? Perhaps, more worryingly, why are so many children and young people living lives characterized by failure to learn and lack of engagement with learning, and why are so many ending up with low self-esteem, poor self-efficacy and limited confidence? It has been a central contention of this text that children fail in their learning because they are not being adequately supported by the adults around them, so why is this continuing?

In looking to the future we must ditch the notion that children fail to learn purely because of within-child factors, because they lack motivation, because they are not that able or because they lack interest, and so on. Thinking like this serves little purpose and extends the type of non-critical and unreflective practice that has meant that so many children in the past have failed to learn as they should have done and have failed to reach their potential. Children in the 21st century will need different experiences to children and young people in previous generations and even recent decades. Children and young people today will, for example, need higher levels of resilience to face the constant changes that are now characteristic of societies across the globe, such as new patterns of employment, job security, the rise in terrorism, and so on. Being highly skilled and knowledgeable with Information and Communications Technology (ICT) will be a prerequisite of success, as will be the capacity to adapt quickly and confidently and to engage in problem solving as a central feature of learning.

CHANGING CONSTRUCTIONS OF CHILDHOOD

There can be little disagreement that childhood is changing at an unprecedented rate. Children are maturing physically at an earlier age and are able to access elements of the adult world that hitherto would have been closed to them. Social websites, mobile telephones, the media, ICT and a rapid growth in materialism have altered the lives of young people. Easier access to birth control is also now available to girls of quite a young age. In this shifting socio-economic context many traditional values and boundaries are being exchanged for new ones and many cultural aspects of learning are changing. Within the UK, communities have become more multicultural. New immigrant families bring with them new ways of thinking about childhood and learning.

Studies of childhood have had a brief history (Gray and MacBlain, 2012) and it is generally recognized that research in this area has been confined to recent times. Ariès (1962/1986) and Zelizer (1985/1994), for example, have viewed childhood in terms of it being a modern concept and suggest that in earlier centuries such as those at the time of John Locke and Jean-Jacques Rousseau (see Chapter 1) childhood was viewed quite differently, not as a separate stage of development, but more in terms of children being 'adults-in-waiting' (Gray and MacBlain, 2012, p. 124). With the onset of industrialization in the UK and the growth in factories new legislation was introduced that was designed to protect children, and with this came the growing realization that children were, in reality, different and childhood was a separate and distinct stage from adulthood. In his important contribution to the literature *Pricing the Priceless Child: The Changing Social Value of Children*, Zelizer (1985/1994), cited in Gray and MacBlain (2012, p. 124), drew attention to the fact that in the years between the 19th and 20th centuries, the perception of childhood moved increasingly from '… economically "useful" to economically "useless" but emotionally "priceless"' with Zelizer proposing that, '… the real "value" of children lies in their ability to give meaning and fulfillment to their parents' lives' (Gray and MacBlain, 2012, p. 124). McDowall Clark (2010) has suggested that there is no universally agreed definition of childhood and that perceptions and practices in relation to childhood vary significantly across the globe and between cultures. Such a view is found elsewhere within the literature. Prout (2005, p. 3), for example, has suggested that the diversity of forms that childhood takes is expanding and becoming increasingly visible through, for example, the media. Because of this, Prout proposes the need to revise our assumptions that childhood is a 'unitary phenomenon'. More recently, Gray and MacBlain (2012, p. 124) have commented as follows:

> Social inequity appears in many guises, not least in global employment patterns. For instance, 14-year-old children can be employed on a part-time basis and 16-year-olds on a full-time basis in the UK. Compare this practice with evidence from a global report by the International Labour Force (2005) which reports that 246 million children worldwide are involved in child labour, and that 179 million children aged 5 to 17 are exposed to forms of child labour that cause irreversible physical or psychological damage, or that even threaten their lives. A further 8.4 million children are trapped in the worst forms of child labour, including forced and bonded labour, pornography, prostitution and armed conflict, and every year 22,000 children die from work-related accidents (Magliano, 2005). Consequently, many children in developing countries find their childhood and education curtailed at an early age by social, cultural and economic conditions. Yet the dominant construction of childhood in the developed world is of childhood as a time of innocence, play, education and economic dependence (Woodhead, 2005).

Despite continued research into childhood the popular perception that many adults hold of this time in the lives of children is that it is a time of playfulness, fun, lack of responsibility, and freedom and innocence (Jenks, 1996). Some two decades ago Schostak (1991, p. 10) commented as follows:

> Society has a picture of the Ideal Family … Within the Ideal Family, however, there is a contradiction since it holds at the same time the proposition that childhood is innocent and the vulnerability of the child should be protected … The Ideal Family is the theme of countless films, television series and novels.

Arguably, this picture of the family offered by Schostak remains relevant today despite the addition to the wider literature of studies and pieces of research indicating otherwise.

Popularized perceptions of childhood in the UK have been radically challenged in the past decade by high-profile cases such as those of Victoria Climbié and Baby P, both young children who were killed by those who had been responsible for their care and who were seen as being failed by the institutions that were in place to protect them. Both cases shocked the general public and led to significant changes

in the way in which, for example, teachers and Early Years practitioners were prepared to work with children. At the time, the notion that children are reared in
stable and loving families came under scrutiny, with a realization by many that
significant numbers of children grow up in poverty, in dysfunctional families and
suffer neglect and in too many cases abuse. Such factors will have enormous
impact upon the learning and cognitive development of children both in school
and outside of school.

Cowie (2012, pp. 1–2) has indicated that:

> In comparison with other countries, children in the UK are more likely to have been drunk.
> Rates of underage sex are high, as is the incidence of teenage pregnancy ... Today's young
> people seem to face severe stresses that were unknown a generation ago. Suicidal thoughts
> are common among young people, as are feelings of hopelessness and futility ... There are
> disturbing statistics on the number of children and young people who run away from
> home or care ... These amount to around 100,000 episodes each year in the UK, with
> around a quarter running away before the age of 13, and one in ten running away before
> the age of ten.

Cowie goes on to indicate that in 2012 the National Society for the Prevention of
Cruelty to Children (NSPCC) was dealing with 30,000 cases, some 0.25 per cent of
the population.

Parents in modern industrialized societies tend to spend much less time with
their children than was the case in previous decades and generations. In part, this
is because of changes in the patterns of working. Recently, James (2007: 273) has
commented:

> Since 1998 the number of people in Britain working more than sixty hours a week has more
> than doubled (from 10 to 26 percent), and full-time Brits work an average of forty-four
> hours, the most in the European Union.

There are some parents nowadays who feel that by spending less time with their
children they need to place much greater emphasis upon the nature of the time they
do spend with their children and the type of activities they feel they should engage
in (Buckingham, 2000). This has been driven in part by an overly exaggerated sense
of needing to improve the quality of their interactions with their children. Indeed,
Buckingham has referred to this perception of time by some parents as being a com-
modity in which they feel that they should be seen by others as being fully engaged
and thus heavily involved with their children. Recently, in the UK, the notion of the
'Yummy Mummy' has emerged and offers a popularized term to account for a certain
type of parenting, characterized by, some would say, exaggerated and competitive
parenting.

Example

Malcolm is 10 years of age and attends a local school, which is considered to be one of the best in the area. In fact, the price of houses in the school catchment area has risen sharply over the past two decades because the school is viewed by parents to be highly successful. Local Estate Agents have little difficulty selling houses to parents of young children wishing to place their children in the school. Malcolm's parents are both professionals and earn well. He is the elder of two children and he has a younger sister who is hoping to start school next year.

Whilst both of Malcolm's parents have been very successful in their careers they would be the first to admit that they have worked extremely hard and at times regret that they did not spend enough time with Malcolm when he was younger. Since attending preschool at the age of four Malcolm has been used to rising early each morning, around 6.00am, to practise his violin. He is now quite proficient with this instrument and is working through his grades to become even better. He plays in a local youth orchestra, which meets every Thursday evening from 5.00pm until 8.00pm. In addition, he regularly plays at weekend events, which normally means having to travel. Often, he leaves home on Saturday morning and does not return until around early evening time. In addition to his music, Malcolm's parents have encouraged him to join the school chess club, which also means staying behind after school and taking time at weekends to travel with members of his school to local and regional championships. Malcolm also attends the local swimming club, to which his parents introduced him shortly after his fourth birthday. This requires weekly attendance on one afternoon each week and each Saturday morning for training. In the past two years Malcolm's parents have encouraged him to take up a second instrument, the piano, and he is making very good progress with this though he finds the amount of practice to be quite tiring at times. As Malcolm faces transition to secondary school and is beginning to show early signs of the onset of adolescence his parents frequently ask themselves and each other if they should have spent more time playing with Malcolm as he was growing up and less time encouraging him to engage in activities outside of the immediate family experience. They resolve to adjust their thinking in regard to Malcolm's younger sister and have actively committed to spending more of their own time with her and being more proactive in playing with her. They have decided that they will go swimming with her as a family at the weekends and spend more time as a family going for walks together and having family outings.

The above example reflects the lives of some families today where parents have perceived a need for their children to be successful in later adulthood and to be involved in activities that will prepare them for such a future time when their success can be measured by economic success and status. In the case of Malcolm his parents appear to be entering a period of reflection when they are attempting to balance the outcomes derived from directing Malcolm into many activities external to the immediate family against those that they might gain from spending more 'natural' time with his younger sister and where they do things together as a family. Older readers of this text who have reared children will be only too familiar with the often heard view that childhood is over too quickly. Whilst Malcolm and his sister have benefited from parents who actively work to provide their children with material benefits and a secure home this is not the case for many children.

A recent report, *What About the Children?*, produced by Ofsted and the Care Quality Commission (CQC) (2013) took evidence from nine local authorities and partner agencies, as well as canvassing the views of parents, carers, children, and practitioners and managers. The report indicated that one in six of the adult population, some nine million individuals, experience mental health problems and that estimates suggest that 30 per cent of those adults have dependent children (between 0 and 18 years of age). The report also indicates that evidence drawn from a number of small studies of individuals with health difficulties suggests that a significant number, 'at least 25% and probably substantially more, especially among young women' of adults in acute psychiatric hospital settings might be parents (Ofsted, 2013, p, 9). The report makes reference to recent findings published by the National Society for the Prevention of Cruelty to Children (NSPCC) (Cuthbert et al., 2011) in which it was estimated that 144,000 babies under the age of one year live with a parent 'who has a common mental health problem'. The report went on to make reference to the National Treatment Agency for Substance Abuse (2011), which collects data on those individuals using drug and alcohol services. This report estimated that around 200,000 adults are currently in receipt of some form of treatment for substance misuse problems and that around 30 per cent of these are parents with children living with them. The recent review undertaken by the NSPCC (Cuthbert et al., 2011) estimated that during the previous year some 19,500 infants under the age of one year were living in a home with a parent who was a user of Class A drugs and that some 93,500 infants under the age of one year lived in a home with a parent who was a problem drinker.

It almost goes without saying that the effect upon young children who live with parents who engage in substance abuse varies enormously and every situation will be different. Research has indicated, for example, that having a second parent or close primary caregiver living in the home who does not engage in substance abuse can lessen the impact of potential neglect and the modelling of undesirable behaviour. For example, young children may frequently observe aggressive and even violent behaviour in those fathers who drink heavily. They may even find themselves on the receiving end of violent behaviour. It is clear, therefore, that many children in the 21st century are living with parents and caregivers who fail them in too many respects. For some of these children the one area of stability that is open to them is their school, and it is at school that they come to observe positive adult behaviours and in doing so learn about themselves and how they can become effective adults.

> **Exercise**
>
> Consider how the role of Early Years practitioners and teachers in primary schools has changed in the last decades and how it might need to change in the future to adapt to the changing nature of childhood.

CREATIVITY, LEARNING AND SUCCESS

It needs to be recognized at the outset that many children in schools who are highly creative and who have the potential to do well are failing to do so because of their learning difficulties. This is especially the case with many children with specific learning difficulties (see Chapter 8). In its review of special educational needs and disability in 2010, Ofsted found that when the learning of pupils with special educational needs and/or disabilities had been outstanding that careful assessment had taken place and teachers had used their assessment to focus their teaching and to take care to address any 'gaps' in their pupils' earlier learning (Ofsted, 2010b). Ofsted also reported that when learning had been outstanding teachers had acted with confidence to 'adjust the lesson' to meet the needs of those pupils whose learning was faster or slower. Lessons that were observed to be the most effective had clear structure, which the teachers took time to carefully explain to their pupils. Focusing upon learning as opposed to keeping their pupils busy was also a key element in achieving success with their pupils' learning. A further important element reported by Ofsted was giving their pupils time to think about what they were doing and to engage in working through problems for themselves. In situations where pupils perceived their own failure in earlier learning, the report stressed that feedback from their teachers was especially important, 'For example, in the outstanding lessons seen, careful, unequivocal feedback built on success and what pupils could do' (Ofsted, 2010b, p. 46).

In reporting its findings Ofsted also identified a number of barriers to learning, which included insufficient preparation and poor use of adults within the classroom:

> In too many examples seen during the review, when a child or young person was supported closely by an adult, the adult focused on the completion of the task rather than on the actual learning. Adults intervened too quickly, so preventing children and young people from having time to think or to learn from their mistakes. (p. 46)

The report suggested that pupils should be 'given a say' when decisions were being made regarding the way in which support was being offered to them, especially in the case of older pupils in post-primary education. In its report Ofsted (2010b, pp. 47–8) concluded that when the learning of pupils was least successful a number of factors were apparent; for example teachers not giving enough time to finding out what their pupils already knew and being unclear about their own expectations of pupils in terms of actual learning outcomes as opposed to completing activities. Ofsted also identified how the work of additional staff such as Learning Support Assistants was not clearly planned, their roles were not clearly understood and agreed, their work with children was not monitored by the teachers and they lacked training. Inspectors also found that when the learning of pupils was least successful, expectations of children with SEN and/or disabilities was low, teachers spent too much time talking and their feedback to children was inconsistent and confusing, with language that was overly complex and challenged the understanding of the children. In addition, they found that interventions and additional activities engaged in by the children were not evaluated by the teachers in terms of their impact upon the learning of the children. Resources tended to be poor, with minimal consideration being given to their purpose and effectiveness. The inspectors also noted, rather worryingly, that when the learning of pupils was least successful, pupils 'had little engagement in what they were learning, usually as a result of the above features' (p. 48).

Ofsted further reported that during the inspectors' visits to providers, in terms of those lessons it observed for disabled children and young people as well as those children and young people with special educational needs, that the 'best' lessons included a number of key characteristics. These 'best' lessons were where teachers had a thorough and detailed knowledge of their pupils, as well as a 'thorough knowledge and understanding of teaching strategies and techniques, including assessment for learning'(p. 45). The best lessons also included teachers having thorough knowledge about the subject or 'areas of learning' they were teaching as well as an understanding of how learning difficulties could affect the learning of children and young people.

In its report, *Learning: Creative Approaches that Raise Standards*, Ofsted surveyed 44 schools made up of nursery, primary and secondary schools and a special school, in addition to gathering additional evidence taken from visits to other schools as part of their more general programme of subject survey inspections. They have offered, amongst others, the following findings:

> ... In a small number of the schools visited, pupils' personal development as creative learners was not matched by their progress in core academic skills such as literacy and numeracy ... Occasionally, teachers failed to grasp that creative learning was not simply a question of allowing pupils to follow their interests; careful planning was needed for enquiry, debate, speculation, experimentation, review and presentation to be productive ... The effective promotion of creative learning depended on the quality of leadership and management and on teachers' subject knowledge being secure and extensive enough to support pupils' enquiry, independent thinking

and debate ... Good professional development within the school was a key factor ... Whole-school commitment to developing and using technology habitually also enhanced pupils' confidence and engagement ... Ways of recording and evaluating pupils' development as learners, rather than their attainment at the end of a unit or a key stage, were not generally well-developed or embedded beyond the Early Years Foundation Stage ... (2010a, p. 6)

The report (p. 7) recommended that all schools should:

- from the Early Years Foundation Stage onwards, ensure that pupils are actively encouraged to ask questions, hypothesise and share their ideas, and that these skills extend into their writing

- in curriculum planning, balance opportunities for creative ways of learning with secure coverage of National Curriculum subjects and skills

- provide continuing professional development to ensure that teachers and support staff have the knowledge, skills and confidence to encourage pupils to be independent and creative learners, and to monitor and assess the effectiveness with which they develop these capabilities

- ensure that all pupils develop skills in technology to support independent and creative learning

- support and sustain partnerships that have the potential to develop pupils of all abilities as confident and creative learners.

The report found that though the term 'creativity' was commonly used in schools there was considerable variation and lack of consensus as to what it meant, 'ranging from an innate attribute to an approach and set of skills that could be cultivated' (p. 7). The report also indicated that teachers and senior leaders were more confident when identifying and evaluating creativity as part of learning when the concept was related to specific activities, for example those identified in the publication *Creativity: Find It, Promote It* (QCA, 2004), rather than expressing it in an abstract form. The report concluded that creative learning was commonly viewed by teachers and senior leaders as being characterized by: questioning and challenging; making connections and seeing relationships; envisaging what might be; exploring ideas, keeping options open; and reflecting critically on ideas, actions and outcomes (Ofsted, 2010a, p. 8).

It is useful at this point to explore creativity and learning within the wider global context and to gain a better sense of those factors that are driving creativity within schools. Craft (2011) has identified three key drivers which she argues are responsible for the increase in creativity, namely, economic, social and technological. She regards the first of these as being the most significant and alerts us to the increase in the numbers of adults over 30 who are currently employed in occupations that did not exist when they attended school. Such a situation, she suggests, is on the increase, with future employment being even less predictable for those young children now entering formal education and who, Craft proposes, will be expected to demonstrate increased capacity to engage in innovation and to respond flexibly to the ever-shifting and uncertain nature of a world characterized by increased marketization and a 'Western mindset' geared towards the increasing desire of individuals 'to possess', and perhaps more worryingly, 'to access'. Creativity, she argues, '… is required to keep the economy changing fast enough to keep up this consumerism' (p. 21).

The second driver identified by Craft, the social driver, offers a most useful perspective from which to view learning. Craft has commented as follows:

> Patterns of social engagement are driven increasingly by individuated preference rather than obligation or tradition, with choice at the heart of change … Education … needs increasingly to be geared toward helping children and young people make sense of the array of choices which face them, exercise creativity in imagining potential, and follow through possibilities. (Craft, 2011, p. 21)

Readers may recall the times when they have heard older members of the public lamenting those past times when children left school and got a trade or an apprenticeship, when traditions were carefully adhered to, and boys and girls generally followed in their father and mother's footsteps. Increased mobility, however, is now a feature of the lives of many children and young people. It is almost expected nowadays that young people when leaving school will take a 'gap year' in which they travel and will, on completing their university studies, consider a year or two working abroad in Australia or New Zealand. Such opportunities simply did not exist three decades ago.

The impact of Craft's final driver, technology, can be observed everywhere and this, she suggests, is most significant in the case of digital technologies. All readers will be aware of the rapid growth in the last decades of technology and how it has come to not only influence, but in many instances, dominate our lives. The effects on children are enormous and it almost goes without saying that schools and teachers at times struggle to keep pace with the changes in this area. Most children now have access to computers and mobile telephones, which can download 'apps' within seconds providing them with quite staggering amounts of information. In previous decades they would have had to visit a library and borrow a book to access such information. This increase in digital technology, coupled with the financial wherewithal to buy it, means that most children nowadays will need to be much more creative in their thinking and learning than was ever the case previously. More importantly, perhaps, it needs to be more fully recognized that access to digital technologies is, for many if not most children, extremely empowering and the means by which they are coming to increasingly define themselves.

> **Exercise**
>
> Consider how young children might define themselves as individuals through the use of different digital technologies. Should schools be involved in supporting or challenging this aspect of learning and development?

LEARNING TO WORK IN SOCIETIES INCREASINGLY DRIVEN BY ECONOMIC FACTORS

Recently, Craft (2011, p. 5) drew attention to the close and inescapable interdependency that exists between children and their families, and society, and the emerging importance of a more global economy, as follows:

> The family, childhood and youth in the early 21st century are harnessed deeply to the globalized economy ... Changes in employment together with speed of economic development and re-development, mean that innovation, creativity, enterprise are all seen as primary to success, alongside traditional skills and knowledge.

This view raises a number of concerns, most particularly perhaps the speed at which change is taking place and the fact that many children are failing to benefit from even the basic opportunities open to other children who are born into affluent homes where enterprise, creativity and innovative thinking are all valued as key contributors to future success. The effects upon the learning and social and emotional development of children growing up in homes where money is in very short supply, where parents are struggling to make ends meet and where even basic amenities might not be readily available cannot be underestimated. A useful entry point here is the work of Urie Bronfenbrenner (see Chapter 5). However, before drawing upon his work let us look at the following two cases, which will help with exploring Bronfenbrenner's views in context:

Examples

The case of Nicola

Nicola, aged eight is described by her teacher as, *'a very outgoing little girl who tries very hard'*. She lives with her mother Janet who was a single parent for six years, her younger brother Michael aged three and Wayne an older step-brother aged 14 who is the son of Darren, her mother's new partner. Janet met her new partner a year ago and after six months he moved into her house with his son. Within a short time of moving in with Janet he became quite aggressive and verbally abusive to Nicola and her children. Nicola and Michael become very frightened when he gets angry. Michael attends a local nursery and is now starting to copy Darren's aggressive behaviours. Nicola's mother has not worked since Nicola was born and before that only ever worked part-time doing occasional jobs for friends. She has lived off benefits since leaving school at the age of 16 when she fell pregnant with Nicola. A recent school report from Nicola's teacher described her reading as extremely poor, with the teacher stressing that Nicola still could not repeat the alphabet in correct sequence and only read when she was made to. Nicola's teacher also reported that she was, 'not good at making and sustaining friendships' and was 'constantly seeking the attention of the Learning Support Assistant'. At a chronological age of eight years and 10 months her reading and spelling ages were recorded by the teacher as being six years and three months, and six years and two months respectively.

The case of Dan

In the same class as Nicola is Dan who is also aged eight and who is described by his teacher as, 'socially very skilled and articulate, always keen to get involved and very hard working.' He lives at home with his mother and father, his two older brothers and his sister Laura who is aged three. Dan's parents are regular church goers and are part of their local church community. They also meet regularly with Dan's teacher and feel that they have gained her confidence. Dan's parents both attended university and now work as well-paid professionals. They have a wide circle of friends and their children are always encouraged to spend time with their friends when they have been invited to each others' houses. Their friends always take time to engage Dan and his brothers and Laura in conversation, inviting them to talk about their school, about what projects they are engaged in and about what sort of things they would like to study in the future and what careers they might choose when they finish education. They frequently share stories about their times at university with Dan and Laura. Dan's parents are very patient with him and enjoy spending time with him and his brothers and sister by taking them to museums, to the park and on adventure holidays where they feel the children can develop not only physically and socially but can also learn about other cultures. Dan was able to read before he went to school and this gave him a great deal of confidence as he was able to move quickly on to higher reading books than most of his peers. By the end of the first year in school his reading and spelling ages were well in advance of his chronological age – at a chronological age of eight years and six months his reading and spelling ages were recorded by the teacher as being 10 years and three months, and nine years and two months respectively. His teacher has described his vocabulary as 'very advanced'. Dan is highly sociable, confident and has lots of friends.

Bronfenbrenner (1979; Bronfenbrenner and Ceci 1994) helps us to understand how children such as Nicola and Dan grow up in modern dynamic societies that are increasingly driven by global economic factors and a rise in consumerism and materialism. Bronfenbrenner, '... emphasizes the importance of studying "development-in-context", or the ecology of development' (Smith et al., 2003: 9). Take, for example, the cases of Nicola and Dan when they are now older and in their first year of secondary school.

Example

Nicola and Dan

Seven years have passed and Nicola and Dan now attend secondary school and are preparing for their formal GCSE examination courses and examinations. Nicola's mother has split with her partner and now lives with a new partner who has two young children aged three and nine. Neither is employed. Nicola has been suspended from school on a number of occasions because of her behaviour and has been cautioned by the police on two occasions for shoplifting. She spends nearly every evening in her room communicating with others on her computer. Dan experienced significant difficulties when his mother died whilst he was in his final year at primary school. His father has remarried and Dan now lives in a large new house bought by his father and step-mother and her two teenage children.

It is clear that Nicola and Dan have experienced significant change in their lives.

From an early age their lives have been very different and the opportunities that have been available to Dan appear to be greater than those for Nicola. The expectations of Dan's parents have always been high, and from birth his parents had assumed that he would do well at school, attend university and seek a professional career. Nicola's parents never considered university for Nicola and have always assumed that she would leave school at 16 and get a job locally, meet someone and settle down.

A further consideration in regard to young people learning to work in modern industrialized societies is the notion that as societies increasingly embrace a therapeutic ethos within education, this is, indirectly, turning significant numbers of young people into vulnerable and anxious individuals as opposed to aspiring and resilient adults (Ecclestone, 2007; Ecclestone and Hayes, 2009; Furedi, 2004). Perhaps now, more than ever before, children need to be supported in developing their resilience, for although children in past centuries experienced acute poverty, children today experience the new stressors of increasing materialism, greater access to the world of adulthood and far greater pressures deriving from a perceived need to succeed and to be accepted. All of these factors affect children's learning and their creativity, as well as their ultimate success as human beings and not as products of a rapidly changing global context. One further, and potentially worrying aspect in regard to creativity, learning and success is the extent to which children actually read for pleasure and how children's learning might be influenced in the future by a lack of motivation to read independently and a diminution in reading for enjoyment in the future.

LEARNING AND READING: LOOKING TO THE FUTURE

At the very core of learning and developing one's creativity is the need to read not only material necessary for passing examination courses but more particularly for enjoyment and self-actualization. One immediately thinks of the creative nature of poetry and drama and the countless books children can now download on technology devices as opposed to having to buy actual books.

Clark and Rumbold (2006) have proposed that reading for pleasure is linked positively to attainments in reading and writing, to comprehension of text, general knowledge and the development of vocabulary, greater understanding and insights into other cultures as well as human nature itself, increased self-confidence as a reader and, perhaps most importantly, greater pleasure in reading during adulthood. Others (Appleyard, 1991; Benton and Fox, 1985; Fisher, 2008) have further suggested that engaging with text at an emotional level contributes not just to the improvement of higher order reading skills but also to social and personal development.

When we consider and fully recognize the important benefits that reading can bring it almost goes without saying that schools and teachers should not overly confine themselves to teaching the skills of reading but should also actively seek to develop within children a love of reading and perhaps more importantly a love of all aspects of literacy. Research (Cremin et al., 2008b, 2009), however, suggests that many teachers are not themselves readers in the sense just proposed. Given this is the case, then perhaps an important first step in creating within children a lifelong love of literacy is to seek to understand why many teachers have turned away from reading for enjoyment and self-actualization in the first place and what perceptions they hold of themselves as readers.

Popular accounts in the media all too frequently present a depressing picture of a generation of children in the UK who fail to read independently and for enjoyment in comparison to children in other countries. Such accounts, however, may not tell the whole story and may even distort the true picture, which, in fact, is one in which many children enjoying reading (Clark and Rumbold, 2006). Indeed, Sainsbury and Schagen (2004) and Sainsbury and Clarkson (2008) have alluded to the fact that it is, in fact, attitudes towards reading that have changed, and in particular the motivation to read that lessened in the five years following the inception of the National Literacy Strategy (NLS) in 1998, which appeared to confine many schools and teachers to a very prescriptive way of teaching reading.

Concerns have been voiced from time to time (Dombey, 1998; Frater, 2000; Sainsbury and Schagen, 2004; Clarke et al., 2008) that the overly prescriptive and overly structured view, with its, arguably, narrow emphasis upon the teaching of phonics and textual analysis, which formed part of the 'Literacy Hour' that became a feature of teaching reading in primary schools in the UK during the 1990s, may have resulted in increased levels of competence in reading, but also, a lowering of the enjoyment of reading. Others (Bearne et al., 2007; Clark and Osborne, 2007; Cremin et al., 2008b) have also alluded to a proliferation of multi-modal texts in children's choice of reading material outside school, which, it can be argued, also played a significant role in the suggested decline in reading for enjoyment.

It almost goes without saying that motivation plays an essential part in influencing the desire of children and young people to read more widely and to incorporate into their reading such aspects of literacy as poetry, plays and drama and novels. Though there has been some debate (see e.g. Edmunds and Tancock, 2003) over the seemingly opposed roles of intrinsic and extrinsic motivation, Wigfield and Guthrie (1997) have, nevertheless, suggested that extrinsic rewards such as a desire for recognition, better grades or the challenge of doing better than their peers) can greatly increase intrinsic motivation where the reward becomes, in itself, a desire to read.

A relatively recent report by Ofsted (2004), *Reading for Purpose and Pleasure*, indicated that few schools were 'successfully engaging the interest of those who, although competent readers, did not read for pleasure' (p. 4), nor were they building upon the children's own interests. Ofsted's subject report *English 2000–2005* went on to paint a picture of teachers who had adopted more of an instrumental view of reading, who were placing much greater emphasis on introducing texts that offered the potential to develop writing techniques in their pupils, often at the expense of taking time to support independent reading amongst their pupils and even of taking time to read aloud to the children, a practice that most, if not all readers of this text will fondly remember from their own days at school.

Lockwood (2008) has pointed towards a number of key features of classroom practice that can be associated with developing reading motivation. Amongst these is the need for children to have ready access to a book-rich environment with opportunities to choose and also discuss reading material, and, very importantly, teachers who model their own reading behaviours and motivation to read to the children. This last feature, however, poses something of a dilemma for if, as was stated earlier, teachers are not, themselves, readers then how can they model such behaviours to their pupils? Equally, without a sound knowledge of children's literature, how can they successfully engage with the reading interests of their pupils? This apparent conundrum requires closer analysis.

Some 50 years ago Chambers (1969, p. 117) made reference to teachers as being 'reluctant readers', suggesting that those who were, indeed, avid and voracious readers would be far more likely to foster positive and purposeful reading habits in their pupils. Chambers' view has continued to be a theme in research into classroom practice. For example, Ofsted (2004, p. 12) in its report, *Reading for Purpose and Pleasure*, endorses the importance of the role that teachers can play in introducing children to literature, for example by introducing them to new authors and variations of text. By doing so, Ofsted proposes that teachers then go quite some way in developing within their pupils much more positive attitudes to reading. More recently, Lockwood (2008), in a survey of teachers from 40 schools, established that English subject leaders continue to believe that book knowledge and understanding of the range and type of texts available on the market are crucial factors.

A report by Cremin et al. (2008c) for the United Kingdom Literacy Association, however, substantiates Ofsted's assertion that many teachers in primary schools continue to be overly reliant upon too narrow a repertoire of authors, including poets. Their findings indicated that more than 50 per cent of their sample of 1200 primary teachers could not name more than two picture book authors, whilst 25 per cent were unable to name any. What children, and indeed their teachers, read is very important. Meek (1988) found that children who read from a range of 'quality' picture books demonstrated different attitudes towards reading than those children whose experience consisted only of a reading scheme and worksheets.

LEARNING AND CYBER COMMUNICATION

There can be little doubt that the internet has had an enormous impact upon the lives of children and young people. Cowie (2012) has indicated that the average age when most children in the UK first access the internet is from seven to nine years. Cowie has also emphasized how children throughout Europe are increasing the amount of time that they spend on the internet away from their immediate family and in privacy (p. 110). She also indicated that, currently in the UK, some 65 per cent of children between 11 and 16 indicate that they have a profile on a social networking site. Rather worryingly, she also indicates that 27 per cent have admitted to supplying an incorrect age. One can only surmise that they will have used an older age.

Texting one another, entering chat rooms, social platforms, and so on, mean that children can have almost instant access to others. With advances in technology comes the acceleration and increased speed of communication. Cyber communication offers enormous opportunities for new learning and the potential to access others far removed from the immediate communities in which children live. Take the case of Nicola and Dan above who both have had access to mobile phones since attending primary school. They both communicate regularly with others on social websites and can link almost instantly with other young people of their own age in other countries. Dan recently entered into a dialogue with three other young people of his own age in the USA. His father speaks regularly with him about the whole aspect of cyber communication and sees it not only as a social activity but also as an opportunity for him to develop his ICT skills and to manage his own social time and learn responsibility for its use. Dan is increasing his awareness of the importance of communicating accurately and in different ways depending upon his audience. Like Dan, Nicola uses social networking via her computer at home and her mobile on a daily basis. They both learn about the lives of others and share their own experiences, as well as exploring the experiences of others. In this way they are exploring cultural aspects of others' societies as well as their own.

Cyber communication means that the social interactions that children and young people have are not limited to their immediate communities, as in the past. Friendships can be established with other children and young people in different communities and even different countries. This can be especially beneficial for those children and young people with sensory impairments such as hearing loss, or those who have a disability that affects their mobility. This said, cyber communication can also lead to a lessening of social interaction and even isolation, and can impact negatively upon family cohesion and the amount of time that families spend together, as in the case of Nicola above who increasingly spent most evenings in her room communicating with others on her computer.

Children are increasingly using the internet as a means of sourcing information in terms of self-help and as a means by which they can express their own feelings and emotions. The extent to which this can support children and young people in their emotional development remains open to question but it must be recognized that the internet is undermining the involvement of parents. Within schools teachers use the internet on a regular basis to work with their pupils. There is now a host of different sites, which teachers can access.

Exercise

Consider how important it is for Early Years practitioners and teachers to have a sound knowledge and skills base in the field of ICT and how their knowledge or lack of knowledge might impact upon children's social, as well as academic, progress in the future.

A most worrying aspect of cyber communication that can have detrimental effects not only on children's learning but also on their social and emotional development is cyberbullying and harassment. In more extreme cases it has been reported that young people have engaged in communications with others about suicide. Cowie (2012) refers to cyberbullying as being a covert form of psychological bullying where electronic devices, most notably mobile phones, are used to harass, stalk, tease, isolate and denigrate others. She cites Smith et al. (2008) who undertook a survey of over 500 pupils in secondary school and concluded that the incidence of cyberbullying was 6.6 per cent, which was around two or three instances in a month, 15.6 per cent around once or twice a week and 77.8 per cent for those who reported never experiencing incidences of cyberbullying. Rather worryingly, Cowie also commented as follows:

> Cyberbullying increased with age and the most reported types of cyberbullying were instant messaging (9.9%), telephone calls (9.5%) and text messages (6.6%) ... The most vulnerable of all were those children who were both cyberbullies and cybervictims. This is in line with studies of traditional bully-victims who tend to be most strongly at risk of a wide range of psychological problems, crime and suicidal thoughts ... Young people now have the power to exclude peers from social networks by means of email or text messaging ... (2012, p. 114)

It is obvious that children who are on the receiving end of cyberbullying will experience significant feelings of discomfort, which will almost certainly impact upon their learning and progress throughout school. Most often such feelings will remain with children throughout their adolescence and into adulthood. For these reasons it is imperative that schools actively engage with this recent and growing phenomenon. Most, if not all, schools will have policies and practices in place to prevent cyberbullying and support children who have experienced it. This said, it continues to happen and schools and teachers must remain highly vigilant.

Many children as they move through school are also affected by specific learning difficulties such as dyslexia and dyspraxia. Typically, many of these children struggle to communicate to their teachers and their peers their true abilities and their natural potential. Take the example of Donna, now aged 17 who, after many years of struggling in school because of her specific learning difficulties, was assessed by an educational psychologist after she had successfully gained a place on a university course. An extract from the educational psychologist's report demonstrates the extent of the difficulties she experienced, but more particularly, the benefits she might gain at university through the use of technology, which could have been put in place by her school to assist her in realizing her potential.

Example

Referral

I met originally with Donna following a request from her parents who wished to have a better understanding of Donna's current level of intellectual functioning and to determine appropriate interventions for her future studies whilst at university. Donna's parents reported to me that Donna had experienced 'major difficulties throughout her time at primary school and in her present secondary school' and that her teachers had described Donna to them as 'a lovely girl who tries very hard and is well meaning', but 'is not really up there with the more academic children'.

Interview with Donna

Donna presented as a most pleasant and highly articulate young person ... who is motivated to achieve ... Within the assessment situation Donna persevered with all of the tasks that were presented to her, even those that caused obvious difficulty.

Intellectual functioning

Psychometric assessment on this occasion offered the following profile:

Table 10.1   Wechsler Adult Intelligence Scale (WAIS III UK)

	Percentile rank	Index score	Confidence level 95%
Verbal Comprehension	99	134	125–139
Perceptual Reasoning	70	108	100–115
Working Memory	1	65	60–75
Processing Speed	1	65	60–78

It is generally agreed that two-thirds of students are considered to function within the average range of ability and this range is represented between the 16th and 84th centiles, where the 16th centile lies at the lowest end of the average range and the 84th centile the highest. The 85th centile upwards represents increasingly higher ability, with the 95th centile representing the top 1 per cent of ability. At the other end of the range, the 1st centile represents the lowest 1 per cent of ability.

Additional assessment of Donna's levels of literacy offered the following results:

It is clear that Donna's levels of literacy are well below what would be expected of someone with her very high level of intellectual functioning, which will have caused her significant difficulties throughout her schooling and even from a very early age.

Discussion of statistical results

Of special note was the significant difference between Donna's percentile scores gained on both the Verbal Comprehension and Perceptual Reasoning Indexes and those gained on the Working Memory and Processing Speed Indexes (see Table 10. 1).

Table 10.2   Wechsler Individual Achievement Test (WIAT-II UK)

	Standard score	Centile
Word Reading	96	39
Reading Comprehension	112	79
Spelling	69	2

Conclusions

In summary … there is a clear and significant discrepancy between Donna's cognitive abilities (Table 10. 1) and her attainments in literacy (Table 10.2) … Assessment would suggest that Donna experiences particular difficulties when attempting to express her level of understanding of a subject in writing. Difficulties with spelling and sentence structure, which affect her ability to produce accurate samples of written work, become apparent, especially where Donna is being asked to work under pressure, for example during examination situations or in timed class-based written assessments. This appears to me to be also the case where Donna is attempting to process a number of operations simultaneously that involve the processing of written symbolic information and oral instructions, for example during whole-class question and answer sessions.

Recommendations

I would recommend that when Donna commences her studies at university she will require a technical assessment in order that appropriate ICT (for example, a dictaphone for note taking and relevant software) can be identified, which will make her academic programme readily accessible. In particular I would suggest that Donna should:

- *Be encouraged to develop her abilities in using a dictaphone and, where possible, record lectures and use this as a means of supporting her with the organization of revision for any examinations or written assignments.*
- *Be actively supported in developing her current knowledge and existing skills base in the area of ICT and extending her thinking in terms of how such an improved knowledge and skills base might help her through her studies at university.*
- *Have regular access to specialist support from Study Skills tutors who are qualified and experienced in working with students with specific learning difficulties such as dyslexia and dyspraxia. Have available to her, the choice of completing her examinations using a computer with keyboard.*
- *Be given additional time (25 per cent) in any formal examination arrangements in order that she can:*

1. *Correctly interpret questions and instructions in a limited time and process written symbolic information efficiently and in a manner that demonstrates her ability and potential.*
2. *Check her accuracy of written work.*
3. *Check the meaning of the text she is reading and responding to.*
4. *Compose and execute written evidence to demonstrate her relevant subject knowledge and understanding in those subject areas that she is being examined in …*

The above example reflects the type of interventions that many children experiencing difficulties with learning can benefit from. What is worrying about Donna's case, as with so many other children and young people, is that she was not assessed until she was nearing the end of her time in formal education and that the benefits that she might have gained from ICT were not made available to her; because of this she spent many years at school being unable to communicate her very high levels of ability.

It is becoming increasingly important that schools and teachers recognize the positive benefits of cyber communication and how it could impact upon the learning of children and young people in ways that would support not only their social development but also their academic development. In the case of Donna, it might be argued that had she been supported at a much younger age in developing her ICT skills she could have used this medium to express her high levels of reasoning and her motivation to do well, and would not have been hindered by, what some might consider, an outdated but persistent belief that children with specific learning difficulties should continue to employ handwriting as the chief means of expressing themselves and communicating their ideas to others.

Summary

This chapter sought to examine the nature of childhood in the 21st century and how it is changing. It is clear that significant numbers of children in the UK and across the industrialized world are growing up in households where they witness substance abuse, domestic abuse and violence. Many children now have access to media that would have been inconceivable about 20 years ago. The impact of this upon children's learning is substantial and will increase in the future and in ways that we currently cannot imagine. The importance of exploring links between creativity, learning and success were also explored and consideration was given to the challenges facing children as they learn to work in global societies increasingly driven by economic factors and quite major shifts in culture.

The growth in cyber communication is changing the way in which children learn, with teachers increasingly becoming facilitators of learning experiences. How learning will emerge in the forthcoming decades is open to speculation and requires that all practitioners working with children are open to the thoughts of those new theorists and philosophers who, like those we discussed in Chapter 1, offer ways of critically engaging with the truth and why, after all, we engage in learning at all. One seemingly worrying development in the UK is an apparent fear that many teachers and Early Years practitioners appear to have in relation to the nature of inspection. In a recent discussion with two academics involved in the training of teachers, the author had this aspect of practice in education and learning described to him as 'ridiculously expensive and non-productive', 'brutal', 'depressing' and 'vile'. Such views, of course, need to be treated with caution. It is for this reason that all practitioners working with children must keep an open mind when they grapple with that most important of all questions, how do children learn?

RECOMMENDED READING

Buckingham, D. (2000) *After the Death of Childhood: Growing up in the Age of Electronic Media*. Cambridge: Polity Press.

Cowie, H. (2012) *From Birth to Sixteen: Children's Health, Social, Emotional and Linguistic Development*. London: Routledge.

Craft, A. (2011) *Creativity and Education Futures: Learning in a Digital Age*. Stoke on Trent: Trentham Books.

Ecclestone, K. and Hayes, D. (2009) *The Dangerous Rise of Therapeutic Education*. London: Routledge.

REFERENCES

Appleyard, J. (1991) *Becoming a Reader: The Experience of Fiction from Childhood to Adulthood*. Cambridge: Cambridge University Press.

Ariès, P. (1962/1986) *Centuries of Childhood: A Social History of Family Life*. London: Penguin Books.

Bearne, E., Clark, C., Johnson, A., Manford, P., Mottram, M. and Wolstencroft, H. (2007) *Reading on Screen*. Leicester: United Kingdom Literacy Association.

Benton, M. and Fox, G. (1985) *Teaching Literature: Nine to Fourteen*. Oxford: Oxford University Press.

Bronfenbrenner, U. (1979) *The Ecology of Human Development*. Cambridge, MA: Harvard University Press.

Bronfenbrenner, U. and Ceci, S.J. (1994) Nature-nurture reconceptualized in the developmental perspective: a bioecological model, *Psychological Review*, 101(11): 568–86.

Buckingham, D. (2000) *After the Death of Childhood: Growing up in the Age of Electronic Media*. Cambridge: Polity Press.

Chambers, A. (1969) *The Reluctant Reader*. Oxford: Pergamon Press.

Clark, C. and Osborne, S. (2007) *Demystifying the Reluctant Reader*. London: National Literacy Trust.

Clark, C. and Rumbold, K. (2006) *Reading for Pleasure: A Research Overview*. London: National Literacy Trust.

Clark, C., Osborne, S. and Akerman, R. (2008) *Young People's Self-perceptions as Readers: An Investigation Including Family, Peer and School Influences*. London: National Literacy Trust.

Cowie, H. (2012) *From Birth to Sixteen: Children's Health, Social, Emotional and Linguistic Development*. London: Routledge.

Craft, A. (2011) *Creativity and Education Futures: Learning in a Digital Age*. Stoke on Trent: Trentham Books.

Cremin, T., Mottram, M., Bearne, E. and Goodwin, P. (2008a) Exploring teachers' knowledge of children's books, *Cambridge Journal of Education*, 38(4): 449–64.

Cremin, T., Mottram, M., Goodwin, P. and Bearne, E. (2008b) Primary teachers as readers, *English in Education*, 42(1): 8–23.

Cremin, T., Mottram, M., Collins, F. and Powell, S. (2008c) *Building Communities of Readers*. Leicester: UKLA.

Cremin, T., Mottram, M., Collins, F., Powell, S. and Safford, K. (2009) Teachers as readers: building communities of readers. *Literacy*, 43(1): 11–19.

Cuthbert, C., Rayns, G. and Stanley, K. (2011) Available at: All babies count: prevention and protection for vulnerable babies: a review of the evidence, National Society for the Prevention of Cruelty to Children, November. Available at:http://www.nspcc.org.uk/inform/resourcesforprofessionals/underones/all_babies_count_wda85568.html

Dombey, H. (1998) Changing literacy in the early years of school. In B. Cox (ed.) *Literacy is not Enough*. Manchester: Manchester University Press and Book Trust.

Ecclestone, K. (2007) Resisting images of the 'diminished self': the implications of emotional well-being and emotional engagement in education policy, *Journal of Education Policy*, 22(4): 455–70.

Ecclestone, K. and Hayes, D. (2009) *The Dangerous Rise of Therapeutic Education*. London: Routledge.

Edmunds, K. and Tancock, S. (2003) Incentives: the effects on the reading motivation of fourth-grade students. *Reading Research and Instruction*, 42 (2): 17–37.

Fenton, B. (2006) Junk culture 'is poisoning our children', *Daily Telegraph*, 12 September, p. 1.

Fisher, A. (2008) The magic of poetry, *English Four to Eleven*, 23: 7–11.

Frater, G. (2000) Observed in practice, English in the National Literacy Strategy: some reflections, *Reading*, 34(3): 107–12.

Furedi, F. (2004) *Therapy Culture: Cultivating Vulnerability in an Uncertain Age*. London: Routledge.

Gray, C. and MacBlain, S.F. (2012) *Learning Theories in Childhood*. London: Sage.

International Labour Force (2005) *A Global Alliance Against Forced Labour: Global Report Under the Follow-up to the ILO Declaration on Fundamental Principles and Rights at Work* 2005. Geneva: International Labour Force Office.

James, O. (2007) *Affluenza*. London: Vermillion.

Jenks, C. (1996) *Childhood* London, Routledge.

Lockwood, M. (2008) *Promoting Reading for Pleasure in the Primary Sc*hool. London: Sage.

Magliano, T. (2005) The world's working children, *Catholic News Service*, posted 06.09.05 at http://www.freerepublic.com/f-religion/1420002/posts (accessed 25 September 2013).

McDowall Clark, R. (2010) *Childhood in Society*. Exeter: Learning Matters.

Meek, M. (1988). *How Texts Teach What Readers Learn*. Stroud: Thimble Press.

Office for Standards in Education (Ofsted) (2004) *Reading for Purpose and Pleasure. London*: Ofsted.

Office for Standards in Education (Ofsted) (2005) *English 2000 – 2005: A review of inspection evidence*. London: The Stationery Office.

Office for Standards in Education (Ofsted) (2010a) *Learning: Creative Approaches that Raise Standards*. London: Ofsted.

Office for Standards in Education (Ofsted) (2010b) *The Special Educational Needs and Disability Review*. London: Ofsted.

Office for Standards in Education (Ofsted) (2013) *What About the Children*? Joint working between adult and children's services when parents or carers have mental ill health and/or drug and alcohol problems. Manchester: Ofsted.

Prout, A. (2005) *The Future of Childhood: Towards the Interdisciplinary Study of Children*. London: Falmer Press.

Qualifications and Curriculum Authority (QCA) (2004) *Creativity: Find It, Promote It*. London: QCA.

Sainsbury, M. and Schagen, I. (2004) Attitudes to reading at ages nine and eleven. *Journal of Research in Reading*, 27 (4): 373–86.

Sainsbury, M. and Clarkson, R. (2008) *Attitudes to Reading at Ages Nine and Eleven: Full Report*. Slough: National Foundation for Educational Research (NFER).

Schostak, J. (1991) *Youth in Trouble*. London: Kogan Page.

Smith, K.S., Cowie, H. and Blades, M. (2003) *Understanding Children's Development* (4th edn). Oxford: Blackwell.

Smith, P.K., Mahdavi, J. and Carvallo, M. (2008) Cyberbullying: its nature and impact in secondary school pupils, *Journal of Child Psychology and Psychiatry*, 49(4): 376–85.

Wigfield, A. and Guthrie, J. (1997) Relations of children's motivations for reading to the amount and breadth of their reading, *Journal of Educational Psychology*, 89(3): 420–32.

Woodhead, M. (2005) Children and development. In J. Oates, C. Wood and A. Grayson (eds) *Psychological Development and Early Childhood*. Oxford: Wiley-Blackwell, pp. 9–46.

Zelizer, V. (1985/1994). *Pricing the Priceless Child: The Changing Social Value of Children*. Princeton, NJ: Princeton University Press.

INDEX

Added to a page number 't' denotes a table.